AN ILLUSTRATED HISTORY OF

ITALY

Endpapers View of the port of Naples by the
Master of the Tavola Strozzi, sixteenth century.
(Museo di S. Martino, Naples)

AN ILLUSTRATED HISTORY OF

ITALY

Edited by Milton Gendel

Introduction by Denis Mack Smith

McGRAW-HILL BOOK COMPANY   NEW YORK   TORONTO

© 1966 George Weidenfeld & Nicolson Ltd

All Rights Reserved

Designed by Felix Gluck for George Weidenfeld & Nicolson Ltd, London

Library of Congress Catalog Card Number 66-21152

58491

Printed in Switzerland by Conzett & Huber, Zürich

Contents

INTRODUCTION

Denis Mack Smith

To follow the history of Italy through the centuries is to penetrate to the very heart of western civilization. The artists, thinkers and statesmen of this small but complex and vital country are part of our own past and have helped to make the present world what it is. What was achieved by the legions of Rome more than two thousand years ago has remained a powerful influence on history ever since, and the cultures of ancient Greece and Israel took their dominant position in our western heritage through the medium of an Italian translation. Christianity was propagated from Rome, the fifteenth century Renaissance from Florence, and the scientific revolution of the sixteenth and seventeenth centuries in great part from Padua. It may be admitted that Italy made less of a contribution than Greece or England to the development of democracy and liberal institutions, less than France to that of the Enlightenment and the great social and political revolution of the eighteenth century, less than Germany and America to the technological and industrial revolution of more recent times; but European history would have been very different without the work of Columbus and Galileo in discovery, Raphael and Michelangelo in art, Aquinas and Vico in philosophy, St Francis and a long list of Popes from Gregory the Great to John XXIII in religion. Italian museums and churches contain what must seem a disproportionate number of the greatest masterpieces of human creativity. This one country often appears to be one great museum of the past, and yet it is far from being only, or mainly, a museum. Italy is a dynamic country which, whether wielding world power or reduced to political insignificance, has at many periods of history been the architect, the initiator, the pace-setter of processes which extended far beyond her own frontiers and became the common inheritance of all humanity.

It would be a mistake to search for a single theme running through the whole intricate network of Italian history, for the only constant factor has been the sea and the Alps which have defined the geographical expression we know as Italy. Mussolini and his official historians tried to force all the centuries into one political pattern tracing the imperial destinies of the Italian race, but this required a good deal of intellectual prestidigitation and distorted the picture to the point of travesty. Politics do not make such a simple pattern, and in any case there is in fact no close correlation between Italy's greatest achievements and her moments of political success. Sometimes it seems as though the very reverse would be much closer to the truth. Political history has often been unkind to her. On the whole she has been more conquered than conquering, yet has not been on this account the less admired, and sometimes the challenge has been stimulating and fruitful. One result of being repeatedly invaded because of her wealth and strategic position was that some careers, which elsewhere would have been channelled into administration and government, were in Italy directed into more creative fields.

Those who came as invaders usually submitted to the *genius loci*; many of them stayed behind to be absorbed and assimilated. This was as true of the civilised Etruscan, Greek and Semitic intruders, as of the crude barbarians from north and east Europe who followed them. Goths, Lombards and Normans were only the most prominent of many northern invaders who came between 400 and 1100 AD to plunder the city of Rome with its glorious relics of antiquity, but they themselves were then captivated and completely changed by what they found. This was one of the most important contributions ever made by Italy to Europe. There is plenty of cruelty and even barbarism in Italian history, but on the whole this country has been the greatest *civilizing* influence of all: and its propagation of *civilitas* was not only by means of the victorious arms of the Roman legions, but also in defeat as the other peoples of Europe came to drink at the fountainhead.

Italy itself was also changed by this process. The Fascist professors claimed to believe that there was an Italian race which had remained more or less unchanged through the passage of the centuries, but few of their pupils can have believed them. The North Africans who emigrated *en masse* into some Italian provinces, the pilgrims who flocked to Rome from all over the world, the slaves who were imported from the Near East by tens of thousands, these did not all return home. Those who came to conquer and pillage were themselves often conquered by something more enduring than military might, and stayed to add their own contribution to the complicated process which produced the infinitely varied Italian people of today.

A second political theme which is sometimes used to give a central meaning to the whole of Italian history describes how many successive generations laboured to join the peninsula into a single state. It is said, for example, that Dionysius of Syracuse in the fourth century BC was aiming at Italian unification, and so were Theodoric in the fifth century AD, the Visconti in the fourteenth century, Cesare Borgia in the sixteenth, and Marshal Murat and Lord William Bentinck more recently, until King Victor Emmanuel finally succeeded in 1861. But to make these into great national heroes, above Virgil and Horace, above Leonardo and Lorenzo, above Monteverdi and Bernini, is better politics than history. The implication would also be that other countries which had been earlier in achieving national unity were in some sense superior. It is a matter of simple historical fact that not even in 1861 was Italy complete: some provinces, including Rome itself, were still excluded, and not until 1919 was the Alpine frontier rounded off by the acquisition of the Trentino from Austria. But to treat the settlement of Versailles in 1919 as the culminating point of all Italian history is to risk an anticlimax and to depreciate the chief glories of the national past.

If political unification took so long in coming, this was by no means due to lack of political skill or of military courage. The simple explanation, and one which is important for an understanding of Italy, is that some of the most vital forces in the country were consistently against it. One distinct characteristic of Italian history has been that loyalties were local quite as much as and usually more than national. No threat from outside, no invasion of a Hannibal or Alaric, was strong enough to make all Italians agree among themselves to resist foreign conquest. Always there were some local factions which welcomed and even instigated the invasion of Arabs, Greeks, Frenchmen, Spaniards, English, one after the other. It seems as though Italians often preferred foreign domination to Italian domination of Italy. As soon as Frederick II, or Gian Galeazzo Visconti, or the Venetian republic, or Pope Julius II came near to establishing a position of peninsular hegemony, the almost automatic policy of other Italian states was to combine in the name of 'Italian liberty' against this threat to their independence. Even the wars of the nineteenth century Risorgimento were largely civil wars in which both sides invoked outside help, and it is not irrelevant to note that the achievement of 1861 was materially assisted by foreign governments, who showed more interest than many Italians in the formation of a single Italian state.

This is not to deny a strong consciousness of 'Italianateness' much earlier in history, at least as early as the time of Dante and Petrarch. One also finds a bitter opposition to the foreign *barbari* who pursued their own private battles on Italian soil. But these feelings were consistent with, and indeed much less marked than, the internal divisions and different regional traditions and interests which struck every observer. The consciousness of *italianità* was something cultural and geographical long before it was introduced into the world of national and international politics. Even the geographical determinants were not quite so compelling as they seemed at first sight. If the Alps seemed to call for political unity, the Apennines spoke in another sense. Was not Sicily perhaps more African than Italian, Apulia more Greek, Piedmont more French? The answer was not always as clear as it is today.

Far from being the leading theme in Italy's history, the consciousness of needing to belong to one single comprehensive state was weaker and arrived later than in some other countries. Much more common was the sentiment which for many centuries made the village of Taormina resent Messina, the province of Messina chafe and often fight against Palermo, and Palermo lock in fierce combat on dozens of occasions with Naples, while the whole of southern Italy continued to

Opposite The stately Italian Mother Earth is represented in a Luna marble relief on the Altar of Peace, which was dedicated in 9 BC to celebrate the pacification of the Empire by Augustus. Peace encourages the Earth's fecundity, thus she is shown with children, domestic animals, flowers, fruit and ears of wheat.

feel utterly different from the north. The creation of a national kingdom did not end the feelings of regional separateness which for so long had been an enduring and often beneficent impulse, and in the 1960s one can still discover traces of *campanilismo*. 'South of Rome begins Africa', is a phrase still heard occasionally from northerners – and some of them have been ready to involve Rome in this blanket exclusion.

Today the south is poor and in many ways backward, though once it was the richest and most civilized region of all. Italy was hellenised from the south before it was romanized, and not until the time of Julius Caesar did the centre of gravity shift decisively northwards. With the fall of the Roman Empire the two halves of Italy developed in different directions. The north was overrun by barbarian tribes and was attached by successive German dynasties to the Holy Roman Empire. The south remained more under Greek and African influence, and was the centre of the Norman-Arab culture of Roger II and Frederick II, which was one of the most brilliant achievements of the Middle Ages; later it was also a colony of Spain for a far longer period than the one century after 1861 in which it has shared a common political history with Lombardy and Venice. This fundamental historical division has still not been eliminated, and other less striking differences continue to survive at a regional level. They show the very variety of Italy's cultural inheritance, as a meeting-place between East and West, between Africa and northern Europe. Her position at the very centre of the Mediterranean forced her into this role.

The influence of Italy has never been greater than under the Roman Empire, and the legacy of ancient Rome made itself felt in every period of later Italian history. The sense of belonging together and the pride of achievement, which are both indispensable to national consciousness, were nourished on these imperial memories in generation after generation as schoolchildren were brought up on the Latin classics and patriotic tales of the Punic wars. Artists in the Middle Ages were continuously confronted with relics and exemplars of classical architecture and statuary. This helps to explain why the work of Andrea Pisano and Giotto was so much more sophisticated and fruitful than that of their contemporaries in northern Europe. The words *Aurea Roma* and *Caput Mundi* recur on medieval coins and in documents, even when Rome

was reduced to being little better than a squalid village in the middle of a malarial marsh. And even in 1341, when not even a Pope was still in Rome, Petrarch was crowned with a wreath as poet laureate by the Roman Senate on the Capitoline hill.

The memory of ancient Rome could sometimes be a depressant as well as a stimulus. It helped to engender the pessimism of those who feared that Italy's greatness lay in the past rather than in the present or the future, and from Boethius to Machiavelli and Leopardi this retrospective vision could inhibit action and depress initiative. Memories of the distant past were an obstacle to Italians thinking of themselves as a new people who might still have a mission to perform. Ancient Rome, anyhow, represented not nationalism but universality, not Italy but an Empire. It had stood for all mankind, for the enfranchisement as Roman citizens of vast numbers of non-Italian people all round the Mediterranean. Even many of the Emperors were not Italians but came from Spain, Africa or eastern Europe. Not only was Rome international, but in particular Latin was an international language and became more so. The painstaking cult of Latin and in particular of Latin oratory had some unfortunate effects on Italian as a language and certainly delayed its development. Dante, the man who almost single-handed created Italian literature, regarded Latin as the normal written language of communication, and Petrarch claimed to despise those of his own poems which had been written in the vernacular.

The popes of Rome were in many ways the successors of the Roman Emperors. Throughout the Middle Ages, though most of the popes were Italian, they presided over the international world of western Europe. Everyone in Christendom looked to Rome as the capital city of their faith, and in this sense the papacy preserved the centre of Italy as an international and sometimes an anti-Italian enclave. It was asserted that the Church could not remain properly autonomous without keeping Rome and most of central Italy as an independent secular state, and in order to maintain this temporal power Pope Hadrian I invited the Franks into Italy, as for the same reason Gregory VII later turned to the Normans, and Urban IV to the Count of Anjou. With repeated recourse to foreign help the Papal State was thus kept in existence, stretching right across the peninsula from sea to sea, and this remained an

Opposite The annual account books of Siena's financial administration from 1258 to 1659 were bound in wooden covers painted with appropriate scenes and the arms of the incumbent officials. They are called *Tavolette di Biccherna* and were painted by the best artists of the republic in each generation, including the Lorenzettis, Sano di Pietro and Beccafumi. This example bears the date of 1467.

insuperable obstacle to any joining together of northern and southern Italy.

Dante and Machiavelli were among those who actively resented that the Church had to play this particular rôle, but most other Italians accepted the fact and were even proud that Rome was the spiritual centre of Europe. Only a few non-Italians became Pope after 1378, and none at all after 1523; the vast majority of the cardinalates and other offices at the headquarters of the Church were also reserved for Italians. One incidental result was to divert a great deal of the available political talent to the ecclesiastical life and away from service of the State, though the significance of this was hardly visible at the time. Much more obvious was the fact that from all over Europe money poured into Rome as alms, tribute and 'Peter's pence', money which became an important factor in the history of Italian art. No doubt Italy suffered in general from the conflict between Church and State, naturally so much more acute here than elsewhere, but there was also a fortuitous and beneficial side-effect in that individual freedoms were more easily preserved in such a divided society. The claims of the State and the counterclaims of the Church also led to a remarkable investigation of the nature and limitations of political obedience. On the one side of this controversy were Marsilio of Padua, Machiavelli, Paolo Sarpi who championed the rights of Venice against the Holy See, and Pietro Giannone who did the same for eighteenth-century Naples; on the other there was a long line of theologians and clerical politicians who, while arguing for the liberties of the Church, also provided arguments for the claims of individual conscience and the right to resist the totalitarian demands of the State.

When Italian patriots blamed the papacy or foreign invaders for preventing national union they were doing little more than trying to find a convenient scapegoat for a largely imaginary offence. It seemed to them that in a world where other nations were taking shape and so becoming powerful, there must be something deficient in their own. Understandably they resented the fact that throughout the Middle Ages the Popes and Emperors fought out their international quarrel in Italy, at Italian expense, lining up Guelphs against Ghibellines, papal city against imperial city, and family against family. But city strife had existed long before this. The protracted dog-fight of Florence against Pisa represented a natural rivalry about trade and political power which would have existed anyway. Not nation states, but city states, were the reality in this world; the Popes in Rome were often no more than one city ruler among many, and no more anti-national than the rest. Lucca, Genoa and Venice were splendid states in their own right, whose loyalties were exclusive and who frequently fought each other; yet the autonomous development of these often tiny political units proved to be one of the conspicuous achievements of Italian history.

Local pride was the greatest possible stimulus to cultural and economic progress. The Florence of the Medici was little more than a large village in size, yet a hundred of the most famous artists and scholars of all time lived and worked there, and in almost every branch of creative activity except science and music they set the fashions for everyone else. Almost as important as Florence was Venice, the wealthiest town in the world, a town which had grown fabulously rich on the profits of eastern trade. Marco Polo visited the court of Kublai Khan in the thirteenth century, and generations of other Venetian merchants created colonies all the way from the Crimea to Cairo and Southampton. The lavish civic pageants depicted by Gentile Bellini and Carpaccio are witness to the wealth and piety but also to the public spirit and civic-mindedness of this hard-headed merchant community in the fifteenth and sixteenth centuries. Writers in France and England held up the unique Venetian constitution as an object lesson in practical politics, and European diplomatists looked on Venice as the very founding home of their art.

The Renaissance in Italy was of course essentially a civic phenomenon. It had little significance in those parts of Italy, for instance Piedmont and south of Naples, where city states took little hold, and it also came to an end when the cities were replaced by much larger territorial units. The various towns in their heyday were ready to make quite extraordinary sacrifices to build a better town hall than their rivals, a larger cathedral, a higher campanile, or to outdo their neighbour in the acquisition of saintly relics for which they would need a reliquary of the finest workmanship. As political domination was impossible, they instead created a compulsive fashion out of this competitive expenditure; and the competition for painters, jewellers and poets between one town and another had a decisive result in raising the social status of the artist.

After the time of Giotto, the painter was no longer an anonymous craftsman. He could even become a rich man, and in the sixteenth century Titian was raised by imperial edict to the nobility.

Civic rivalry thus led to a great expenditure on works of art, just as in politics it led to anarchy. In a sense these were reverse sides of the same coin, complementary to each other, and their reciprocal influence explains a good deal about the waxing and waning of a whole culture. Much of the wealth which paid for the Renaissance was accumulated out of the profits of this political anarchy and from war between one town and another. The Dukes of Urbino, whose tiny and impoverished state was the home of Raphael, Bramante and Castiglione, were professional soldiers who had few other sources of revenue. Here at the court of Urbino was laid down the standard of behaviour between gentlemen which became an international code of conduct. Here the plunder of war was used with infinite patience and taste to build up the finest manuscript library of the day. Later the Popes, who were rival bibliophiles as well as political enemies, annexed Urbino and transferred these priceless manuscripts to the Vatican library. This was one small example of how political anarchy was to destroy the civilization of the Renaissance, for the very vitality and self-consciousness of these city states made it hard for them to agree, and it was their animosities which as much as anything else condemned Italy to a century of war and destruction. The individualism which Burkhardt discerned as the chief characteristic of the Italian Renaissance was the same human quality which brought the Renaissance to an end. The same sense of individualism and independence which in the first place had made the city states possible, in the end led to their destroying each other.

In modern history after 1500 Italy played a far less prominent part in Europe than before. The hostile feelings between one region of Italy and another eventually broke up the precarious balance of power in the peninsula which Lorenzo de' Medici had done so much to maintain, and this opened up the way to invasion by the nation states which were being formed elsewhere. A French army had recently been able to move through the whole length of Italy with astonishing speed, meeting little opposition, and indeed this French intervention was actively instigated by the Sforzas who ruled Milan, as well as by Neapolitan barons, by the anti-Medici faction in Florence, and by the future Pope Julius II who wanted French help to advance his career and depose the Borgias. In reply the armies of the Habsburgs invaded from the south and made Milan, Naples, Sicily and Sardinia into colonies of Spain. Spanish now became the main language of government. Even in Tuscany the Medici became the champions of Spain, just as the Sforzas had welcomed the Valois; and the Dukes of Savoy, whose heirs much later were to unite Italy, cheerfully served as generals in the Spanish armies which kept Italy in thrall. Family rivalries and social cleavages inside each city were such that an invader could always rely on local help.

The result was that in some regions almost every village and town was sacked at one time or another in the sixteenth century, and the worst event of all, the prolonged plundering of Rome in 1527, was the great shock which brought the flourishing world of the Renaissance to a close. The financial capital which had been invested and accumulated over centuries was thus dissipated quickly in war and depredation. Invading armies were often unpaid and had to live off the countryside: they burnt the woods and killed off herds of cattle: they broke aqueducts and in a single day could ruin vital irrigation works which had taken centuries of patient work to construct. The damage done in this period was impossible to repair.

In a very real sense Italy was exhausted. Intolerance by the Church—as witness the attitudes toward Veronese's religious pictures, Palestrina's early music, and the burning alive of Giordano Bruno—was something which reflected a new lack of self-confidence in Christendom. The same fear was experienced by others who realised that Italy was moving into a different world where former assumptions of natural superiority no longer applied. In each state military commitments now required the allocation of an increasing proportion of the available resources, and these resources were less plentiful than before. Caught up in the fierce religious feeling of the Counter-Reformation, Italians were drafted to fight on Spanish orders against Protestantism in the north, and against Islam in Africa and throughout the Mediterranean. As servants of the Habsburgs they had to fight frequently against France and with no profit to their own country. In this much more uncharitable world the Turks, and the Algerian and English 'pirates', naturally reacted by making trade as difficult as possible and doing their best to destroy Italian shipping. Venice remained independent but no more 'held the glorious east in fee'. Italy was no longer in the centre of the known world and the meeting-ground of cultures; it was rather a frontier territory fighting for survival.

In fact the economic axis of Europe was rapidly shifting away from this inland sea towards the Atlantic seaboard. Italy's pre-eminence hitherto had been in a civilization which was primarily Mediterranean, but this could not survive the revival of Islam under the Turks and the discovery of a New World across the Atlantic. The ironic fact was that some of the admirals in the hostile Turkish fleet and some of the explorers who took service with Spain and Portugal were by origin Italian. It was Spain and not Genoa or Venice who encouraged and financed Columbus, and he was only one of many Italian seamen who had emigrated to Spain in the past century to find an outlet for their talents. Cabot, Amerigo Vespucci, Toscanelli, and many others who helped to discover the new trans-atlantic world were likewise Italians, yet Italy in the sixteenth and seventeenth centuries was unwilling or unable to exploit their achievement.

Technological and economic backwardness was one aspect of the relative decline in the importance of Italy during modern times. There was still inventiveness in plenty, but new knowledge was not organized mathe-matically or applied in practice with enough system. Leonardo's sketchbooks are full of insights into the new world of hydraulic power, the steam engine and the flying machine, but his attempts to employ his know-ledge as an effective engineer were either half-hearted or outrageously impractical. The tactless and essen-tially unnecessary condemnation by the Church of Galileo was another sign of the times, for in this less expansive age speculative science was not encouraged. Long after the Dutch had pioneered an altogether new type of ocean navigation, oared galleys continued to be built for the Italian navies. Agricultural methods and tools changed little or not at all when they were being revolutionized in northern Europe. Italy, it is true, lacked the raw materials to compete in the new environment created by an industrial revolution. Even the tin needed for Renaissance bronzes had been im-ported from England. Italy had individual skilled crafts-manship in abundance, but not the water power, not the canals, not the coal and iron which were going to trans-form the whole globe. Suddenly she found herself at a tremendous disadvantage. Even the nature of her phy-sical geography was unconducive to the road-building

which was indispensable for creating a larger internal market and a more immediate sense of *italianità*.

Nor, as the population suddenly began to increase, could Italy produce enough food for her needs. Her wealth in ancient and medieval times had made people forget their economic dependence on the outside world and the difficulty of using much of her mountainous land for agricultural purposes. The countries of the Medi-terranean have always been close to famine. By 1550 we find that the feeding of the bishops at the Council of Trent was a serious problem. How to pay for imported food was indeed shortly to become a regular preoccu-pation of nearly every Italian government. Locusts, a hot sirocco, unexpectedly heavy rains or wheat rust, might at any moment create real starvation. This was an important cause of the continual peasant unrest, of the tension between countryside and town, between shepherds and farmers, mountaineers and plainsmen, that kept rural areas unnecessarily poor and always on the verge of revolution. In a country where agricul-ture provided most of the national income, it did not leave much capital for investment in art on the same scale as before. Still less was there much left over for the conquest of political power in the fierce competition between nation states.

Political differences and even civil wars nevertheless did not at any time destroy the feeling among at least the intellectuals of the peninsula that they had an essential quality in common. Even those who served other nations and died in exile knew that they were Italians, and indeed the feeling of oppression by Spanish, French and Austrian governments had the effect of making *italianità* the obvious expression of a widely mixed bag of political discontents.

It has been the experience of almost all countries that a common language is the surest binding force and the clearest evidence for the existence of a nation. In Italy the Tuscan dialect gradually emerged as the national language. This was due in the first place to Dante and Petrarch, reinforced later by the writings of Boccaccio, Machiavelli, Michelangelo and Galileo, all of whom came from this one region and possessed remarkable gifts in either prose or poetry. Tuscan had to contend for a long time not only with Latin but with a dozen other regional dialects whose current use made most Italians quite unintelligible to one another. The influence of Greek was still clear in the Calabrian dialect, that of Arabic in Sicilian, and Spanish in Sardinian. Only one Italian in twenty was Italian-speaking at the time of national unification in 1861, and at the start of the twentieth century the State schools were still often using dialect as the general medium of instruction. As late as the 1950s, more than two-thirds of Italians normally spoke in dialect. Quite apart from this, French was still used in Piedmont, German in the Italian Tyrol, and Slavonic in Venice by many people who had not been wholly assimilated.

This diversity of speech was of course the chief symptom and the most obvious cause of regional separateness. In some areas a lively dialect literature has continued to grow down to our own day. Except in Tuscany the Italian language was for a long time the language only of intellectuals, something written rather than spoken. The art of the novel, for example, was made especially hard by the fact that the language of ordinary speech could not be rendered in generally intelligible prose, while the written language of Italian, to those who understood it, sounded cumbrous and stilted. To the Venetian playwright, Goldoni, in the eighteenth century, as to the Lombard Manzoni and the Sicilian Verga in the nineteenth, this fact presented very special problems. Alessandro Manzoni, after considering briefly whether Milanese or Venetian could be made a more widely used literary medium, set himself late in life to learn and propagate the use of Tuscan, and the enormous success of the revised edition in the 1840s of his novel, *I promessi sposi*, was worth more to Italian patriotism than any battle of the Risorgimento.

With the spread of education, the experience of the Napoleonic wars, and the arrival of a fashionable liberalism and romanticism in the early nineteenth century, gradually the sense of belonging to a shared culture became part of the common inheritance of a wider and wider group of people, and at last it was possible to translate the vague aspirations of a Dante and a Machiavelli into practical politics. Mazzini, the greatest prophet of nationality, addressed himself directly to the common people, and in the face of every kind of opposition from his own countrymen and others, often in the teeth of the facts, he dedicated his life to preaching to ordinary Italians that their country must be united. In Mazzini's view municipal rivalry had been the great cause of economic, social and political backwardness, but a united nation would

change Italians into a 'Messiah people', whose destiny was to initiate a new epoch and once again make Rome the moral centre of the civilized world. After the Italy of the Roman Emperors, and the Italy of the medieval Popes, there was to be a Third Italy of the people. Much of what he said was nonsense, but it was an inspired nonsense, which restored the sense of self-confidence that had for so long been lacking; and by 1861 it had succeeded in preparing a sufficient number of people to accept the united kingdom which Cavour and Garibaldi won by diplomacy and force of arms. When Mazzini died – tragically as a fugitive from his own people and living under the assumed name of John Brown – Italy could once again claim to be one of the great powers of Europe and Rome was the capital of a nation as well as of Christendom.

In the years since the Risorgimento Italy has continued to make her own special contribution to the history of the western world. Sometimes, as in an earlier period, individualism led to a political anarchy which made many Italians despair of liberal parliamentarism. Yet at the same time names of Italians were prominent in every field of human endeavour: to single out even a long list of them would be merely invidious. On the one hand an anarchic individualism finally led to the rise of Fascism; on the other hand the same individualism made Italian Fascism for all its horrors little more than a paper tiger. 'I am the most disobeyed man in history,' said Mussolini. But other would-be Italian tyrants had said much the same in their day, and for the same reason.

No doubt it would be wrong to regard Fascism as a parenthesis in Italian history, a mere episode unconnected with the struggle for national unity. But nor should its significance be exaggerated. Mussolini's twenty-three years of power are no longer a subject merely for political reprobation; they can be studied as history, and a period of history which had important results. Politics aside, however, it is essentially an uninteresting and unrewarding period to dwell upon. Once free government had been restored in 1945, it is astonishing to see how the energies which Mussolini had suppressed were suddenly reactivated. Once again the challenge of the barbarians had been met and overcome. Individualism was again encouraged. A false view of history, which thought in terms of racialism and imperialism, was repudiated, and the legacy of many centuries was brought to bear in a more hopeful direction for Italy and the world.

ANCIENT ITALY   FROM PREHISTORY TO 476 AD

Michael Grant

Italy, inhabited for hundreds of thousands of years, comes into history in the first millennium BC as the land of the Etruscans, Italic and other tribes, Greek and Carthaginian colonists. Influenced by Greece and, through Greece, by the civilizations of the near east, the gifted but bloodthirsty Etruscans, organized in loosely federated city-states in Tuscany and Umbria, converted these influences into something profoundly original and individual, giving Italy its first great native civilization. The Etruscans, sometimes in alliance and sometimes in conflict with the vast Carthaginian, semitic empire centring on Palermo, clashed with the Greek settlers on the southern Italian coast. The Greater Greece of these colonists from all over the motherland became a network of independent city-states which contributed brilliant poetry, philosophy, architecture, science and coinage to Hellenism. The beginnings of Rome are legendary; uniting at this fortunately situated trading post on the Tiber the Latins and Sabines created a confederacy which in the course of three centuries, by diplomacy and military skill, law and engineering, inexorably subjugated the rest of Italy. Even more significant to the five-hundred-year span of the Republic, was Rome's success in establishing the first stable and well-balanced constitution of antiquity. But with imperial expansion on a Mediterranean scale, political as well as economic problems became acute, and power rivalries led to civil war that ended in autocracy, temporarily under Sulla and Caesar and on a permanent basis under Augustus. The Principate established by him lasted for five centuries, of which the last three brought immense prosperity to Italy. But when the Empire became a prize contended by its own generals, Rome lost its unique status and was rivalled as imperial capital by Milan and Ravenna, while paganism and the mystery religious gradually gave way to Christianity. When Constantine moved to Byzantium, Italy became a provincial territory of the empire it had created.

Italy without the Romans

Geography has placed special obstacles in the way of Italian unity. The islands have often had histories of their own. The Alpine frontier, too, has been described as a splendid traitor, since its passes (sixteen now, half as many in antiquity) have often made it ineffective as a bulwark. Inside the peninsula three-quarters of the land is a continuation of the European mountain zone, its unification retarded by the Apennines, which extend southwards into an irregular series of ridges and limestone massifs separated by gorges. Only one-fifth of the country is plain; two-thirds of this is the fertile Po valley, transitional between the Mediterranean climate and central Europe's more rainy weather. The other most notable plainland is the dual region of Latium and Campania, around Rome and to its south: ventilated by moist south-westerly winds, fertilized by volcanic ash just before the beginning of history, its soil intractable enough to challenge and invite an energetic response. Rivers, except the Po, Tiber and Arno, are brief, fierce and capricious. And there is a lack of harbours—especially to the east, nearest Greece, from which civilisation had to come.

Palaeolithic remains are found in the south-east near Otranto, in the north-west (Liguria), and near the later

Boldly carved hunting scenes like this relief have been unearthed in the early Iron Age cemeteries between Pesaro and Novilara. Similar finds have been made across the Adriatic in Istria.

Twenty-five thousand years ago these 'Venuses', as they are called because of their monumental femininity, were made over a vast area from South Russia to France. This example from Italy was found at Savignano (Panaro).

A hut-shaped burial urn for the ashes of the dead, from an early Iron Age cemetery at Grottaferrata. Such sites in the Alban Hills near Rome date from the ninth century BC onwards, the time when several of Rome's hills were also settled—no doubt with huts like this.

Above Canopic, or human-shaped, cinerary urns of the seventh century BC are a feature of the arts of Chiusi (Clusium), which developed as a leading Etruscan centre later than the more southerly cities of Caere and Vulci.

Left A tribal chieftain with staff and rough cloak. These Sardinian bronze statuettes are uniquely informative about the customs and clothing of the non-classical world during the early first millennium BC.

Posidonia (Paestum), founded about 600 BC by Greek settlers on the flat Lucanian plain, still has
the ruins of superb early Doric temples. The so-called Temple of Ceres (c 530 BC) is seen here from
the fifth century 'Temple of Neptune'.

Right Bronze statuette of mounted warrior, *c* 550 BC, from Grumentum in Lucania, one of the numerous settlements established by the Greeks in the south of Italy.

The relief of a girl offering a cock and a libation, *c* 450 BC, comes from Locri, in the toe of Italy, founded by Locrians from Central Greece. These small clay plaques were placed as offerings in temples and shrines.

site of Rome. Comparison of the earliest and the latest of these palaeolithic objects has prompted the reflection that there was very little material progress in nearly half a million years: 98 per cent of the human span, so far, upon earth.

The first decisive advance came in the mid-third millennium BC, when neolithic peoples (conceivably influenced from North Africa or Spain) no longer flaked and chipped their implements, but ground or polished them. Pottery was made, though not yet on the wheel, and a needle was invented with an eyelet. Passo di Corvo, near Foggia, is probably the largest known neolithic site in Europe.

Copper came to Italy in the second half of the third millennium BC, though it did not supersede stone tools to any great extent. This chalcolithic epoch, continuing after 2000 BC and apparently coinciding with the introduction of cremation, is represented in the southerly parts of central Italy; and its northern manifestations included dwellings raised above piles (palafitte) on the lakes and swamps which then abounded in the valley of the Po.

Later peoples, who introduced bronze, again lived in pile-dwellings – on what had become dry land by now (c 1600). This has been called the 'terramare' culture, from the rich heaps of compost or black earth (terra marna) which survive from such settlements. Those, however, are only characteristic of the Po valley – which was perhaps subject to Transalpine influences – and there are other bronze-age remains all the way down to Taranto. Some of them, notably in Liguria, indicate that waggons and ox-drawn ploughs were in use.

The progress of the Italian islands during these epochs was striking and peculiar. The Stentinello culture of Sicily – named after one of its fortified villages – employed an agrarian economy, pottery bearing imprinted designs, sling bullets, and tools of flint and obsidian, a product of the strategically placed Aeolian (Lipari) islands. Bronze-age cemeteries in southeastern Sicily such as Castelluccio display elaborate burials in rock-cut graves, continuing until 1500 – 1400 BC. Sicilian harbours, unlike most of those on the mainland, looked out towards the Aegean, and were enriched by commercial and artistic contacts with the Mycenaean world. Sicilian finds also reveal analogies with the vigorous cultures of Spain.

The earliest known dwellings of Sardinia contain flint implements and a few bronze and stone ornaments of Aegean type. The Sardinians call them *Domus de Janas*, or witches' houses. Then the islanders began to build their huge, many-storeyed, polygonal basalt watch-towers or *nuraghi*, such as those grouped round Barumini (c 1270). From c 950 to 500 BC, as sea-borne traffic increased, their constructions evolved a new sophistication and complexity. Large parts of the island were now studded with great many-towered fortresses possessing curtain walls, parapets, terraces and massive central keeps – the most imposing monuments to survive from prehistoric Europe.

Iron appeared in the Po valley soon after 1000 BC. Its utilisers practised cremation like their bronze-age forerunners in the same area. They correspond to the early iron-age Hallstatt culture across the Alps, and may well have been immigrants, or the descendants of immigrants, from Bohemia and Hungary. Within a few hundred years Bologna became a flourishing producer of bronze and iron exports. A nearby settlement, Villanova, has misleadingly been allowed to give its name to Italian iron-age cultures in general. But the early iron-age communities of Italy pushed down the east coast as far as Rimini, where they seem to have been stopped by peoples who still practised the pre-metal-age (neolithic) custom of inhumation; though racial differences, or similarities, can rarely be deduced from burial customs. In any case, the iron-users appear to have been forced westwards, and so they settled in Tuscany and Latium, extending as far towards the south as the Alban Hills. At least by the eleventh century BC they were using that marshy depression between hills, which later became the Roman Forum, for the burial of urns containing the ashes of their dead.

These settlers in the centre of the peninsula spoke an Indo-European language divided into two distinguishable groups of dialects – the branch that came to prevail in coastal Latium and developed the language subsequently known as Latin, and the Sabellian (Oscan, Umbrian) tongues spoken by less advanced tribes which occupied the hill-top villages of the central and southern Apennines. These peoples said 'pod' when the Latins said 'quod', a difference also found between the Brythonic and Goidelic Celts who were their distant relations.

In north-western Italy, the Ligurians are among the many puzzles that perturb students of origins. They acquired Indo-European speech, but the archaeologist can trace no abrupt cultural changes, and the Ligurian hillmen of historic times may possibly have been descendants of neolithic peoples, thrust back into the mountains by later arrivals. In the north-eastern extremities of the peninsula, the Latin type of Indo-European tongue prevailed among the Veneti, between the Adige and the head of the Adriatic. Este (Ateste) in particular became the centre of a flourishing iron-age community from about 900 BC, importing metal skills from the Danubian area and gradually superseding Bologna.

Further down the east coast, the area of Picenum (Rimini – Vasto) had a long neolithic and cuprolithic prehistory. Then, missing out the bronze age, it developed a distinctive iron-using culture. Large eighth-century cemeteries are full of weapons reflecting a warlike, wealthy ruling class, conservative in their practice of inhumation. Concerning 'Illyrian' incursions or influences or infiltrations from across the Adriatic there have been endless theories, hampered by varying definitions of who the Illyrians were; but there do appear to have been contacts with the Balkans. Again, if we move southwards down the Italian coast and come to the Messapians in the heel of the peninsula, it does seem legitimate to connect the tribe of the Iapyges with the Iapudes the other side of the Adriatic. We have some two hundred Messapic inscriptions to work upon, and (like the 150 left to us by the Veneti) they are usually thought to belong to an Indo-European tongue.

From the Sicels, who gave their name to Sicily, only a very few inscriptions survive. These too are apparently Indo-European. But 'Sicel', 'Siculi' have become almost meaningless words, since there are nearly a score of conflicting ideas about their origins. Whoever they were, they joined for mutual protection in large communities such as Pantalica, west of the later Syracuse; probably it was the legendary Hybla, famous for its honey. Little of Pantalica survives except 5,000 tombs, but the contents of these show that it flourished from the thirteenth to eighth centuries BC. Sicels also apparently inhabited not only these Sicilian regions but the toe of Italy. (Since the middle ages this has been known as Calabria, formerly the name of the heel.) Its southern portion gave the name of Italia to the whole peninsula; it is probably a graecised form of 'Vitelia', meaning 'the land of calves'.

It was, however, the Etruscans, 'Rasenna' to themselves, who from c 800 BC developed Italy's first great civilisation in their loosely federated city states of Tuscany and Umbria. Ruled first by monarchs and then by republican regimes, they derived their strength from copper mines, and particularly from the iron of Elba; and they introduced the Italians to a formidable new war-weapon, the horse-chariot.

In the seventh century BC the cities of southern Etruria, each not far from a harbour, were particularly rich in resources and sea-power – Caere, Vulci, and Tarquinii, the country's religious centre. Then Clusium, farther to the north, became strong. But there were also important Etruscan-controlled regions beyond both the extremities of Etruria itself. As far away as Campania (the area—south-east of the present Campagna—of which Naples is the modern capital), there was an Etruscan federation dominated by Capua. In the Po valley, too, there were powerful Etruscan communities. Bologna, settled under the name of Felsina, became their chief city north of the Apennines; and another strongpoint was Melpum (Milan).

The Etruscans were a piratical and dangerous people. Blood-thirsty games seem to be one of the many institutions that they handed down to Rome. They also possessed pathologically unpleasant religious customs, including divination by animal entrails and human sacrifice; and they became morbidly interested in posthumous punishments and tortures. Their language, to a large extent incomprehensible, seems to be non-Indo-European. Their racial origins are another well-known mystery: did they or did they not comprise immigrants from the Near East? But the racial origins of many communities in Italy (as elsewhere) are irremediably obscure.

At all events the Etruscans' exceptionally inquisitive artistic taste seized upon the art-forms which successively came to their notice, whether by trade or immigration, from the orient.

Not only did they absorb these art-forms, but they absorbed them creatively and transformingly: first bringing life and vigour to middle eastern styles – Assyrian, Syrian, Phoenician, Anatolian (c 650–600 BC) – and then modifying archaic Greek artistic models by an un-classical tension, spontaneity and dynamism which were peculiarly Etruscan. Political and economic eclipse came to Etruria before the classical maturity of Periclean Greece could exercise its influence. Yet what survived and developed instead was a complex of traditions based on their own peculiar experiences. One of the results was an expressive, concrete, realistic portraiture which, through Rome, became Etruria's most durable and influential legacy to the medieval and modern worlds.

Opposite A gold pendant of the late sixth century BC representing the river god Achelous as a bull-headed man. Inspired by a Greek theme, this minute ornamental mask is a masterpiece of the Etruscans' unrivalled technique of granulation in goldwork.

The Etruscans clashed with Greek settlers on the Italian coasts. Already from *c* 1600 BC Minoan (Cretan) and Mycenaean traders had arrived both in the islands round Italy and on mainland sites such as Scoglio del Tonno opposite Taranto. But thereafter, as Greece sank into a 'dark age', contact was broken.

Vases found in excavations indicate that it was renewed early in the eighth century BC. Before long the explosive economic and population problems of Hellas caused Greeks not only to trade in Italy but to settle there. Eretria and Chalcis, cities of the Aegean island of Euboea, sent colonists round to the west coast island of Pithecussae (Ischia), and to the steep, defensible acropolis of Cyme or Cumae (*c* 750), accessible to the coast and to Etruscan-controlled inland trade.

Soon afterwards other Euboeans sought and found places to settle in eastern Sicily. At the site with the most opportune harbour for their commerce, they founded Naxos (Capo Schiso); Leontini and Catana were established nearby. The straits of Messana (Messina) received further colonies at Zancle on the Sicilian, and Rhegium (Reggio di Calabria) on the mainland, shore. Corinth founded what very quickly became the greatest city of the western Greeks, Syracuse (*c* 733), with the best harbour of all; and, although the colonies were politically independent of their founders and motherlands, the Corinthians almost monopolized western commerce for 150 years, until Athenian traders superseded them. Another region of Greece, Achaea in the Peloponnese, at an early date provided colonists for the eastward-facing zones of south Italy. Pre-eminent among their settlements was Sybaris (*c* 720), chosen for its rich plain and its accessibility to both seas. Achaean settlers at Sybaris, Croton and Metapontum built roads which enabled traders to avoid sailing round the toe of Italy. Fine, though imitative, temples and sculptural reliefs and handsome silver coins appeared in Italy and Sicily from early in the sixth century BC.

Away to the north and west were other Greek colonies such as Massilia (Marseilles, *c* 600) and then Alalia in Corsica (Aleria, *c* 560), founded by emigrants from Phocaea on the coast of Asia Minor. These settlements not only traded with the Etruscans, but confronted them in a fashion that they found distasteful. The implied bid for a Greek monopoly of these seas was equally unattractive to the second great western power, Semitic Carthage on the sea-board of what is now Tunisia. Themselves colonists of the Phoenicians who,

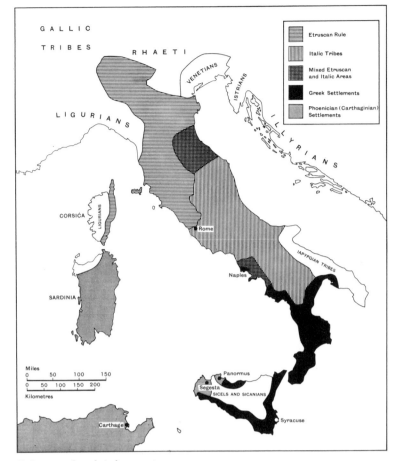

Italy: seventh and sixth centuries BC

from their Levantine cities of Tyre and Sidon, had dominated the Mediterranean while Greece was still in its dark age, the Carthaginians in the sixth century BC took over the Phoenician positions in western Sicily. With their capital at Panormus (Palermo), they began to establish their empire, which lasted for three centuries; no city state had ever created such an empire before. It was founded in order to guarantee the maintenance of Carthage's trade-routes to mineral-rich Spain – just as, at the other end of the Mediterranean, it was the cardinal policy of Athens to keep open the corn-route to the Black Sea.

Under the quasi-monarchic Magonid dynasty (later succeeded by an aristocratic regime) Carthage allied itself with the Etruscans in order to eliminate Greek influence from Italian lands and waters. The naval superiority of the Phocaeans was broken by the two non-Greek powers in a battle off Alalia (*c* 535), which confirmed Carthaginian domination of Sardinia and brought the coast of Corsica under Etruscan control.

Nevertheless during the next sixty years Hellenic Cumae, in various coalitions, got the better of Etruria; and Carthage never succeeded in ejecting the Greeks

Opposite One of the frescoes depicting dancers from the Tomb of the Bacchant, at Tarquinia, *c* 520 BC. Music played a large part in the Etruscan way of life.

from eastern Sicily. In the latter region, powerful dictatorships were founded early in the fifth century BC at Syracuse, Acragas (Agrigento), Messana and Himera. Himera called upon the Carthaginians to come to its help; but they were heavily defeated beside its walls by Gelon of Syracuse and Theron of Acragas. Gelon's successor Hiero helped to put an end to the Etruscan menace, though war between Greeks and Carthaginians in Sicily remained for centuries chronic and indecisive.

Yet Syracuse, moving from dictatorship to democracy, developed an immensely prosperous economy. Like the whole of Italian Greek civilization, it was sometimes showy and vulgar. But it produced artistic masterpieces – notably the city's brilliantly designed coinage. Intellectual triumphs were by no means new among the western Greeks. Before 600 BC Stesichorus of Himera had created novel and glorious worlds for lyric poetry. In c 531 the philosopher, mathematician and political medicine-man Pythagoras had moved from Samos in the Aegean to south Italian Croton, which he ruled as Calvin ruled Geneva. Croton obliterated its rival Sybaris in c 510. Elea or Velia, further west, produced Parmenides, who with his fellow-citizen Zeno (the alleged founder of dialectic) rejected the ostensible diversity of the cosmos, substituting a concept of eternal immobility. But then, in the mid-fifth century, Empedocles of Acragas took the contrary view that the universe is a perpetual battleground of opposites – thus anticipating the dualist heresies that sapped medieval Christendom. Empedocles was also known as the inventor of rhetoric, basis of the literary educational system that pervaded the classical civilizations. The most spectacular rhetorician, however, was another Sicilian, Gorgias of Leontini, who during his long life (c 483–376) did much to polish Greek prose. He contributed as well to the current 'sophistical' attack on too easy beliefs, by suggesting that nothing exists – but that if it does there is no way of knowing what it is.

Gorgias was also an early believer in the doctrine that Greeks should unite. The unrealizable nature of this pan-Hellenism was proved on Sicilian soil when, during the Peloponnesian War, an Athenian expeditionary force sent against the Syracusans met with the catastrophe (415–13) which Thucydides so harrowingly described. Not long afterwards Dionysius I (406–367) plundered Etruria and occupied Corsica. Exploiting all the arts of dictatorial appeal to the proletariat, he made Syracuse for a time into the largest empire the Greek world had ever known.

The Rise of Rome

Meanwhile Etruscan influence and rule helped Rome to become a city. Strategically and to some extent defensibly placed, its hills were not too far from the salt deposits at the Tiber's mouth; and they were at the river's lowest crossing-point, linking the two sub-areas of the fertile coastal plain – Etruria and Latium. The habitations on these Roman hills at first developed as normal, distinct hill-top towns. Archaeological evidence suggests partial occupation during the second millennium BC. Then, though not necessarily in direct continuity, there followed iron-age villages upon the same slopes and crests, analogous to earlier counterparts (c 1100–1000) at Tolfa (S. Etruria) and on the Alban Mount.

By c 800 BC there were settlements on several of the hills of Rome: the Palatine – regarded later as the city's original nucleus – on which the most important cremation tombs are to be found, as well as traces of huts; the Esquiline, site of the most numerous graves, almost all of inhumation type; the Quirinal; and perhaps also the Caelian. In each case, apparently, the first inhabitants were speakers of Latin or of an earlier stage of that language. But then probably the northern spurs also received immigrants, from the second of the two main strains in the Indo-European-speaking Italic population, the Umbro-Sabellian group (p. 21). These settlers belonged to its westernmost branch, namely the Sabines, who thus came to form the second main constituent in the historic Roman population.

Tradition tells of the union of Latins and Sabines, effected by an eighth century 'Romulus'. Archaeology, however, speaks decisively of a true creation and urbanization of Rome in c 575 BC, when the marsh-logged cemetery was reclaimed and laid out as a market-place (Forum) serving several of the hills between which it lay. The legends, in which the city was so rich, mirror a period of Etruscan domination when they speak of the two monarchs named Tarquin – founders of the great sixth-century BC Capitoline temple of Jupiter, the most splendid shrine in Italy outside Greek lands. Probably there were more than the seven or eight Roman kings of tradition. One of these, sandwiched between the Tarquins, was Rome's quasi-magical second founder Servius Tullius, a modernizer (like the slightly earlier Athenian Solon) who curbed rising aristocratic anarchy with a middle-class 'hoplite' infantry army.

Two warriors in helmets support the dead body of a comrade, so forming the handle of a fourth century BC engraved bronze casket from Praeneste (Palestrina).

A sixth-century bronze statuette of an Etruscan ploughing with two steers. He wears hat, tunic, hide, and perhaps boots, and his plough is made of a one-piece wooden share-beam, metal share and wooden handle.

Roman military equipment is worn by the warriors, probably representing Hermes and Hercules, on this ivory plaque from Praeneste, third century BC. It was originally painted and adorned a wooden casket.

Interior of the Tomb of the Leopards, Tarquinia, showing frescoes of banqueters and musicians. Tarquinia, the religious centre of Etruria, is famous for its underground burial chambers, which provide most of our knowledge of Etruscan painting, especially of about 500 B C.

Top right Well preserved grave mounds at Cerveteri (Caere), a great Etruscan centre close to Rome. The city attained its highest prosperity after 700 BC, but the thousands of tombs of its necropolis, one of the most impressive monuments of the Mediterranean world, were built over many centuries.

Vulci, the greatest Etruscan city-state, reached its peak in the later sixth century BC, but four hundred years later was still producing important art works like the celebrated François Tomb. This savage picture from the tomb shows the double fratricide of Polynices and Eteocles.

This war elephant (with baby) carrying two armoured soldiers in a turret on its back portrays one of the twenty brought to Italy by King Pyrrhus of Epirus; they were said to be responsible for his victory at Heraclea. Early third-century BC painted clay dish from Capena (Leprignano).

Opposite Priam (seated) and Antenor, represented on the François vase from Chiusi, *c* 570–65 BC, which was signed by its Greek painter and potter. Etruscan finds of Greek pottery have been of outstanding importance.

These are saga-encrusted topics, and so is the revolution which supposedly drove out Tarquin 'the Proud' in c 510 and established a Roman Republic. Much is controversial, yet it does seem that Etruscan control ceased, here as elsewhere, at about that time or soon afterwards and that the Roman monarchy gave way to the two consuls who continued to be elected each year (except for dictators in the occasional emergency) until the end of the Republic 500 years later – and even under the imperial regime which became its successor.

During the first two and a half centuries of its Republic, Rome carried out two vast tasks which add up to the most startling achievements of the ancient world. One of these achievements was the solution of an internal problem. Patricians and plebeians had become separated, at least by the early days of the Republic, and not improbably before the monarchy had come to an end. In the transitional period of the fifth century BC came the legal code of the Twelve Tables, which by its concise and penetrating precision foreshadows the whole marvellous heritage of Roman law. These Twelve Tables reveal a combination of primitive religious practices, aristocratic influence, and a trend towards liberalism. This last is evident in clauses on sale, which reflect external commercial relations, notably with Greek traders on the Aventine hill.

To the Aventine, also, more than once seceded the rebellious plebeians, as they fought for office, economic improvement, and relief from debts and from the imprisonment and slavery to which such debts could lead. The youthful state was almost riven in half. Yet the rebels gained their way through their own representatives, the 'tribunes of the people', who successfully asserted the plebeians' claim to an Assembly of their own. In the following century plebeians achieved admission to the main offices of state (366, 351), and when their Assembly's decisions were given the force of law (c 287) popular sovereignty had come into being. Thus the Romans worked out by constitutional means the solution of a problem which the Greeks, although quicker of wit, had found insoluble. The 'tribunes' attended – and co-operated with – the Senate in a spirit of mutual compromise which the world had not seen before.

This success was one of the causes of early Rome's other outstanding performance. This was the gradual but remorselessly complete reduction of all neighbouring peoples as far as the Po in the north and the Greek territories to the south. After repeated wars of attrition, Etruscans, Latins and Umbro-Sabellian tribes alike succumbed. The strongest of these last were the Samnites, who were finally subjugated in 272.

Gibbon has sarcastic things to say about an empire ostensibly won in self-defence. And it is certain that skilful diplomacy ranked high among Roman assets. Another was a remorseless perseverance – often after initial, amateurish catastrophes. Always ready to learn new military tactics from enemies, the Romans seemed quite unable to accept defeat as final; and their discipline was extraordinary. A principal method of their aggrandizement was colonization. This started in the later sixth century BC with boundary fortresses founded in association with the Latins, as bulwarks against the menacing Volscian (Umbro-Sabellian) tribesmen who had settled south-east of the Alban Hills. The fourth century BC witnessed a further crop of settlements planned to meet state needs. Although themselves reduced to subordinate status (338), the Latins continued to contribute contingents to autonomous colonies, federal in name but in fact extensions of Roman power. One of them, now excavated, was Alba Fucens (303), an advanced base in the Second Samnite War, settled by 3,000 families and dominating five valleys. Moreover, because of reluctance to maintain a permanent fleet, purely Roman colonies of about 300 families were founded to garrison the coastline at Ostia, Antium (Anzio) and Tarracina (329). The structure of these towns was methodical, regimented, arbitrary: such was the cost of peace.

The other great weapon of expansion was the Roman road, ruthlessly straight and effective. The Via Latina had reached Cales (Calvi), the first Latin colony in Campania, by 334. The Via Appia led to Capua (312), and the Via Flaminia to Ariminum (Rimini); both were later extended. Before long there was a great network of roads. The pioneer aqueducts had also been built, the Aqua Appia (312–308) and the Anio Vetus (279–69) – pioneers of many others which brought water to Rome, at first mainly underground, and then upon elevated arches.

By 260 BC the confederacy had spread over 52,000 square miles – a larger area than all contemporary Mediterranean empires except that of the Seleucids in the middle east. Rome's system of government was clever and patient. Conspiracy against her was prevented by agreements on a bilateral or unilateral (never multilateral) basis. Italians were rather grudgingly awarded either the full Roman franchise or an incomplete version of it. Citizens paid direct taxes; allies contributed

Opposite A wall-painting from Paestum in Lucania showing a Samnite soldier returning from battle. This probably dates from the fourth century BC, when Samium was at the height of its power and defeated both the Romans (at the Caudine Forks) and the Greeks.

military service which supplied half of Rome's armed force – though they had no say in deciding peace or war. But they escaped detailed interference, and enjoyed some of the loot. As the Latin language and Roman law lowered cultural boundaries, the romanization of Italy proceeded.

To the north of the Roman confederacy there were now Gauls, who early in the fourth century BC had seized Rome itself (apart perhaps from its Capitoline citadel) before withdrawing with a ransom. These marauding bands, lacking coherent purpose, were offshoots of the vast Celtic nucleus in central Europe, representing the La Tène culture of the later iron age. Utilising their rich metallurgical resources, they ornamented their chariots and weapons and harnesses with a lively rhythmical art which, borrowing from Scythians, Orientals and Etruscans, reduced classical motifs to curvilinear abstractions. Their contact with the Etruscans erupted into violence when the Celtic Insubres, entering Italy by the Ticinus valley, captured and occupied Etruscan Melpum (Milan). Then the Boii, who reputedly reached Italy across the Great St Bernard Pass, pushed beyond the Po and took Felsina (Bologna). Though the Veneti beat off Gaulish attackers, the populations of the Po basin had mostly succumbed before 300; the Senones, last to settle, ousted the Umbrians from the 'Gallic Land' between Rimini and Ancona. Though defeated by the Gauls at Arretium (Arezzo) in 284, Rome won in the end, but not completely for nearly another hundred years. In the meanwhile the Gauls were ceasing to be noisy naked warriors and became good peasant farmers.

In the Greek south, Syracuse had only fitfully maintained, against Carthage and internal dissensions, the formidable grandeur of Dionysius I. After a period of democracy under a Corinthian general, Timoleon (344 – 37), the dictatorial violence of Agathocles (317 – 289) defeated its own ends. Far greater was the city's distinction as birthplace of Theocritus (c 310), who, moving to the world's new cultural capital Alexandria, conceived the novel *genre* of pastoral poetry, partly from his rural Sicilian memories. And another Syracusan was Archimedes (c 287), the outstanding mathematician and engineer of antiquity.

In one of its periodic scares caused by Carthage, Syracuse appealed to Pyrrhus, the half-Hellenic king of Epirus (280). Another appeal came to him, but this time directed against Rome rather than Carthage, from the most powerful Greek city in southern Italy, Taras

(Tarentum). A Spartan foundation (c 700) governed by a moderate democracy in which fishermen predominated, Taras traded far and wide, as finds of its splendid gold coins as far as the Po valley indicate. The rich Tarentine pastures produced the best fleeces in Italy, which were made into fine woollen cloths and dyed with purple from mussel-beds in the city's harbour. Taras' acclimatization and knowledge of vegetables and fruits were among the most lasting gifts of the Italian Greeks to civilisation. Rising as Croton declined, Taras had been at its height under the fourth-century administration of Archytas – philosopher, mathematician, theorist of music, and reputedly the founder of mechanics.

A hundred years later the western Greeks' most dangerous enemy was no longer Carthage but Rome; and the first Greek city to find Roman proximity perilous was Taras. Pyrrhus invaded Sicily and Italy (280 – 72) on its behalf. But he was a chivalrous adventurer without staying power, and did not save the western Greeks from gradual Roman domination.

Nor did the mighty clashes between Rome and Carthage which followed. After the first of these Punic Wars (264 – 41, 218 – 201), in which the Romans had inaugurated their navy, the Carthaginians lost Sicily and Sardinia. The Second Punic War was Rome's severest trial; Hannibal inflicted shattering defeats (Trebia, Trasimene, Cannae), and remained in Italy for fifteen years. But the Roman confederacy held together, a Carthaginian relief force was annihilated on the river Metaurus (207), and the final outcome – of which the principal architect was Scipio Africanus – saw the elimination of Carthage as a major power (202). An earlier casualty of the war was western Greek independence; for Syracuse, which had finally backed the wrong horse, fell to Rome in 212. The same fate befell the relatively few Italian cities which had taken advantage of Rome's crisis to rebel – for example Campania's rich industrial metropolis Capua (211).

An incidental effect of the Punic Wars had been to broaden the minds of Roman soldiers, as they marched and fought and sacked. In particular, some of them were introduced to Greek culture. Accordingly, the Victory Games after the first Punic War witnessed the performance of Latin versions of Greek plays, written and produced by a freed slave from Taras who may have been wholly or partially Greek, Livius Andronicus. Ennius, 'father of Roman poetry' and founder of the national epic, was a trilingual (Latin, Greek, Oscan) from Rudiae near Lecce. There were also crude

Left A majestic portrayal of Julius Caesar. In the first century BC Roman portrait sculpture under Greek and native influence achieved the heights which it long maintained.

Right In the masterly propaganda portraiture of Augustus, he was represented variously as monarch, Roman first citizen and Italian individual. Here, pensive and poetic, he is Pontifex Maximus, the title later inherited by the Popes.

Menander, the Greek poet of the New Comedy, is shown talking to a Muse in this relief of the first century BC. His incisive characterization and brilliant handling of the love theme greatly influenced Roman and later comic dramatists.

Some of the victims of the eruption of Vesuvius in AD 79 are seen in casts preserved in the museum of Pompeii. The impressions left by bodies in the deposits of ashes and stones that suffocated and overwhelmed the inhabitants were injected with plaster to form the casts.

Left A death's head, the Wheel of Fate, and other symbols of death figure on this mosaic from Pompeii as if presaging the destruction of the city.

Opposite One of the most noteworthy ancient Italian portrait paintings, from the House of the Terentii at Pompeii, *c* AD 60. The man, who has been identified as Terentius Neo, carries a scroll; his wife holds a stilus and writing tablets.

theatrical traditions in Etruria; and the Umbrian town of Sarsina (Mercato Saraceno) was the birthplace of the supreme Latin comic dramatist, Plautus (c 254 – 184). Miraculously, at so early a date in Latin culture, Plautus transformed the charming, minor-key Athenian New Comedy of Manners into the racing farcical robustness that befitted a Roman audience and their vigorous language. His quieter and more sophisticated successor Terence, reputedly from North Africa, belonged to the circle of the enlightened Scipio Aemilianus, whose protégés also included a decisive figure in the satirical tradition which Romans found so greatly to their taste, Lucilius from Suessa Aurunca (Sessa) on the borders of Campania.

As Rome won extensive conquests overseas culminating in the wealthy province of Asia (West Asia Minor, 133 BC), Italy became a very different sort of place. The rich became much richer and more numerous, and a whole new financial class of 'knights' came into existence, forming joint-stock companies which lucratively farmed taxes for the state. These knights joined the senators as members of the ruling class—though relations soon deteriorated. Senators were ostensibly debarred from such financial operations; but they managed to obtain a good share of the profits. They also went from strength to strength as political managers, their prestige enhanced by the successful wars against Carthage (destroyed in 146 BC) and various Greek states.

From Anarchy to Imperial Prosperity

But meantime the poor in Italy became poorer. The wars had partially depopulated large parts of the country, and small holdings were replaced by enormous ranches on which it was more profitable to graze cattle than to grow cereals. The brutalities callously inflicted upon the huge gangs of slaves who were employed on these estates – mostly prisoners of foreign wars, or their descendants – provoked savage outbreaks by armies of deserters. Large areas were plunged into anarchy so grave that the whole structure of Mediterranean society seemed to be cracking. In Sicily, 70,000 slaves under the Syrian Eunus, taking the royal name Antiochus, temporarily seized several towns, including Tauromenium (Taormina) and Catana (135 – 2). A second slave war (103 – 1), which gravely embarrassed Rome owing to its coincidence with external invasions,

consisted of two separate risings on the south and west coasts of Sicily, under 'King' Salvius and the Cilician Athenion respectively. Finally the Thracian gladiator Spartacus led another revolt throughout the length and breadth of Italy (73 – 1). Again, this was only stamped out by the employment of large Roman armies, one of which cornered Spartacus in Apulia.

Between the first and last of these rebellions, Roman and Italian politics had veered from relative stability into chaos, augmented by the drift of destitute unemployed to the cities. Violence had begun when two enlightened young aristocratic brothers, Tiberius and Gaius Gracchus, sought to relieve agrarian distress by land-laws, which Gaius wanted to follow up by extending the magic circle of Roman citizenship in Italy. But when the Gracchi, more well-intentioned than diplomatic, were both in turn murdered by their opponents, a new and sinister era was in being.

From now on discernible, though fluid, left and right wings replaced the previous free-for-all. And soon large sections of the Roman army started to display allegiance, no longer to the government – which was failing to rise to its new large-scale responsibilities – but to individual generals. In order to suppress a kinglet (Jugurtha) who aimed to succeed Carthage as a North African power, Marius, under protest from the aristocracy, employed a partially volunteer army. His prestige rose again when Italy itself was threatened by two huge migrating waves of Germans, emanating originally from Jutland. After Marius had defeated one of these hordes, the Teutones, at Aquae Sextiae (Aix-en-Provence), the other, the Cimbri, skirted Italy and penetrated the Po valley, where Marius annihilated it at Vercellae (101).

In the disturbed period that followed Rome's unwise neglect of those numerous discontented Italians who did not possess the franchise, there were four years of unparalleled, catastrophic civil strife. In this Social or Marsian War (91 – 87), the rebel coalition established its capital successively at Corfinium (near Pentima), Bovianum Vetus (Bojano) and Aesernia (Isernia). The northerly Apennine tribes fought for citizenship, but as the war went on it became clear that the Oscan-speaking Samnites were striving for the independence they had lost two centuries back. Rome won, by fighting and by quite early conceding (at least in words) the less inflammatory of the points at issue: every man south of the Po received citizenship, and certain rights were extended to those beyond the river.

Yet Rome's own political chiefs also fought each

Opposite A philosopher on a mural fresco from Boscoreale, a villa near Pompeii.
He gazes reflectively at a group (in a neighbouring painting) of the Hellenistic royal personages who encouraged the presence of these learned men at court.

other openly and forcibly as Marius, backed by knights and Italians, and Sulla, with greater senatorial support, contended for a profitable eastern command against Mithridates VI of Pontus. Sulla set an ominous precedent by marching on Rome (88); then, after his withdrawal to the east, the vengeful Marius and Cinna did likewise. Sulla's return from the Levant (83) again plunged Italy into full-scale civil war, in which he and his supporters were victorious near Praeneste (Palestrina) and Faventia (Faenza) and finally in a bloodthirsty holocaust outside Rome's Colline Gate.

Sulla mobilised the ancient emergency office of dictator for quasi-monarchical rule, yet employed it to bolster up the traditional system of senatorial control against his democratic opponents. Then followed the three decades of the Republic's death throes, immortalized by Cicero's letters and speeches. After Pompey had joined Caesar and the millionaire Crassus in the First Triumvirate directed against the traditional Establishment (60), Crassus was killed fighting against the Parthians in Mesopotamia, and Caesar's completion of the conquest of Gaul precipitated the breach between Pompey and himself. Caesar moved into Italy across what was then its border, the river Rubicon ten miles north-west of Rimini; Pompey fell back from Rome to Capua. His supporter Ahenobarbus foolishly allowed himself to be trapped at Corfinium, but Pompey evacuated his army across the Adriatic, and Italy belonged to Caesar. He moved its geographical limits northwards so as to include the Po valley and Cisalpine Gaul.

Caesar's subsequent victorious campaigns are not Italian history; but it was in Italy, at Rome, that he met his death, because the new title *dictator perpetuus*, and all that it implied, was unacceptable even to his own Roman entourage—including Brutus and Cassius whom he had pardoned and favoured.

In the struggle for power that followed, one of the first scenes took place at Mutina (Modena), where Antony besieged a Republican garrison without success (43). But then he allied himself with Caesar's young official heir Octavian (the later Augustus) and with Lepidus. Wiping out some of their political enemies such as Cicero by massacre, and eliminating Brutus and Cassius at the battle of Philippi in Macedonia, this Second Triumvirate divided the Roman world. In Italy—following the example of generals from Sulla onwards—they arbitrarily earmarked the territory of eighteen cities to provide a million acres of land for demobilised soldiers. In order to carry out these allot-

ments Octavian, to whom the task fell, had to starve Antony's brother Lucius into surrender at Perusia (Perugia); but Antony himself conferred with Octavian and reached precarious agreement at Brundusium (Brindisi) and again at Tarentum. Sicily and the adjacent seas were temporarily lost to the late Pompey's son Sextus, whom after major naval hostilities Octavian's admiral Agrippa crushed off Naulochus (Venetico) near the straits of Messina (36).

Six years later, Antony and Cleopatra were defeated and dead, and Octavian master of Egypt's wealth and the whole Roman world. The Republic was at an end; the 'restored Republic', which replaced it concealed the efficient rule of an autocrat, the *princeps* or emperor.

The upheavals of the previous century had left their mark on Italy. The rich—men like Crassus and Atticus—had become very rich indeed. Cicero was not rich but even he found it necessary, in order to maintain political appearances, to live on credit and keep up many mansions. At the other end of the scale the Roman proletariat had become enormous, heavily subsidised by the state and menacingly available to strong-arm politicians. Civil war had inflicted many wounds upon the countryside, and there were extensive changes in landownership. Many of these changes were due to the settlement, first, of about 50,000 – 75,000 destitute Romans (133–109 BC), and then of the ex-soldiers for whom military leaders had provided.

Although not all of these veterans succeeded as farmers, a policy of land-allotment meant that large areas of the Italian mainland—though not Sicily—were reconverted from ranches (for which fewer foreign prisoners of war were now available) into small holdings. Cicero's contemporary Varro, encyclopaedist and agriculturalist, describes the typical farm of his time (c 67–54) as a property of 100 – 200 acres, cultivated intensively, with growing diversification.

Campania now outstripped Etruria as an agricultural centre. Its oil, already a large-scale industry in the previous century, was dispatched overseas from the harbour-city of Puteoli (Pozzuoli). The oil and vines of this region were unequalled, and a century and a half later Italy was reported by Pliny the younger to be producing two-thirds of the finest wines in the world. Soft, delicate wool came from Apulia's grazing lands, and the best of all from the sheep of Tarentum. Wool, as well as honey, was exported from Brundusium.

The densely populated north of Italy, full of rich cities

Painting of a harbour scene from the wall of a house at Stabiae
(Castellamare) which was swallowed up by the eruption of Vesuvius.
The rendering of the passing play of sunlight upon the buildings
anticipates Pissarro and the French Impressionists.

Right Part of a Dionysiac series, probably depicting the initiation
of a bride, this scene belongs to a magnificent painting cycle
of the first century BC which covers several walls of the Villa of the
Mysteries near Pompeii. A seated priestess hears a child read
from a liturgical scroll.

This animated Maenad and Satyr scene, made in honour
of Bacchus (Dionysus), is in marble inlay called *opus sectile*.
The worship of Bacchus, at first repressed by the Senate, became
very popular owing to its promise of immortality.

Left Romulus and Remus suckled by the wolf. The foundation myth is still repeated on this bronze coin of the early Christian empire (fourth century AD).

Right Shown on a coin, the Colosseum, begun by Vespasian in AD 72, was completed and opened in AD 80 during the reign of Titus. No building had a greater influence on the architects of the Renaissance.

and potential Roman soldiers, also abounded in corn, oil, millet, herds, wine and wool. Mutina (Modena) was famous for wool, and the exceptionally wealthy community of Patavium (Padua) spun it into clothing, blankets and rugs for Rome. At the head of the Adriatic, Aquileia exchanged such Italian goods for iron, steel and hides from across the Alps, and controlled the trade passing along the Danube and the Save. Iron from Elba and elsewhere was shipped for manufacture to Puteoli, which exported these products as it had exported the bronzes of Capua. Its imports, larger still, included Sicilian grain (Rome needed 180,000 – 190,000 tons of wheat yearly), Spanish silver, and slaves from the international market on the Aegean isle of Delos. By the end of the Republic all Italian centres were linked by good roads – though Caesar did not live to complete his barge-canal linking Rome, Ostia and Puteoli, or to drain the Pontine marshes and the Fucine Lake.

Marble came from Luna and Carrara, 'Travertine' from Tibur (now Tivoli), and another building stone from Gabii. The second century BC had initiated a revolution in building methods, inspired by Greece but carried through by means of the specific Roman mastery of large spaces and curved surfaces. This talent was given magnificent expression by the newly exploited, thrust-eliminating material of concrete.

Rome was transformed by lofty tenements and by public buildings of all kinds, including temples, bridges, houses, quays, and new aqueducts. The typical, axial town-forum was evolved from Hellenistic models. It comprised colonnaded porticoes, and an aisled and clerestoried *basilica* (market and law-court). The first of these buildings at Rome (184 BC) was due to Cato the elder – usually thought of as a reactionary rather than an innovator. The ornamented Roman ceremonial arch also made its appearance (120). Near the Campanian coast at Pompeii, a township grown rich on the sale of textiles, the earliest identifiable houses display a colonnaded *atrium* recalling the residences of Greek or Italian businessmen on Delos, but un-Greek in the greater symmetry of its design. Pompeii's domed Stabian Baths were small-scale predecessors of countless enormous constructions elsewhere.

Sulla, systematizing the architecture of a large part of Rome, was a great sponsor of these exciting adaptations of Hellenistic ideas. In the reconstructed sanctuary of Fortune at Praeneste (Palestrina) – as on a much smaller scale at pre-Sullan Fasolo and Gabii, and at Cagliari in Sardinia – a whole mountainside was transformed into a dynamic composition of terraces. Another art which rose to remarkable achievements during the last century BC was portrait sculpture. Great hauls of statuary had come in as loot from Volsinii (265), Syracuse, Tarentum and especially Corinth (146). Now, prompted by Hellenistic and Etruscan achievements and by a native Roman tradition of preserving death-masks, Greek and Oriental portraitists exploited the financial resources, the love-hate feelings towards Hellenic culture, and the emphatic physiognomies, of their Roman patrons.

In spite of political anarchy, Roman law had become one of the greatest masterpieces of the human mind, the very principle of an ideal order, conceived in terms of practical, vital common sense and treated with an unprecedentedly scientific technique. Outstanding jurists used Greek ideas to fertilize a national talent Already in the second century BC the Roman *ius civile* began to be overlaid by the *ius gentium* – a composite code pieced together from the usage of surrounding states – and theorists borrowed from concepts of natural law that had been formulated by Stoic philosophers at Athens. But it was the Romans themselves who created a practical tradition, based upon a legal profession and upon a habit of interpreting and applying the laws as each particular instance arose, in accordance with recorded precedents.

Writers gradually emerged to rival in other fields the achievement of the long-dead Latin dramatists. Caesar was a Roman nobleman; Cicero and the historian Sallust came from Arpinum and Amiternum (San Vittorno), respectively, in central Italy. Poetic achievement was largely in the hands of north Italians. The birthplace of Lucretius, the Epicurean who was as fanatical as his master had been mild, is unknown. But Catullus, whose love-poetry is of a lyrical imaginative intensity beyond imitation, came from Verona, and his friends and immediate forerunners, among them Valerius Cato, all stimulated by a two-century-old perfectionist movement from Alexandria, were from the same region.

Octavian's new name (Augustus, 27 BC) carried an odour of sanctity hinting at the new autocracy which successive constitutional settlements framed in carefully Republican terms. Though related to Caesar, Augustus was at heart a bourgeois Italian with tastes derived from his native Velitrae (Velletri).

Although his enormous reorganization of the empire

achieved general prosperity, Rome and Italy – now a concept with national, emotional undertones – were deliberately given the primacy and, amid a huge building programme, flourished unprecedentedly. Agriculture remained the principal industry, and was extended. Supported by a magnificent coinage, commerce and manufacture advanced apace. Italy led the world with new factories for woollen goods in Pompeii and the north; there was great demand for the red pottery of Arretium (Arezzo), the glass blown in Campania, and the metalwork of Rome. Exports increased and luxury imports multiplied, carried over seas that had been made safe and Alpine frontiers where recalcitrant tribes were one after another 'pacified'.

Italian religion, strengthened by feelings of guilt and anxiety due to prolonged civil war, was exploited and given new life. So was Italian art, cunningly blended with Hellenic ideals. This new synthesis was expressed in a monumental extension of the forum-concept, the Forum of Augustus grouped round its temple of Mars the Avenger. There was also skilful and effectively propagandist sculptural and numismatic portraiture of the Emperor.

Rich men's houses at Pompeii and Herculaneum were full of vivid floor-mosaics, and of colourful mural frescoes executed in rapidly evolving styles which exploited the combined resources of mythological tradition, landscape techniques and architectural illusionism. Other parts of Italy likewise reveal novel and distinctive artistic trends, notably the north where a school of sculptors based on Aquileia employed simplified modelling which aimed at internal coherence rather than exact representation.

From the north too – from Mantua and Padua respectively – came both the greatest poet and the leading historian of the age and the regime, Virgil and Livy. Their unequalled and infinitely influential artistry was accompanied not only by belief in Augustus, who for all his grimmer side was the bringer and only guarantor of peace, but by a fervent Italian patriotism which, although Virgil early moved south to Naples, contains something of the frontiersman's emotional attachment. Maecenas, Virgil's friend and patron and Augustus' principal civilian adviser, was an Etruscan, claiming descent from the princely Cilnii of Arretium. Other members of Maecenas' circle included the incomparably lapidary lyricist and poetic essayist Horace, the son of an ex-slave, who transferred his devotion from Venusia to his Sabine farm. Another

associate of Maecenas was the most haunting of elegiac poets, Propertius from Assisi. A second elegist, Tibullus, equalled Virgil in his love of the Italian countryside and its traditions. But the most famous exponent of this sort of verse was Ovid, who although utterly metropolitan in spirit came from Sulmo (Sulmona) in the mountainous centre of Italy. His *Metamorphoses*, a quasi-epic collection of stories in hexameters not elegiac couplets, gave both the Middle Ages and the Renaissance much of their learning and entertainment.

Despite an occasional financial crisis the prosperity of Italy continued for two centuries; its material remains are to be seen on all sides today. The easy tenor of life was not greatly influenced by the political convulsions which, as Tacitus and Suetonius stress with macabre relish, gradually decimated the Roman court and aristocracy. Campagnia had suffered from the restless wanderings of Tiberius, before he settled permanently off its coast at Capri.

Meanwhile the bronze pots and pans of Cipus Polybius of Capua made their way as far as the Black Sea, and to Wales and Scotland. Ostia began to rival Puteoli, and Claudius and Nero went to immense expense to develop its harbour so as to secure the corn-supplies upon which the Emperor's popularity at Rome depended. It was off the Campanian coast that Nero arranged for a collapsible ship to destroy his mother; she succeeded in swimming ashore to Bauli, only to be murdered there.

The end of Nero himself (AD 68) meant the end of the Julio-Claudian line, and prolonged civil war. In the Year of the Four Emperors that followed, north Italy was the worst sufferer. Second only to Padua among north Italian cities, Cremona, twice a battlefield, was savagely plundered; and the whole region was impoverished by Vitellius eating his gargantuan way through its cities. Yet under his conqueror and successor Vespasian, a humorous and sensible middle-class Italian from Sabine Reate (Rieti), recovery was swift, with Padua and Aquileia in particular greatly profiting from their Danube trade.

Province-based armies had fought and won the civil wars, but for a time Italy remained supreme. Under the new Flavian dynasty its worst trials were the eruption of Vesuvius, which in the reign of Titus destroyed Pompeii and Herculaneum (AD 79), and an agrarian crisis under Domitian due to the over-production of wine. The same epoch witnessed grandiose advances

Opposite A cemetery outside Rome's port of Ostia on the road to Laurentum. Inscriptions show that most of the ashes lodged here were those of liberated slaves (freed men) who had been prominent in the town's commercial life.

The Emperor Claudius (AD 41–54), who was extremely ugly and looked ridiculous, caused artists a problem. While some attempted a realistic approach, this sculptor infused a strong element of idealism.

Antonia, daughter of Marcus Antonius and half sister of the Emperor Claudius, was probably the subject of this first-century marble head springing from a flower. Asian and Greek sculptors working in Rome achieved brilliant representations of women and children as well as men.

Nero (AD 54–68) portrayed on a brass coin. Portraiture on Roman imperial coinage, the finest the world has ever seen, reached its zenith in brilliant interpretations of the heavy features of Nero.

The head of the Emperor Trajan (AD 98–117), the most formidable and popular of conquerors. His portraiture does not try to individualize but aims at imperial grandeur.

Relief from the Tomb of the Haterii, found near Centocelle, late first century AD. This is a scene of burial in a family mausoleum covered with symbols of an immortal afterlife. The large crane is operated by a treadmill worked by slaves.

Opposite A baker's shop in a wall painting from Pompeii. Two men and an eager small boy stand in front of a counter piled with loaves, similar to those discovered black and charred in the ruined town. This scene may represent a free distribution of bread.

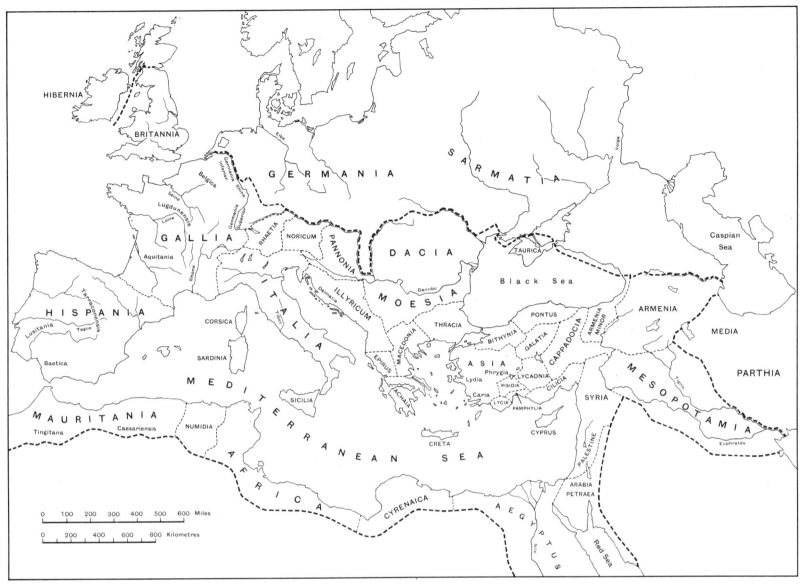

The Roman Empire early second century AD

in monumental architecture. In Rome, the reliefs of the Arch of Titus are cunning in their chiaroscuro, the Colosseum towered to a four-storeyed grandeur which decisively influenced the Renaissance, and the Golden House of Nero was equalled or outdone by the throne-room – once barrel-vaulted – of Domitian's Palatine palace. The two Plinies, who illustrate the epoch, were from Comum (Como), and the poet Statius was from Naples. Yet most good Latin writers now came from Spain – Seneca, Lucan, Martial, Quintilian; a province could eclipse Italy in Italy's own language.

In addition to lavishing huge sums on the Roman population's food and amusements, emperors took careful, humanitarian steps to eliminate abuses and anomalies throughout the peninsula. For example Nerva (AD 96–8) relieved Italian municipalities of the expenses of the imperial postal service, and he and Trajan and their successors developed a new experiment in public assistance (*alimenta*), by which Italian landowners received capital loans on condition that they paid 5 per cent interest into municipal treasuries, for the maintenance of poor children in the area.

Amid abounding prosperity, there were, perhaps, disturbing portents – but only for the very thoughtful – in an increasing reluctance among well-off citizens to accept the chores and expenses of municipal office. More immediately noticeable in its effects upon Italy was the successful industrial competition of the most advanced western provinces; for example the potteries of Arretium were now superseded first by Gaulish and then by Rhineland wares. Italians too, may have been shocked when Hadrian – of provincial (Spanish) origin,

Opposite, below Nereid and seahorse from Stabiae. The wall-paintings of this town, which suffered the fate of neighbouring Pompeii and Herculaneum have an uninhibited freshness of line and delicacy of colour.

Opposite, above This fresco painting from a funeral monument at Ostia depicts a small merchant ship, the *Isis Germiniana* taking in grain. Farnaces is the captain and Abascantus probably the owner of the ship and tomb. A porter says '*Feci*': I have done the task.

like his predecessor Trajan – conceived each province as possessing a quasi-national or federal entity and value of its own, not wholly dependent upon Italy. However, the coins of his successor Antoninus Pius (although likewise a non-Italian, of a family from Nîmes) show a reversion to the doctrine of Italy's supremacy.

Hadrian's ideas had not prevented him from enriching Italy with even grander and more noteworthy buildings than the Forum and Column of his predecessor Trajan. Trajan's Column still stands, and so does Hadrian's Pantheon, with its marvellous monolithic concrete dome 142 feet wide and high. Of his group of palaces and pavilions extending over seven square miles at Tivoli, enough survives to suggest the baroque daring of their domes and half-domes and vaults and niches and pendentives.

The Transformation: Rome, Milan, Ravenna

Most of the wars of the second century AD had been comfortably far away; and one at least, Trajan's conquest of Dacia (Rumania), had brought in the traditional spoils of gold. But a grave shock was in store for Italy under Marcus Aurelius (161 – 80), the philosopher who by a sad irony spent most of his reign fighting. At a time when the Empire was ravaged by plague, enormous groups of south German tribes, under pressure from others behind them, broke across the frontiers – brushing aside a static defence system supported by too few reserves. After they had penetrated the Julian Alps into Italy, the Germans besieged Aquileia, and stormed and burnt Opitergium on the way to Verona.

Levying funds by unfamiliar emergency measures, Aurelius repaired the breach. But the deeply engraved, emotional relief-work of the Column of Aurelius shows that a new age of anxiety had begun. The people of Rome and Italy were turning to mystery religions from the east – Isis, Cybele, Mithras – that would console their worries or their boredom; under Aurelius' son Commodus, there is often a hint that Jupiter is no longer seen as president of an Olympian pantheon but rather as a pantheistic or single god. In the civil wars (193–6) that followed the failure and murder of Commodus the victor was Septimius Severus. His homeland was North Africa, which also produced the outstanding Latin

literature of this epoch; but it was the Danube army with which Severus marched on Rome and put down all contestants. In order to remain supreme at home and on the frontiers, the new Emperor replaced the comparatively liberal second century regime by a totalitarian system. The army, by now composed largely of non-Italians, received extraordinary sums and favours. Italy's aristocracy, amid extensive confiscations, became less preponderant in the Senate. The Italians lost their privilege of providing the Emperor's praetorian bodyguard and their immunity from garrisoning. Gone was their ancient superiority over the provinces, home of this formidable Emperor who tried to strike a realistic equilibrium between Italy and other imperial lands. Commodus had already conceived the whim of calling Rome a 'colony', named after himself; Severus stationed a legion at Albanum. He himself avoided living in Rome, feeling that residence in Campania was less demoralizing for his unstable sons, Caracalla and Geta.

Lawyers of unprecedented talent such as Papinian and Ulpian developed the humanitarianism of the previous century into a general levelling process, dramatically symbolized under Caracalla by the empire-wide diffusion of Roman citizenship – and tax obligations – to almost all who were not slaves. (Papinian himself was an easterner, and so probably was Ulpian.) But as so often happens after egalitarian measures, there soon emerged a new class structure, distinguishing senior officials from the masses of the population, of whom many, in a period of crushing taxation, soon became very nearly serfs. Yet the Severi made even greater endeavours than their predecessors to conciliate the population of Rome, as is indicated by Caracalla's Baths which surpassed all previous models in their gigantic luxury. But before the death of Caracalla (217) Italy was placed under an official who virtually became its governor, so that the equation to a province went further still.

The government of the young, mild Severus Alexander (222 – 35) showed a desire to return (or at least to seem to return) to the old fairly liberal sort of Senatorial government. But this was impossible owing to an abundance of acute financial problems. These, combined with the jurists' views on supreme imperial power, led to a continuance and even an increase in the state's intervention in private affairs.

Meanwhile, a menacing power (Sassanian Persia) had risen beyond the eastern borders of the Empire;

Left Hadrian (AD 117–38) was one of the most complex characters of antiquity, who made the empire an efficient organic whole. In this marble head he is represented with a subtle plastic infusion of the Hellenic culture he so greatly admired. He brought beards back into fashion.

Right Antoninus Pius (AD 138–61), the beneficent high-minded ruler whose propaganda, on coinage, reflects a return from Hadrian's Hellenism to redoubled emphasis on mythical Virgilian Italy.

A bust of the bearded emperor Caracalla (AD 211–17), son of Severus, who aped Alexander the Great and abased Italy's privileges. In his expression his tiresome, dangerous nature is realistically portrayed. He died at the hands of an assassin.

Opposite One of the chief oriental mystery religions imported into Italy was the worship of the god Attis and of Cybele, the Great Mother of Asia. A eunuch priest of the cult is shown with ritual symbols and vestments on this second-century votive bas-relief found at Lanuvium, near Rome.

Stevedores carry sacks down a gang plank, while they are checked off by three men. Detail of a relief showing a port scene.

Interior of a shop on a relief, *circa* first century AD. The wall is hung with pillows or rugs, belts and cloth. Two assistants, in the presence of the owner, open a box for two seated customers.

Opposite Marcus Aurelius (AD 161–80) is shown on horseback, receiving the surrender of barbarians in a panel from a triumphal arch. Although a lover of philosophy, he spent nearly all his reign at war.

and its northern defences were breaking again—with no Roman to mend them for half a century, owing to a series of violently disputed imperial successions. Italy was far from secure. Alexander's successor Maximinus (235–8), a ruthless Thracian peasant who had fought well on the northern frontiers, was assassinated by his own soldiers while besieging disaffected Aquileia, and very soon afterwards two imperial colleagues set up by the Senate (Balbinus and Pupienus) were murdered in the praetorian camp.

The sculptural and numismatic portraits of these monarchs who followed one another in a rapid, violent succession are first-rate realistic masterpieces, so important was it to present the Emperor's features, however hard-bitten and careworn, to his subjects. Another art now at its climax was that of the sculptural reliefs upon sarcophagi, which had first reappeared in the second century AD as inhumation replaced cremation. Their deeply incised and highlighted, tortuous, restless patterns range from philosophical and religious compositions – the latter merging from pagan into Christian ideas – to violent scenes of battle and hunting which symbolize spiritual victory; and styles oscillated between Hellenism and novel or oriental expressionist ideas. The vast constructional projects of Gordian III (238–44) have not come down to us. Nor have the unprecedentedly grandiose Baths completed by the Illyrian Trajanus Decius (249–51), persecutor for patriotic reasons of the rapidly rising community of Christians whose underground catacombs covered miles beneath the city.

His Arab predecessor Philip had celebrated Rome's millennium. Decius killed him in a battle near Verona (249), and other Italian localities, probably Interamna (Terni) and Spoletum, witnessed the deaths of the next emperors, Gallus (who came of an ancient Etruscan family from Perusia) and his successor Aemilian. A fearful pestilence was abroad, and a brutally debased coinage flooded the market, raising prices a thousand-fold in just over two decades and causing untold misery. Invaders and usurpers were endless – one of them, Postumus, ruled over all the western provinces – and it seemed that the end of Italy and the Empire was at hand. It was impossible to defray both external hostilities and civil wars of imperial succession; and neither could be stopped.

Yet when things were at their very worst, Gallienus (in addition to patronizing a philhellenic renaissance of the arts) somehow formed a corps of heavy cavalry which he employed to eject the German Alamanni from north Italy (258 or 259). Gallienus' idea was to supplement the fixed frontier defence by a system of protection in depth provided by this mobile army at strategically located, heavily fortified cities behind the line. Conspicuous among them were Mediolanum (Milan), Aquileia (Philip, anxious to defend the peninsula, had already stationed troops there), and Verona. These centres began to eclipse Rome in power. Moreover, the same northern area had also become much the richest region in wine and oil, produced for export on large estates (*villae rusticae*) such as Brioni Grande.

The successive commanders of this new cavalry corps became the second men in the Empire—and a great danger to the throne. One of them, Aureolus, rose against Gallienus at Milan (268); and Gallienus, though successful against him, fell to the next commander Claudius II (Gothicus). But then a gradual miraculous recovery began at the hands of emperors from the Balkans – military geniuses who fortunately regarded the protection of Italy as the precondition for saving their homelands. First, Claudius Gothicus stopped the Alamanni at Lake Garda (268). Then he died of the plague, and his brother ruled briefly at Aquileia (270). The next emperor, Aurelian, recovered from a German defeat at Placentia (Piacenza) to overwhelm a horde of Scythians in successive battles near Fanum Fortunae (Fano) and Ticinum. Aurelian went on to start building a great wall round Rome, twelve miles long and with 381 towers and eighteen portcullised gates, of which nine survive. Except for Dacia which was sacrificed, Aurelian reunified the Empire with a new oriental-style autocracy and Sun-cult as its bases. He also re-cast the public services, and to provide for the food-supply of Rome created extensive plantations in the east and north-east of the peninsula.

The reorganization of the Empire on a savagely authoritarian, bureaucratic basis, calculated to guarantee survival, was carried much further by Diocletian (284–305). Owing to the many tasks in hand, he, like others before him, appointed a fellow-emperor, Maximian (286), who was allotted the western regions of the Empire. When not fighting, Maximian resided at Milan or Aquileia – nearer the front than Rome – while Diocletian established his capital at Nicomedia in Asia Minor, and two emperors of secondary rank, making up the 'Tetrarchy', resided at Trier and Salonica. The two main rulers had a meeting at Milan, where the new oriental ceremonial of the court was

Opposite A startling change in Roman portraiture is felt in this head of Constantine the Great (AD 306–37). All realism abandoned, his gaze appears fixed on infinity: this is the colossal, inscrutable, inhuman face of God's vicegerent.

very much in evidence. Soon a far-reaching overhaul of the administration gave official shape to the gradual reduction of Italy to the level of a mere province: or rather of two provinces, since the country was now divided into two separate territories or *dioeceseis* (out of the twelve in the Empire as a whole). So there was a second Italian capital at Milan – though this northern part of the peninsula was made subject to taxes in kind, which Italians had not previously experienced.

However, the system of four rulers rapidly disintegrated, and for a time six Augusti reigned side by side. Maximian's son Maxentius ruled at Rome (306), ostentatiously but unsuccessfully reviving its ancient claims to honour. But his regime came to an end when Constantine – son of one of Diocletian's secondary emperors – struck across the Alps over the Mont Genèvre Pass. Aquileia, Verona and Mutina fell to him, and he overwhelmed Maxentius at the Milvian Bridge on the outskirts of Rome (312).

But the defeated ruler had left a monument, which Constantine completed. The largest hall in the ancient world (outdoing even the unprecedentedly enormous Baths of Diocletian), this Basilica of Maxentius has three gigantic vault-spans suggestive of Persian influence; and its aisles, apses and side-chapels pointed the way to the churches of many centuries to come. Also, perhaps, of fourth (or fifth?) century date is an enormous palatial complex at Piazza Armerina in Sicily, exploiting architectural space in strangely restless designs – clover leafs, ellipses, apses. The floor-mosaics of Piazza Armerina display hunting and circus scenes that are remarkable examples of this traditional art. Mosaic-making likewise flourished in the Romagna and the Veneto. Milan, especially, was an artistic as well as a governmental and administrative centre; its imperial palace must have been superbly grandiose, though the remains have almost vanished under today's city.

It was at Milan that Constantine and his colleague Licinius now conferred (313), and decided to apply the edict of tolerance towards Christianity which their predecessor Galerius, formerly an arch-persecutor, had promulgated at Serdica (Sofia) shortly before his death two years earlier. Christians received back their confiscated property and civic rights, and Constantine, presiding over theological congresses, moved far towards making their faith the state religion. Himself an Illyrian, he moved his capital outside Italy into his own native land, establishing it first at Sirmium (Mitrovica), next at Serdica, and then finally, after he had become sole ruler, at his mighty new foundation of Byzantium (Constantinople) (330), which for 1,100 years was to take over the imperial task of Rome. But one of the three prefects among whom the administration of the Empire was divided had his residence at Milan.

Yet Rome also was in the forefront of the great new opportunities afforded to Constantinian architects by Christianity. The secular basilica-form (p. 43) was developed into resplendent churches such as St John Lateran and the five-aisled transepted St Peter's, forerunner of the present building. The tradition of centralised construction was likewise drawn upon, for baptistries, martyrs' shrines, mausoleums, and churches such as the domed and columned S Costanza just outside Rome (c 320 – 37). The vaulting of its ambulatory is covered with graceful, non-representational mosaic decoration which shows how this art-form, already found occasionally on walls and ceilings (in addition to floors) during previous centuries, was now beginning to produce unprecedently fine work on these surfaces.

As Constantine's sons and joint heirs came to grips with one another, the first to fall was Constantine II, killed at Aquileia (340). The final survivor, Constantius II, often resided at Milan, only briefly visiting Rome (357), whose Senate was now equalled in privilege by the Senate of Constantinople. Constantius II was an Arian (Unitarian) but sought compromize with Athanasian Trinitarianism at the Conference of Ariminum (Rimini) (359).

After a short pagan revival under Julian, the Empire returned to Trinitarian Christianity – and to a more or less permanent political division. Although the western Emperor, Valentinian I, resided outside Italy (at Trier), the independence of the church was asserted by St Ambrose (373), Bishop of Milan and prototype of politically vigorous churchmen, and it was at Milan that St Augustine experienced his final conversion (386). At Rome, in spite of strong pagan reactions, the Emperor Gratian removed the Altar of Victory from the Roman Senate-house, suppressed the Vestal Virgins, and handed over to the Popes the title of 'pontifex maximus'. With the scholarly, ascetic St Jerome as his secretary, Damasus, though his papacy was due to Ambrose's influence, worked hard like many of his successors to establish the ecclesiastical primacy of Rome. Yet it was in Milan that Gratian (*d*. 383) and Valentinian II (*d*. 392) established their courts. So did Theodosius I (*d*. 395), who though more powerful than his predecessors came

Opposite Wearing the colours of his faction, a circus charioteer stands beside his horse in this mosaic from Baccano. Numerous other mosaics of charioteers and gladiators have preserved to our day the ephemeral popularity of Roman athletes.

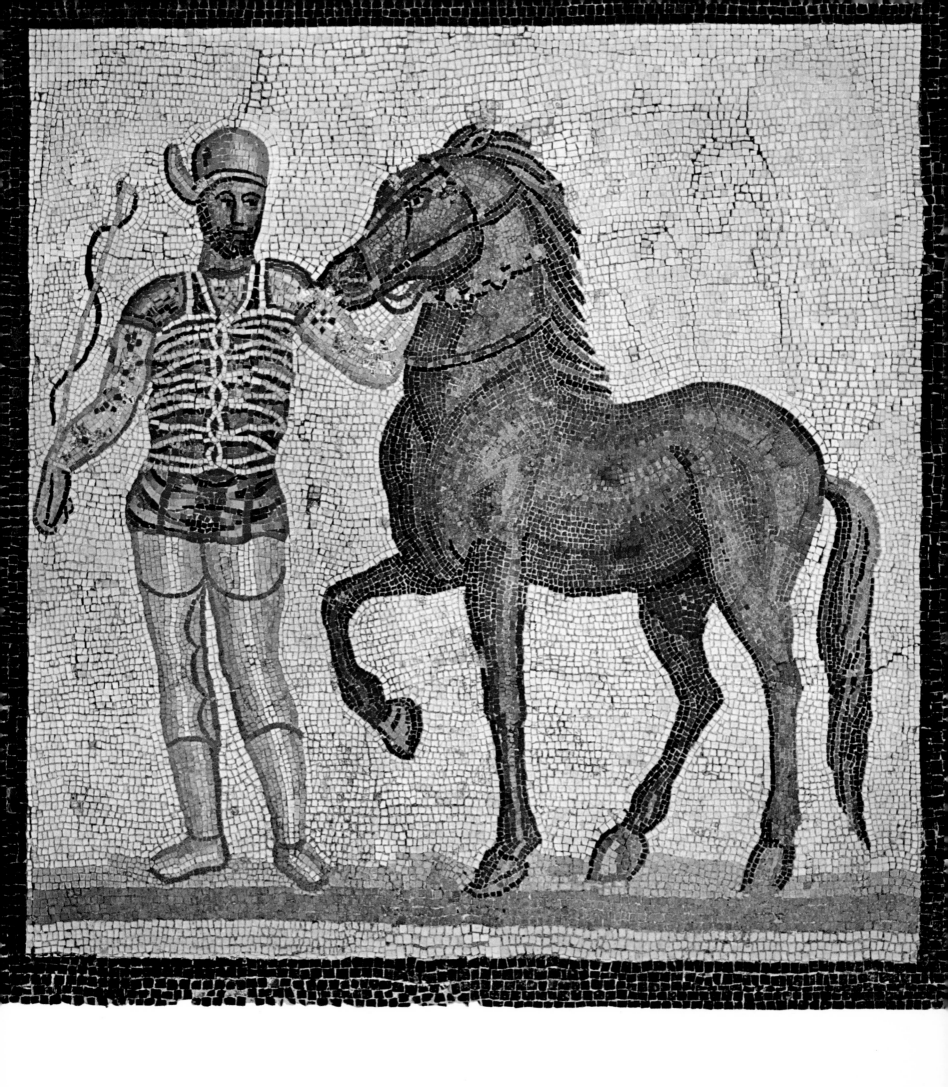

Above A dove incised on marble, from the catacomb in the Via Latina, Rome, *c* AD 300. The dove, represented by itself or with a praying woman, was often used by Christians to represent the soul.

Right Stairs leading to the catacombs of Domitilla (or St Nereus and St Achilleus). The alcoves in the walls originally contained the tombs of Christians serving the first-century imperial family of the Flavians.

Opposite This small round temple which overlooks the 'Vale of Tempe' is one of the buildings of Hadrian's Villa at Tivoli, 'the most fantastic of Roman material creations'.

Below The Multiplication of Loaves was, like the Miraculous Draught of Fishes, a favourite Christian miracle, recalling the bread of the Eucharist. This gold painting on glass reflects a fashionable trend in late Roman minor art.

The column of the Byzantine Emperor Phocas, in the Roman Forum, was described by Byron as the 'nameless column with the buried base', but has since been disinterred. It was erected in AD 608 by the Governor Smaragdus to celebrate the return of peace to Italy.

A delicately formal representation of the Western Emperor Honorius ennoble this wing of an ivory diptych which celebrates the inauguration of Anicius Probus as Consul. The earliest dated of the consular diptychs, it was made in AD 406.

off worst in a clash with Ambrose. Theodosius momentarily reunified the Empire by putting down, on the Carso, a last pagan rally under Eugenius (394). But after the death of Theodosius in the following year, the emperors based on Italy were less and less successful in defending the peninsula from northern invaders. Indeed, their chief generals often tended to compromise, being themselves Germans, and surrounded by courtiers and soldiers who were likewise Germans and were not permitted to inter-marry with Italians—but coveted their land. In 401 the Visigothic invader Alaric was before the walls of Milan. He was pushed back by the imperial general Stilicho, a Vandal (Visigoths and Vandals were two major branches of the German stock). But Alaric returned in 407 and Stilicho's murder at Pavia in the following year enabled him to seize Rome temporarily, and put it to the sack (410).

St Augustine, with the partial detachment of a North African, argued in his *City of God* that such external happenings, however disastrous, could not touch a true Christian. Moreover at Rome, as Pope succeeded Pope, mighty churches continued to be built. S Sabina on the Aventine (425–32) is a dignified aisled basilica in which great rows of columns (taken from pagan temples) lead irresistibly to the altar in the eastern apse. Probably of this date, too, are the wall-mosaics of S Maria Maggiore, which are midway between classical naturalism and Byzantine stylization.

There were now three courts in Italy: the court of the Pope, the court of the western Emperor's chief German military adviser, and the court of the western Emperor himself. After Stilicho's murder, fear of Alaric induced Theodosius' son Honorius to take up his residence at Ravenna on the Adriatic, a harbour-city protected by the sea and marshes. Here Valentinian III spent most of his long reign (425–55), inaugurating the remarkable building projects which made the place a forerunner and model of Byzantine art. A small domed mausoleum, now bearing the name of Galla Placidia (c 450), is decorated with wall- and ceiling-mosaics against a background of deep blue. The octagonal Baptistry of the Orthodox or Neon (451–73) glows richly with a wider range of colours.

But meanwhile northern Italy was faced with its gravest menace, the terrifying mounted commandos of the Huns, of Asian origin. Breaking the Germans and compelling them to flee before him or to join his army, Attila sought to extend his gigantic central and east European empire by sweeping down from the Danubian territory into Italy (452). Aquileia, one of the world's largest cities, fell to him; and its inhabitants, in flight, settled on the safer site of Venice. However, after negotiating with Pope Leo I before the gates of Milan, Attila was induced to withdraw—and his death in the next year was followed by the disintegration of his realm. For Rome, however, the respite was brief, since it was almost immediately pillaged again, by the Vandal Genseric landing from Africa (455).

Twenty years later, Attila's former secretary Orestes proclaimed his own young son Romulus 'Augustulus' as Emperor at Ravenna. But soon afterwards, in the pine-woods nearby, their troops were defeated by the Romano-German army of Milan. The victorious force now brought an end to the western Empire, declaring its German commander Odoacer monarch of Italy or 'king of the nations' (*rex gentium*) in his own right (476). Odoacer promised his barbarian soldiery one-third of all Italian lands (though the laws against inter-marriage between the two communities were not repealed). The new king also sent the west Roman imperial regalia to Constantinople, saying that one emperor was enough. Yet it was in alliance with an East Roman (Byzantine) emperor Zeno, and as his titular inferior, that another German, Theodoric the Ostrogoth, marched round the head of the Venetian gulf into Italy and overthrew Odoacer. Five years of warfare culminated in the capitulation of Ravenna and the treacherous murder of Odoacer (493).

Surprisingly enough, the reign of Theodoric lasted for thirty-three years; under him Italy enjoyed a peace and prosperity which in recent centuries had been rare indeed. But although the eastern Emperor Anastasius sent the symbols of power back to Theodoric (497)—thereby recognising him as a king ruling outside the Empire—neither Italy nor Rome were any longer at the centre of the world.

John Julius Norwich

After driving out the Gothic invaders, Byzantine power faltered before the Lombards who succeeded in conquering a large part of Italy. An important consequence of the Byzantine withdrawal was the new status of the Pope who, in the person of Gregory the Great, became the political ruler of Rome. With the papacy now a state, the Pope resorted to foreign alliances to protect his territories, and with the Roman coronation of Charlemagne in 800 AD the long history of precarious relations between pontiffs and Germanic emperors began. While empire and papacy struggled for supremacy, the maritime republics and mercantile cities of Lombardy and Tuscany remained independent, continuing a Roman tradition of municipal freedom. In southern Italy Norman adventurers in a few generations established an opulent monarchy compounded of Latin, Greek and Arab civilizations, which merged with the Empire of Frederick II — the 'Wonder of the World' — and then passed to the House of Anjou. French control of the papacy and the unending strife of Guelfs and Ghibellines led to the Popes' seventy-two years of voluntary exile in Avignon, while Rome shrank to the size of a village. With the return of the papacy to Rome in 1377, and in the painting of Giotto, in the sculpture of the Pisani, and in the writings of Dante, Petrarch and Boccaccio, fourteenth century Italy became the harbinger of the Renaissance.

Goths, Lombards and Franks

When, in 476 AD, the people of Italy witnessed the downfall of the Roman Empire of the West, few can have suspected that the whole course of Italian history had been changed. The greatest political institution the world had ever known had long been a hollow mockery; the new conquerors preserved the Senate and civil administration and continued to pay assiduous lip-service to the Emperor at Constantinople. Surely, men thought, this was just a sensible regularization of the existing state of affairs. They were wrong. When Odoacer's barbarians settled the callow young ex-Emperor into his Neapolitan villa, they were in fact sentencing Italy to fourteen centuries of division and suffering; and the first nine of those centuries form the subject of this chapter. There is scarcely a year among them in which Italian soil was not drenched in blood — the blood of Vandal and Goth, of Greek and Lombard; of Frank and Latin, Norman and Saracen, Angevin and Spaniard; all bitter struggles, yet all overshadowed by the huge, remorseless contest of Emperor and Pope. These were the purgatorial years, and they left the land exhausted and cruelly torn; but it is in them that the key, not only to the Renaissance but to the whole character of modern Italy, is to be found.

Opposite The three Magi — part of a mosaic from Theodoric's church of S. Apollinare Nuovo, Ravenna. It dates from Justinian's rededication of the church in the later sixth century; the costumes, often described as those of Ostrogothic noblemen, were more likely meant to give a generally oriental flavour.

+SCS BALTHASSAR +SCS MELCHIOR +SCS GASPAR .

His enemy Theodoric had all the advantages Odoacer lacked. He had spent his boyhood and adolescence as an honoured hostage at Constantinople, and though he had gained little intellectually from the experience—throughout his life he would stencil his signature through a perforated gold plate—he had managed to acquire a remarkable understanding of Byzantine psychology. This made it easy for him to obtain the authority of the Emperor Zeno (474–91) for the expulsion of Odoacer from Italy, while his superb leadership and unquestioned supremacy over his people did the rest. Here was not a military campaign so much as the migration of an entire race, perhaps a quarter of a million men, women and children, who swept south in the winter of 488–9. Against such a tide Odoacer's kingdom had no hope.

The murder by Theodoric of his conquered ex-enemy in the middle of a banquet held to celebrate their new friendship was hardly an auspicious beginning; but Italy soon settled down to enjoy the benefits he brought her. What could not be forgotten—at least in Constantinople—was his Arian faith. Arianism—according to which Christ was not truly divine, but merely a creation of God the Father and therefore inferior to Him—had long ago been condemned as heresy; it had, however, unfortunately been professed by the first Christian missionaries with whom many of the barbarians had come in contact, and it was still staunchly upheld by nearly all the tribes of Europe. Theodoric himself was a tolerant man, protecting all shades of religious belief and decreeing particularly severe penalties for anti-Semitism; but the faith of his people made them fair game for Byzantine ambitions and so ultimately brought about their downfall.

A darker stain on his reputation was his treatment of Boethius, that gentlest and serenest of thinkers whose *Consolations of Philosophy*, almost pantheistic in its suggestion that happiness makes man into God and that evil does not exist, could never have obtained ecclesiastical approval had its author not been executed by the Arian Theodoric and thus obtained a martyr's crown. Centuries ahead of its time, it emerged from the dungeons of Pavia to become the most popular speculative work of the Middle Ages. The only other contemporary to have a comparable effect on future generations was St Benedict of Nursia, the father of western monasticism. Sweeping away the squalor and exaggerated ascetic self-humiliation which had characterized so many of the early fathers from St Jerome

downwards, Benedict in 529 established at Monte Cassino the first ordered monastic rule, austere yet moderate, suited to the western way of life.

In 535, nine years after Theodoric's death, Justinian began the reconquest of Italy in earnest. It proved a long and bitter struggle as the Byzantine armies, led at first by the brilliant Belisarius and later by the septuagenarian eunuch Narses, battled their way up and down the peninsula. Rome alone changed hands five times; all her aqueducts were cut, turning the surrounding country into the malarial swamp which it remained for a millennium to come. But at last Narses annihilated the Gothic army of King Totila among the foothills of Vesuvius, and at the close of the year 551 the last thousand Goths, armed with an imperial safe-conduct, had vanished across the Alps.

The Gothic War ushered in a dark age. Justinian's exarchs (governors) did their best to restore prosperity, but they had little success. Italy was a desolation; Rome, Milan and Naples empty shells. And now, within a few years of the Goths' departure, a new Germanic horde appeared on the scene—the Lombards, spreading relentlessly over north Italy and the great plain that still bears their name and finally setting up their capital at Pavia. Their line of advance was checked by Rome and the Exarchate of Ravenna, but two spearheads pressed through to set up the great southern duchies of Spoleto and Benevento. From here they might have gone on to conquer the rest of the south, but they were few and insufficiently united; Apulia, Calabria and Sicily remained under Byzantine control.

That Rome herself did not succumb to the Lombard tide was a miracle hardly less extraordinary than that which had saved her from Attila in the preceding century. Once again it was wrought by a Pope—this time one of her most outstanding medieval statesmen, Gregory the Great (590–604). Gregory was no intellectual—like most churchmen of his day he cherished a deep suspicion of secular learning—but he was autocratic and utterly fearless, and through these troubled times it was he alone who preserved the prestige of the city.

Yet even Gregory recognised the Emperor at Constantinople as his temporal overlord, and Rome under his successors became steadily more Byzantinised as the seventh century took its course. Greek refugees from the Middle East and North Africa poured into Italy as their lands were overrun, first by the Persians and then, from about 640, by the Moslems,

Opposite The most detailed picture of beekeeping in the twelfth century, from a south Italian Exultet Roll. These rolls, containing the service for blessing the beeswax Paschal candle, were illustrated with pictures drawn upside-down so that they would appear correctly to the congregation when the upper sections hung over the front of the ambo.

Italy 476–1377

now carrying all before them on the first irresistible surge of their enthusiasm. In 663, Italy received an unusually distinguished Byzantine immigrant—the Emperor Constans II, determined to shift his capital back again to the West. Rome he found as uncongenial as Constantinople, but Hellenistic Sicily proved more to his taste and he reigned five years in Syracuse until one day a dissatisfied courtier, in an access of nostalgia, surprised him in his bath and felled him with the soapdish.

The Court returned to the Bosphorus and Italy to her own problems. The most serious was still the Lombards who, as they increased in strength and numbers, were casting ever more covetous eyes over neighbouring territory. Their actual progress was slow, since the Exarchate constituted a moderately effective bulwark; but pressure on the frontiers never diminished. This uneasy equilibrium lasted over the turn of the century; then, in 726, came crisis. The Emperor Leo III ordered the destruction of all icons and holy images throughout his dominions. The effect of his decree was immediate and shattering. Men rose everywhere in wrath; monasteries, in particular,

were outraged. In the Eastern provinces, where the cult of icons had reached such proportions that they frequently served as god-parents at baptisms, a puritan reaction had been inevitable and thus Leo found some measure of support; but in the more moderate West, which had done nothing to deserve them, the new laws could not be tolerated. Italy, under energetic papal leadership, refused to comply, Pope Gregory III going so far as to excommunicate all iconoclasts. The resulting quarrel between Rome and Byzantium gave the Lombards their opportunity. Playing one side off against the other, they steadily gained ground until at last, in 751, they captured Ravenna. It was the end of the Exarchate. Such Byzantine lands as remained in Italy – apart from Venice, safe and semi-independent among her lagoons – were cut off by the Lombard duchies of the south and thus powerless to help. Rome was left naked to her enemies.

Not, however, for long. Before the end of the year, beyond the Alps to the West, the Frankish leader Pepin the Short had obtained papal approval for the deposition of the Merovingian figurehead Childeric III and his own coronation. He could not now ignore the Church's appeal. In 754 Pope Stephen II travelled to St Denis, where he confirmed and annointed Pepin and his two sons Charles and Carloman as kings of the Franks; two years later, in response to a letter said to have been miraculously penned by St Peter himself, Frankish troops swept into Italy and brought the Lombard King Aistulf to his knees. Pepin now established the Pope as head of an independent state, snaking across central Italy to embrace Rome, Perugia and Ravenna – roughly the lands of the defunct Exarchate. He may have been basing his action on the so-called *Donation of Constantine*, by which that Emperor was supposed to have granted to the papacy temporal rule over 'Italy and all the Western regions'; if so, he was seriously misled. The *Donation* was later shown up as a forgery, shamelessly concocted in the papal Curia; but the Papal States which it brought into being, however shaky their legal foundations, were to last over a thousand years until 1870.

Rome was saved; but warfare continued, and for the next forty years Pepin and his son Charles found themselves the chief protectors of the papacy against all its foes. It was no easy task. The Lombard kingdom came to an end after Charles took Pavia in 774, but the duchies of Spoleto and Benevento—soon

Queen Amalasuntha, Theodoric's daughter, who after his death acted as regent for her son Athalaric. She was always pro-Byzantine in her sympathies, and it was her murder by her second husband Theodahad that gave Justinian his excuse for invading Italy in AD 535.

A bronze coin of the Emperor Justinian (482–565), who reconquered Italy from the Goths and controlled the Empire's domestic and foreign policy from 527 until his death. A brilliant lawgiver, administrator and builder, he was responsible for the construction of S. Sophia at Constantinople and S. Vitale at Ravenna.

Right Theodora, daughter of a bear-keeper in the hippodrome and in her youth a notorious courtesan, later married Justinian and played an important part in imperial affairs. Though she herself tended towards the monophysite heresy, she is hieratically represented in mosaics of S. Vitale where, like here husband, she wears a halo.

Right The Iron Crown of Lombardy. Forged, according to tradition, from a nail of the True Cross, it may well have been sent from Constantinople for the coronation of Theodoric in 493.

Far right, above Gregory the Great with his parents. He was the first Pope (590–604) to become the real political ruler of Rome, and the first to demand unquestioning obedience from the hierarchy. Before his day the Bishop of Rome had been respected by his colleagues only as *primus inter pares*; thenceforth he was supreme.

Right This pectoral cross, made of gold and studded with fifty-six precious stones around its great central sapphire, is said to have been given by King Berengar, and was used, with the Iron Crown, for the coronation of his successors.

Far right, below A horse — or perhaps a deer — grazing. This eighth-century relief in the church of S. Saba, Rome, is an engaging example of Lombard art; the church itself was founded in the seventh century as a monastery for Basilian monks, fleeing from the Arab and Persian invasions of the Levant.

The throne of Archbishop Maximian at Ravenna, the most superb complex of carved ivory known in Europe. The plaques on the sides are probably of Alexandrian workmanship, while the five front panels are in the manner of Constantinople. About 550.

to be joined by Salerno and Capua – proved worthy successors to its old traditions, promoting themselves to principalities to stress their independence. Even in Rome itself the Popes had their enemies. The throne of St Peter was too exalted and too profitable a seat ever to prove comfortable to its occupant, and thwarted ambitions all too often led to corruption and conspiracy. Surprisingly, it was one of these countless petty intrigues on the part of the disgruntled Roman aristocracy, rather than any cataclysmic event on the European stage, that led to the most far-reaching single political development of the Middle Ages – the coronation of Charlemagne in 800 AD by Pope Leo III and the consequent foundation of a new and independent Empire of the West.

Charlemagne always maintained, probably truthfully, that his imperial coronation had taken him entirely by surprise. Throughout his reign he strove to uphold the supremacy of the law, and Leo's action was by any standards flagrantly illegal. Frankish apologists might argue that the Byzantine Empire had lapsed through iconoclasm into heresy and that the reigning Empress Irene, even though she had rescinded the hated decrees, was a woman and a usurper who had blinded her own son and thus forfeited all claims to allegiance; the fact remained that the Roman Empire had passed down an unbroken line of Emperors at Constantinople, and that it belonged to them by right. It was hardly for the Franks to talk about usurping.

On the other hand, the old order was becoming more and more of a contradiction. Constantinople may have been the theoretical repository of Roman law, civilisation and imperial traditions; but in spirit it was now entirely Greek. Rome, shattered by the barbarians, demoralised by centuries of near-anarchy, was still the focal point of Latin culture and it was Charlemagne, not his fanatical Byzantine counterparts, who upheld the *Pax Romana* in the West. For the chaotic Europe of the Middle Ages, one Emperor was no longer enough. Perhaps, subconsciously, the Byzantines knew it, for it took Charlemagne only twelve years to obtain their official recognition. The price he paid was Venice.

It was four hundred years since the first refugees from Attila had sought shelter in the north-western corner of the Adriatic, among that cluster of little islands which lay, protected by sandbanks and shoals, inaccessible to all but their own native pilots. Successive barbarian invasions had overrun the rest of Italy, but here the natural defences had always held; and

thus Venice, alone among the North Italian towns, had managed to escape Teutonic contamination. She had been a largely autonomous republic ever since the election of her first Doge in 697, and after the fall of the Exarchate found herself the only power left in North Italy which still remained loyal to Byzantium. She was already rich, her trade was fast developing, her navy one of the best in the Mediterranean. Charlemagne at once saw her strategic importance and her value as a diplomatic pawn. His first attempt at conquest was repelled by the Byzantine fleet. A second, by his son Pepin, partially succeeded; but, though most outlying districts (and the Doge himself) fell into Frankish hands, the islands of the Rialto continued their resistance until Pepin, dying of fever, was forced in 810 to withdraw. Venetian national pride later transformed his retreat into a historic victory, but the Byzantines, less starry-eyed, were ready to negotiate. Thus the seventy-year-old Charlemagne received the recognition he needed; and Constantinople retained her links with Venice while allowing her, in gratitude for her loyalty, still more privileges than before.

In achievement as in physical stature, Charlemagne was well over life-size; but his achievement was short lived. This extraordinary figure, immoral, illiterate, more than half barbarian, kept his newly forged Empire together by the strength of his personality alone; after his death in 814 its story is one of steady decline, with virtual disintegration following the extinction of his family in 888. Now North Italy became once again a battleground of faceless princelings, squabbling over a meaningless crown, dragging their land ever deeper into chaos. In the south also, new dangers arose. In 827 the Saracens of North Africa invaded Sicily in strength at the request of the Byzantine governor, rebelling against Constantinople in an effort to avoid the consequences of having eloped with a local nun. Four years later they took Palermo. Henceforth the peninsula was in constant danger. Taranto and Bari fell in 840, and in 846 it was the turn of Rome itself. An Arab fleet sailed up the Tiber, sacked the Borgo and plundered St Peter's, even wrenching the silver plate from the doors of the basilica. Again the city was saved by her Pope. Summoning the combined navies of his three maritime neighbours, Naples, Gaeta and Amalfi, and himself assuming the supreme command, Leo IV in 849 destroyed the Saracen fleet off Ostia. The hundreds of captives were set to work building an immense rampart round the Vatican and down as far as

Opposite Queen Theodelinda of the Lombards chose Agilulf, Duke of Turin, as her second husband. 'When they had met,' writes Paul the Deacon, 'she ordered wine to be brought. He receiving the cup, kissed her hand; but she with a blush and a smile, said: "He should not kiss my hand who has the right to kiss my lips".'
A sixth-century episode seen through the fifteenth-century eyes of the Brothers Zavattari.

the Castel Sant' Angelo – the Leonine Wall, considerable sections of which still remain today.

Leo IV and his second successor, Nicholas I, were the last two outstanding Popes to occupy the throne of St Peter for a century and a half – unless we include the Englishwoman Pope Joan, who apparently managed to conceal her sex throughout her three-year pontificate until, by some unhappy miscalculation, she gave birth to a baby on the steps of the Lateran. Joan belongs, alas, to legend; but her story is symptomatic of the decadence and chaos of a period in which many of the historical Popes seem scarcely less fantastic – John VIII, for example, hammered to death by his jealous relations; Formosus, whose dead body was exhumed, brought to trial before a synod of bishops, stripped, mutilated and cast into the Tiber, then miraculously recovered, rehabilitated and reinterred in its former tomb; John X, strangled in the Castel Sant' Angelo by his mistress's daughter so that she could instal on the Papal throne her own bastard son by Pope Sergius III; or John XII under whose reign, according to Gibbon, 'We learn with some surprise...that the Lateran palace was turned into a school for prostitution; and that his rapes of virgins and widows had deterred the female pilgrims from visiting the tomb of St Peter, lest, in the devout act, they should be violated by his successor'.

But if John XII marked the nadir of the papal pornocracy, he was also responsible for Italy's deliverance. In 962, powerless against the Italian 'King' Berengar II, he appealed for help to Otto, Duke of Saxony, who had recently married the widow of Berengar's predecessor and was by now the strongest power in North Italy. Otto hurried to Rome, where John hastily crowned him Emperor. This act was the Pope's undoing. Debauchery was bad enough, but when two years later he also proved insubordinate to the Emperor he had created, Otto summoned a synod and had him deposed, obtaining a promise from the bishops that they should henceforth obtain prior imperial approval for any Pope they elected. Berengar soon surrendered, leaving Otto supreme; and the Empire of the West was reborn, to continue virtually uninterrupted until the age of Napoleon.

Otto's title of 'the Great' was not undeserved. He had but one ambition – to restore his Empire to the power and prosperity it had enjoyed under Charlemagne – and he came close to achieving it. In the eleven years of his reign, spent largely in Italy, he brought to the North a measure of peace unparalleled in living memory. Rome was more of a problem; flash point in the heat generated by constant papal intrigue was never far off, and in 966 Otto was faced with serious riots which he was able to quell only after he had hanged the Prefect of the City by his hair from the equestrian statue of Marcus Aurelius before the Lateran. (The statue was subsequently moved by Michelangelo to his newly designed Campidoglio, where it still stands.) It was in the South, however, that the Emperor found himself in real difficulties. He knew that he could never control the peninsula while Apulia and Calabria remained in Byzantine hands, but the Greeks' hold on their Italian provinces was too strong for him. When war failed, he tried diplomacy, marrying his son and heir to the lovely young Byzantine princess Theophano; her dowry was generous, but it did not include south Italy. Otto died a disappointed man. His former allies, the Lombard duchies, were left more powerful than ever, and Apulia and Calabria were as Greek as ever they had been.

Like his hero Charlemagne, Otto the Great was unfortunate in his successors. His son Otto II did his best but, after a hair's-breadth escape from a Saracen expeditionary force which had trounced his army in Calabria, he died in 983, aged only twenty-eight. (He is the only Roman Emperor to be buried in St Peter's.) His son by Theophano, Otto III, proved a strange contrast to his forbears, combining the ambitions of his line with a romantic mysticism clearly inherited from his mother, and forever dreaming of a great Byzantinesque theocracy that would embrace Germans, Italians and Slavs, with God at its head, and Pope and Emperor His twin viceroys. This extraordinary youth had hardly left Rome after his imperial coronation in 996 when the city rose once again in revolt; but two years later he returned in strength, re-established order, restored the young German visionary Gregory V to the papacy and built himself a magnificent palace on the Aventine. Here he passed the remaining four years of his life in a curious combination of splendour and asceticism, surrounded by a court stiff with Byzantine ceremonial, eating in solitude off gold plate, occasionally shedding his purple dalmatic for a pilgrim's cloak and trudging barefoot to some distant shrine. In 999 he elevated his old tutor, Gerbert of Aurillac, to the papacy under the name of Sylvester II. Gerbert was not only a distinguished theologian; he was also the most learned scientist and mathematician

Opposite Pope Leo III and Charlemagne, whom he crowned in 800, are shown as deriving their respective spiritual and temporal authorities from St Peter. But the struggle for dominance between popes and emperors was to last for centuries. A major step in resolving the conflict was the Concordat of Worms, signed in 1122 by Calixtus II and the Emperor Henry V who are seen holding the parchment. Old drawings from the medieval mosaic in the Lateran Triclinium and from a destroyed fresco.

The martyrdom by Roman soldiers of St Magnus, a saint whose legend is confused but interwoven with fearful memories of Saracen incursions in southern and central Italy. The twelfth-century fresco in the Cathedral of Anagni shows a stylistic fusion of Byzantine currents from Monte Cassino and a more naturalistic vein stemming from Rome.

Opposite Doge Ordelaffo Falier (1102–18). A portrait detail from the Pala d'Oro, the huge altarpiece of gold, enamel and precious stones that is one of the chief glories of St Mark's in Venice. Much of it, though since reworked, was commissioned from Constantinople by Falier during his reign.

The Emperor Otto III is portrayed on a marble well-head in the church of S. Bartolomeo, which he founded on the Tiber Island in Rome to en-shrine the body of the apostle. The well may mark the site of a healing spring in an ancient temple of Aesculapius.

REX ROGAT ABBATEM MATHILDIM SUPPLICAT ATQ;

of his time, and is generally credited with having introduced Arabic numerals and the use of the astrolabe into the Christian West. For a Pope of such calibre the Romans should have been grateful to their Emperor; but Otto tried their patience too hard and in 1001 they expelled him from the city. He died the following year, twenty-two years old and leaving, as might have been expected, no issue.

Emperor and Pope

The year 1000, roughly coinciding with the extinction of the Ottonian line, provides a good opportunity to pause for a glance at Italy as a whole at this stage of her political development. Certain patterns are already formed, others are slowly taking shape. First and most important is the interrelationship of Italy, the papacy and the Empire of the West. Italy was once again an integral part of the Empire, united with Germany under a single ruler, but subordinate in that she had no say in his election. He was thus always a German prince, never an Italian. On the other hand this ruler, though technically King of the Romans, could assume the dignity of Emperor only after his coronation by the Pope in Rome; and the imperial claim to the right of papal appointment was not generally accepted in Italy – least of all by the Curia and the Roman aristocracy. Even the journey to Rome through Lombardy, Tuscany and the Papal State could be made difficult for an unpopular candidate; while the cities of north Italy were growing steadily stronger and more self-willed. The chaos of the ninth and early tenth centuries had given them a taste for independence; and the peace which they had known under the Ottos had favoured their commercial development and made many of them already rich – particularly Milan, the first great crossroads south of the Alpine passes, and the swelling sea-republics of Genoa, Pisa and Venice.

In Rome and the Papal State the old mixture of turbulence and turpitude still prevailed as the great rival families – the Crescenti, the Counts of Tusculum and the rest – circled ceaselessly round the throne of St Peter. Yet even here and within the Curia itself a new spirit was beginning to appear, an awakening consciousness of the Church's need, if she were to survive, to shake off the shame of the past century and somehow to regain her moral and intellectual ascendancy. This was the spirit of Cluny, the great French mother-abbey of reform. A Cluniac dependency had existed in Rome for the past fifty years; at the start it had had little influence, but now at last its example and teachings were beginning to take effect.

Thus, so far as north and central Italy were concerned, the tendencies which were to shape the course of events in the eleventh century – the quickening of the struggle between an arrogant Empire and a resurgent papacy, with the increasingly self-reliant Lombard and Tuscan cities playing off the one against the other – were already discernible as the century opened. In the south, on the other hand, the situation in 1000 AD gave no clue to the momentous developments which lay in store. Of the four tenth-century protagonists in the region, two had now withdrawn; the Western Empire had shown no further interest since Otto II's *débacle* and the Saracens, while continuing their pirate raids from Sicily, seemed to have renounced the idea of establishing permanent settlements on the mainland. This led to a polarization between the two remaining parties, Lombard and Byzantine, whose desultory fighting might have been expected to drag on interminably had they been left to themselves. In the event, however, they were now joined by newcomers from the north, superior alike in courage, energy and intelligence, by whom they were outclassed and, in little more than fifty years, overthrown.

The story of the Normans in South Italy begins around 1015 with a group of about forty young pilgrims at the shrine of the Archangel Michael on Monte Gargano. Seeing in this underpopulated, unruly land both an opportunity and a challenge, they were easily persuaded by certain Lombard leaders to remain there as mercenaries against the Byzantines. Word soon got back to Normandy, and the initial trickle of footloose, adventurous younger sons rapidly swelled to a steady immigration. Fighting now indiscriminately for Lombard and Greek alike, the Normans soon began to exact payment for their services in land. In 1030 Duke Sergius of Naples, grateful for their support, invested their leader Rainulf with the County of Aversa; henceforth their progress was fast, and in 1053 at Civitate they defeated a vastly superior army, raised and led against them by Pope Leo IX in person. By this time the supremacy among the Norman chiefs had been assumed by the family of Tancred de Hauteville, an obscure Norman knight of whose twelve sons eight

Opposite The struggle between Empire and Papacy reached a climax in the reign of Gregory VII. The emperor Henry IV, excommunicated in 1076, was prepared to humble himself and later, in St Nicholas' Chapel, at Canossa, he asked Countess Matilda of Tuscany and Abbot Hugh of Cluny to intercede on his behalf.

had settled in Italy and five were to become leaders of the first rank. After Civitate papal policy changed; Robert de Hauteville, nicknamed Guiscard (the crafty) was in 1059 invested by Pope Nicholas II with the Dukedoms of Apulia, Calabria and Sicily. Of these territories much of Apulia and most of Calabria remained Greek, while Sicily was still in the hands of the Saracens; but Robert, strengthened by his new legitimacy, could not be checked for long. Two years later he and his youngest brother Roger invaded Sicily, and for the next decade they were able simultaneously to maintain the pressure there and on the mainland. Bari fell in 1071, and with it the last remnants of Byzantine power in Italy. Early next year Palermo followed, and the Saracen hold in Sicily was broken for ever. In 1075 came the collapse of Salerno, the last independent Lombard principality. By the end of the century the Normans had annihilated foreign opposition. In all Italy south of the Garigliano they reigned supreme; while in Sicily they were well on their way to establishing the most brilliant and cultivated court of the Middle Ages.

The Western Emperors of the eleventh century had been less preoccupied with Italy than the Ottos. Henry II 'The Holy' (1002–24) was passionately interested in ecclesiastical reform, but he could do little for the papacy in face of the worldly and unscrupulous family of the Counts of Tusculum which had entrenched itself at the Lateran, and neither he nor his successor Conrad II (1024–39) left an appreciable imprint on the peninsula. Nor, in the political sphere, did Henry III (1039–56); but Henry's life was dedicated to the concept of a strong reformed papacy working in close collusion with the Empire, and through a combination of good fortune and his own outstanding ability he achieved it. For the first six years of his reign he was mainly occupied in Germany; but when in 1045 matters had deteriorated to the point where no less than three rival Popes were squabbling over the papal crown, he delayed no longer. Hurrying to Rome, he immediately deposed all three, setting up in their place his friend and compatriot Suidger, Bishop of Bamberg who, as Pope Clement II, forthwith crowned him Emperor. Even now the trouble was not entirely over, for Clement lived less than a year and Henry's next appointee, Damasus II, expired after a pontificate of only twenty-three days in circumstances that suggested poison. Suitable candidates were now becoming hard to find, but in December 1048 a great council of bishops held at Worms called unanimously for the Emperor's second cousin – Bruno, Bishop of Toul.

With Bruno's installation as Leo IX, the Papacy recovered its self-respect. Here at last was a Pope worthy of his throne, a man who combined genuine saintliness with immense administrative ability and reformist zeal. The dreadful spell that had so long degraded Rome was broken; and though Leo died after only six years, never really recovering from his humiliation at the hands of the Normans, he had already laid the foundations of a reformed and revitalized papacy. In this task, however, he had had the wholehearted support of his Emperor – an advantage which his successors were never to enjoy, for with his death in 1054 and Henry's two years later, the fleeting era of harmonious co-operation between Emperor and Pope was at an end. It was the irony of Henry's life that, in striving to build the papacy into an ally, he succeeded only in creating a rival. The Church, having regained her virtue, now began to seek power as well – a quest which was bound to bring her into conflict with imperial interests, especially when pursued with the inflexible determination of prelates such as Archdeacon Hildebrand.

For nearly thirty years before his election as Pope Gregory VII in 1073, Hildebrand had played a leading part in Church affairs. He had been one of Leo's most trusted lieutenants, but had later been largely responsible for the reconciliation with the Normans, whose armed assistance he had twice sought at moments of crisis over the papal succession. For him, however, the Normans were never more than a means to an end, and that end was to impose upon all Christendom, from the Emperor down, an unwavering obedience to the Church. This could clearly not be achieved while the Pope was dependent on the Emperor for his election; and already in 1059 he had persuaded Nicholas II to promulgate a decree placing the responsibility for papal elections squarely upon the College of Cardinals, and virtually excluding the possibility of imperial intervention.

It was Hildebrand's good fortune that Henry III's son and heir, the young king and future emperor Henry IV, was still a child and that these courageous measures therefore escaped the opposition which might otherwise have been expected. As Henry grew up, however, he became increasingly resentful of the new attitude of Rome. A clash was inevitable; it came, unexpectedly, in Milan. Nowhere in Lombardy did

Opposite above The tenth-century church of La Cattolica at Stilo, Calabria. Unlike Apulia, Calabria was never invaded by the Lombards and so retained its Byzantine churches and traditions in a far purer form. A curious dialect of Greek is still spoken in some villages.

Opposite below The Piazza del Mercato in Lucca preserves the outline of the classical amphitheatre which stood on the site in the second century AD. It reveals the gradual organic transition from the antique to the medieval pattern of life.

Above S. Giovanni degli Eremiti, Palermo, was founded in 1132 by Roger II, the first Norman King of Sicily. Its five red domes and little open cloister exemplify the perfect fusion of Moorish and Romanesque characteristic of Norman Sicilian architecture.

Below An emperor and a builder, who is shown working on S. Sophia in Benevento, converse in this miniature from a twelfth-century south Italian MS. Byzantine influence on the Norman monarchy is reflected in the robe of Sicilian silk, the crown and the cushioned throne.

the spirit of independence burn more brightly than in this old capital of the North, where a special liturgical tradition had been jealously preserved since the time of St Ambrose; nowhere were the new reformist decrees, particularly those relating to simony and clerical marriage, more bitterly resented by the ecclesiastical die-hards. On the other hand, the city government was now dominated by a radical left-wing party known as the Patarines, fanatical supporters of reform. Such a situation would have been explosive enough without imperial interference; but in 1073, during a dispute over the vacant archbishopric of Milan, Henry had aggravated matters by giving formal investiture to the anti-reform candidate while fully aware that Pope Alexander II had already approved the canonical election of a Patarine. Here was an act of open defiance which the Church could not ignore; and in 1075 Hildebrand – now Pope Gregory VII – categorically condemned all ecclesiastical investiture by laymen, on pain of anathema. Henry, furious, immediately invested two more German bishops with Italian sees, and added for good measure a further Archbishop of Milan, although his former nominee was still alive. Refusing a papal summons to Rome to answer for his actions, he then called a general council of all the German bishops and, on 24 January 1076, formally deposed Gregory from the papacy.

He had badly overplayed his hand. The Pope's answering deposition, accompanied by the excommunication of the King and the release of all his subjects from their allegiance, led to revolts throughout Germany which brought Henry literally to his knees. Crossing the Alps in the depth of winter with his wife and baby son, he found Gregory in January 1077 at the castle of Canossa and there, after three days of abject humiliation, he at length received the absolution he needed. The story of Canossa, usually enlivened by an illustration of the King, barefoot and in sackcloth, shivering in the snow before the locked doors of the castle, has been a perennial favourite with the writers of children's history books, where it is apt to appear as an improving object-lesson in the vanity of temporal ambitions. In fact Gregory's triumph was empty and ephemeral, and Henry knew it. He had no intention of keeping his promises of submission and in 1081, after incurring a second but less effective sentence of deposition and excommunication, crossed into Italy once again – this time at the head of an army. At first Rome held firm, but after two years' campaigning

against the Pope's staunchest ally, Countess Matilda of Tuscany, Henry managed to break through its defences. A few half-hearted attempts at negotiation were soon abandoned and on Easter Day, 1084, Henry had himself crowned Emperor by his nominee anti-Pope Clement III.

Even now Gregory, entrenched in the Castel Sant' Angelo, refused to surrender. He had one more card to play. The Normans, to whom he always appealed when in trouble, had this time been slow to respond, Robert Guiscard being occupied with a Balkan campaign against the Eastern Empire; but in May 1084 Robert suddenly appeared with an army of 36,000 at the walls of Rome. Henry, hopelessly outnumbered, withdrew just in time. The Normans broke through the Flaminian Gate, and for three days the city was given over to an orgy of pillage and slaughter; when at last peace was restored the whole district between the Colosseum and the Lateran had been burnt to the ground. Rome had suffered more from the champions of the Pope than she had ever had to endure from Goth or Vandal. Robert Guiscard, not daring to leave the unhappy Gregory to the mercy of the populace, escorted him south to Salerno where, in the following year, he died. His last words have come down to us: 'I have loved righteousness and hated iniquity, therefore I die in exile.'

It was a bitter valediction; but Gregory's achievement had been greater than he knew. He had finally established papal supremacy over the Church hierarchy – the practice of lay investitures, already losing ground, was to die out early in the following century – and even if he had not won a similar victory over the Empire he had at least asserted his claims in such a way that they could never again be ignored. The Church had shown her teeth; future Emperors would defy her at their peril.

The Normans, Barbarossa and the Lombard League

The events of the eleventh century, and in particular the weakening of the imperial hold on Italy as the investiture struggle gained momentum, provided a perfect climate for the development of the Lombard and Tuscan city-states. This was a characteristically Italian phenomenon. All over Western Europe, the revival of trade and the beginnings of organized industry

Opposite Abbot Desiderius of Monte Cassino with St Benedict. Abbot from 1058–81, builder, patron of the arts and a skilled diplomat, he ended his life with a short and undistinguished pontificate as Victor III.

had set in motion that slow drift from the country to the towns which still continues today; but in Italy, where there was no embryonic concept of nationhood to override that of municipal solidarity, the process was quicker and more self-conscious than elsewhere. For most of the north Italian towns the Emperor was too remote, his local representative too weak or irresponsible, to constitute a serious brake on their independent development. The result was that the towns took advantage of the growing discord between Empire and Papacy to play one off against the other, some using papal support to sever their allegiance to the Emperor, others pledging him their continued steadfastness against the Pope's blandishments in return for an imperial charter. Thus during the eleventh and twelfth centuries were born the city-states of Italy, self-governing according to a communal system often consciously based on the Roman model, strong enough both to defend their independence against all-comers — including each other — and to exert an increasing gravitational pull on the local landed aristocracy. And thus, simultaneously, were sown the seeds of that grim conflict, later associated with the names of Guelf (papalist) and Ghibelline (imperialist), which was to lacerate north and central Italy for centuries to come.

While these fissile and republican tendencies were shaping the destinies of Lombardy and Tuscany, the south was developing on precisely opposite lines. Here the energy of the Normans had welded the land together for the first time in five centuries, imposing on it an autocratic feudalism stricter than anything the north had ever known. Robert Guiscard died in 1085, leaving his mainland dominion to his son but effective control in Sicily to his brother — now Count Roger — who had been largely responsible for its conquest. It was a fortunate decision, since it enabled the Count to consolidate the Norman hold on the island, where in certain areas Saracen resistance was still alive. In the sixteen years that he was to survive his brother, Roger laid the foundations of a secure, well-organized state — foundations on which his son, Roger II, was so triumphantly to build.

In Roger II Europe saw one of the greatest and most colourful rulers of the Middle Ages. Born of an Italian mother; raised in Sicily where, thanks to his father's principles of complete religious toleration, Greek and Saracen mingled on equal footing with Norman and Latin; in appearance a southerner, in temperament an oriental, he had yet inherited all the ambition and energy of his Norman forbears and combined them with a gift for civil administration entirely his own. In 1127 he acquired the Norman mainland from his incapable and feckless cousin, thus becoming in his own right one of the leading rulers of Europe. Only one qualification was lacking before he could compete as an equal with his fellow-princes: he needed a crown.

His opportunity came in February 1130, in the all too familiar guise of a dispute over the papal succession. Pope Honorius II was dying. His obvious successor was Cardinal Pierleoni, former Papal Legate to Henry I of England, a cleric of outstanding ability and irreproachable Cluniac background — who, however, being a member of a rich and influential family of Jewish origins, was unacceptable to the extreme reformist section of the Curia. While the majority acclaimed Pierleoni as Anacletus II, this group therefore elected their own candidate, who took the name of Innocent II. Within a few days, Innocent's position became so dangerous that he was forced to leave Rome. His departure proved his salvation. Once over the Alps, his cause championed by one of the greatest and most disruptive political influences of his age, St Bernard of Clairvaux, he rapidly gathered support from all Christian Europe. Anacletus was left with only Rome — and Roger. Roger's terms were simple — Norman support in return for a crown. Hastily, the Pope agreed. So it was that on Christmas Day, 1130, in conditions of unprecedented splendour, Roger was crowned 'King of Sicily and Italy' in Palermo Cathedral.

His troubles, however, were not over. Anacletus died in 1138 and the following year Innocent, at last secure on his throne, himself led an army against the new kingdom. It was always a mistake for Popes to meet Normans on the battlefield; Innocent was captured at the Garigliano just as Leo IX had been at Civitate, and received his liberty only on formally recognizing Roger's title to the Crown. But Roger constituted too dangerous a threat to the southern frontier of the Papal State to allow of any real reconciliation. Neither were his relations with the two Empires any happier. Both saw him as a challenge to their own sovereignty, and in 1146 even Roger's superbly tortuous diplomacy failed to prevent an entente of all three powers against him. He was saved only by the Second Crusade, that humiliating fiasco which was the price the princes of Europe had to pay for allowing St Bernard to meddle in their affairs.

Yet with all his problems, foreign and domestic — for

Opposite Innocent II, arch enemy of Roger II. From the apse mosaic of the church of S. Maria in Trastevere which he rebuilt, and of which he holds a model in his hand.

Above S. Pietro, L'Aquila, is a fine example of the continuity of classical forms in Italian Romanesque architecture. The twelfth-century church, restored after a devastating earthquake in 1915, shows the adroit re-use of classical columns, probably taken from nearby Alba Fucense, combined with the sparkling contemporary Cosmatesque ambo and altar screen.

Right Mermaid with gryphon. Romanesque art always preserved a strong tradition of the fantastic, as in this relief from the church of S. Pietro, L'Aquila. Early twelfth century.

the powerful vassals in Apulia maintained a state of almost constant insurrection through much of his reign – Roger's power continued to grow, as did the magnificence of his court. The navy that he created under his brilliant admiral George of Antioch soon became, despite the hostility of the Italian sea-republics, paramount in the Mediterranean. Malta he conquered, and much of the North African coast; Constantinople itself was raided; so were Corinth and Thebes, centre of the Byzantine silk-weaving industry, whence captive artisans were brought back to staff the royal workshops in Palermo. Here, in his palaces and pavilions among the orange-groves, Roger spent the last ten years of his life, working with his polyglot chancery (Latin, Greek and Arabic were all official languages of the kingdom), discussing science and philosophy with the foremost international scholars of his time (Sicily was now the main channel through which Arab and Greek learning passed into Europe), or taking his ease like any oriental potentate with his splendidly stocked harem. Here, also, and at his great foundation at Cefalù, he built those churches in which the Romanesque and Arabic styles seem effortlessly to coalesce and which, further embellished with Byzantine mosaics as fine as any of their date in existence, constitute one of the glories of Europe.

Meanwhile the wind of change which had already swept through North Italy was moving slowly south to Rome. In 1143 a civil insurrection broke out and a Senate was once again established. The papacy fought back – in 1145 Pope Lucius II actually died of wounds received while storming the Capitol – but the communal movement steadily gained ground, particularly after the arrival in Rome of a certain Arnold of Brescia, a fiery young monk in whom the extreme asceticism of the Patarines was buttressed by a new approach to religious thinking – scholasticism. This had grown up during the past century in France, under theologians such as Arnold's old master Peter Abelard, and it was now taking root in Italy. Essentially a trend away from the old mysticism towards a spirit of logical, rationalistic enquiry in spiritual matters, it was one of the two dominant influences in Arnold's life. The other was the revived interest in Roman law now being expounded at Bologna University. From these two influences he had developed his theory, preached tirelessly through the streets and piazzas of Rome, that the Church should subject herself entirely in all things temporal to the civil authority of the state, renouncing all worldly power

and reverting to the pure and uncompromising poverty of the early fathers. Here was dangerous stuff; to St Bernard, who preached diametrically opposite views with equal force and who had already condemned Arnold, with Abelard, at the great council of Sens in 1140, it was anathema. But not even Bernard could shake Arnold's hold on Rome. This was to be the joint achievement of two other towering figures of their century, Frederick Barbarossa and Nicholas Breakspear who, as Pope Adrian IV, was the only Englishman ever to occupy the throne of St Peter.

Adrian made it clear from the outset that he intended to take orders from no one. When, therefore, he found that the Roman commune, supported by Arnold, was barring him access to the Lateran, his reply was swift. Early in 1155 all Rome was placed under an interdict until Arnold should be expelled from the city. No Pope had ever dared to take such a step before, but it proved triumphantly successful. Holy Week was approaching, a godless Easter was unthinkable; popular feeling rose sharply against the commune. Suddenly Arnold disappeared, and Adrian found himself at last free to leave the Leonine City. On Easter Day he presided, as planned, at High Mass in the Lateran.

Frederick of Hohenstaufen, King of the Germans since 1152, kept the feast at Pavia. He had recently received the Iron Crown of Lombardy – in a ceremony even more symbolic than usual since several of the Lombard towns, led by Milan, were now in open opposition to the Empire – and was heading south to his imperial coronation in Rome. Near Siena he was met by papal legates with an urgent request – his assistance in capturing Arnold of Brescia, who had taken refuge in a neighbouring castle. For Frederick's army this caused no difficulty. Arnold soon gave himself up and was returned to Rome; condemned by the prefect of the city, he was hanged then burnt, and his ashes cast into the Tiber.

But the speed of Frederick's advance was beginning to cause concern in the Curia. Not without difficulty – for neither party trusted each other an inch – a meeting was arranged between King and Pope near Sutri. It nearly ended in fiasco when for two days Barbarossa refused to perform the symbolical act of holding Adrian's bridle and stirrup as he dismounted; but at last agreement was reached and the two rode on south together. They were soon intercepted by envoys from the commune; if Frederick wished to enter the city he would have to pay tribute and guarantee all civic liberties. The

Opposite Head of an eagle, holding a jewel in its beak. This powerful detail from the cope of St Alboin, in the Diocesan Museum of Bressanone (Brixen), shows the vigour of Byzantine textile design in the eleventh and twelfth centuries.

King angrily refused and the envoys returned to Rome; but Adrian, scenting trouble, quickly dispatched a heavy advance force to take over the Leonine City. The next morning at first light he and Frederick slipped into Rome; and a few hours later the new Emperor had been crowned. The news reached the commune while they were meeting to discuss how best to prevent the coronation. Furious at having been tricked, mob and militia together attacked the Vatican. All day the fighting went on, with heavy slaughter on both sides; but by evening the imperial forces had prevailed and the remaining attackers withdrew across the Tiber.

Frederick, having got what he wanted, now returned to Germany. For Adrian, however, it had been an empty victory. Without the German troops to protect him he could not remain in Rome; and he had failed to mobilize imperial support against King William I 'The Bad' of Sicily, Roger II's son and successor, whom he still refused to recognize. His best hope of achieving the downfall of the Sicilian kingdom now lay in the Apulian barons, once again in revolt and this time supported by a Byzantine army. But his luck had deserted him. William did not deserve his nickname; lazier and still more pleasure-loving than his father, he had retained the Hauteville gift of galvanizing himself and all those around him when faced with a crisis. He now swept up from Sicily at the head of his Saracen shock-troops, smashed the Greeks and the Norman insurgents at Brindisi, and then went on to besiege Adrian at Benevento. For the third time the Normans had a great Pope at their mercy. In June, 1156, forced to capitulate, Adrian confirmed William in his Sicilian kingdom.

Humiliating as it was, the Pope soon had cause to be glad of his action; for Barbarossa was proving more of a menace to the papacy than William had ever been. During the summer of 1158 he returned to Italy in strength, and at the Diet of Roncaglia left the Italian cities in no doubt as to his own concept of imperial sovereignty, as four celebrated savants from Bologna (a university to which he had always shown especial favour) demolished all their beloved ideals of municipal independence as pipe-dreams, totally devoid of legal foundation. Henceforth every city would be subjected, through a foreign *podestà*, to complete imperial control. Throughout Lombardy, the effect was electric; but Frederick had come prepared for trouble. In 1159, at Crema, he tied 50 hostages, including children, to his siege-engines to prevent the defenders from counter-attacking; in 1162 he at last brought the Milanese to

their knees and razed their city to the ground, so that for five years it lay deserted and in ruins. But he only stiffened the resistance. Past rivalries now forgotten, the cities formed the great Lombard League to defend their liberties; Venice, Sicily and the new Pope Alexander III lent their active support; and soon Frederick began to feel, for the first time, the full weight of the Italian opposition.

Soon too, his luck began to turn. In 1167 a march on Rome was brought to nothing when plague broke out in the imperial army; the Emperor was forced to retreat, almost defenceless, through hostile Lombardy, and barely managed to drag his pale survivors back over the Alps. In 1174 he returned, but the momentum had gone; on 29 May 1176, his German knights were routed at Legnano by the forces of the League. It was the end of Frederick's ambitions in Lombardy. At the Congress of Venice in the following year he publicly kissed Pope Alexander's foot in St Mark's Square and in 1183, at Constance, the Venetian truce became a treaty. Though imperial suzerainty was technically preserved, the cities of Lombardy (and to some extent Tuscany also) were henceforth free to manage their own affairs. It was hardly the solution Frederick had foreseen at Roncaglia, but consolation was soon at hand. In 1184 his son Henry became betrothed to Constance, posthumous daughter of King Roger II and sole heiress to the Sicilian kingdom. The Empire, which had fought so vainly and so long for control over Lombardy, was now to acquire Sicily with hardly a struggle.

Hohenstaufen and Angevin

William II 'The Good' of Sicily (1166–89), had proved himself as bad a king as his father, William I 'The Bad' had been a good one. His popularity was based on his youth, his beauty and on a genuine religious devotion which is reflected in his Cathedral of Monreale, the richest and most grandiose of all the Norman foundations in Sicily; but although William had inherited all his grandfather's territorial ambitions, he possessed none of Roger's political judgement or diplomatic finesse. Had he been endowed with either, he would never after seven years of childless marriage – to Joanna, daughter of Henry II of England – have pledged his Aunt Constance to Barbarossa's son.

Opposite The coronation by Christ of Roger II of Sicily, in the Martorana, Palermo, is the work of Greek mosaicists, brought to Sicily by the King. Roger's brilliant mingling of the diverse elements existing in his kingdom made Norman Sicily a model of efficient administration.

Frederick I, Barbarossa, Emperor of the West (1155–90), never managed to bend the cities of Lombardy to his will. Here he is shown as a Crusader. He was one of the leaders of the Third Crusade, and was drowned crossing the River Calycadnus in Cicilia on his way to the Holy Land.

Above, right 'Behold a monkey is crowned' jeered Peter of Eboli when Tancred of Lecce became King of Sicily in 1189. In this illustration from Peter's MS at Bern, Tancred, top left, is given an ape's face. Below is Count Roger of Andria, his unsuccessful rival, whom he imprisoned the year after his accession.

Right The Empress Constance, on horseback, led by two soldiers, displays her newborn son Frederick, later Frederick II, to his future subjects. Another illustration from the MS of Peter of Eboli.

Opposite A merchant bargaining with two customers, and another merchant, seated, recording the price of grain in the presence of two purchasers. An early fourteenth-century miniature from the *Specchio Umano* by Domenico Lenzi.

Galen and Hippocrates, the two great fathers of classical medicine, in medieval dress. This thirteenth-century fresco at Anagni reflects the influence throughout south Italy of the School of Salerno, centre of European medical studies.

Below A deed granting concessions to the people of Benevento, in July 1265, signed by Charles I of Anjou. His campaign to claim the Sicilian crown marked a turning point in Italian history when the French replaced the Germans as the predominant power in Italy.

Right Frederick II was called 'The Wonder of the World' by his contemporaries. Scientist, statesman, general, poet, architect, sportsman, he was perhaps the most gifted intellectual ever to wear a crown. Like other sculpture of Frederick's reign, this portrait closely follows classical models.

For Norman Sicily it was the beginning of the end. Three years after the marriage William died, still childless. He was succeeded by Tancred of Lecce, an illegitimate grandson of Roger II, but in 1194 Tancred also died and Constance's husband, now the Emperor Henry VI (1190–7), descended with an army to Sicily to claim his inheritance. More than ever the Sicilians had cause to regret the Hohenstaufen marriage. Tancred's son, the seven-year-old William III, was deposed, castrated and blinded, and all the Sicilian nobles who had supported Tancred's own coronation were burnt alive. The Norman kingdom was over.

Henry was crowned on Christmas Day. On 26 December, which marked the beginning of the massacre, the Empress Constance was delivered of her only child. She had stopped in the little town of Jesi on her way from Germany to join her husband, and to avoid any dangerous gossip about the genuineness of the boy's parentage – for she was now forty and had been married eight years – the birth took place in the main square of the town, under a hastily erected tent to which any local matron was allowed access. They were wise precautions; before her son Frederick was four years old he found himself orphaned, and the ward of the greatest of all the medieval Popes – Innocent III (1198–1216).

Innocent succeeded where Hildebrand had failed; in the eighteen years of his pontificate he made his authority supreme through the length and breadth of Europe – even in Rome itself where, only ten years before his accession, the Commune had wrested from Pope Clement III the last shreds of temporal power over the city; even in Constantinople, sacked and smouldering after the treachery of the so-called Fourth Crusade which enthroned a crew of Frankish thugs on the Bosphorus and made 1204 the blackest year in the history of Christendom. Only once did Innocent make a serious tactical mistake: in 1212 he gave reluctant consent to the election of young Frederick as King of the Romans. No one was more conscious than he of the danger of allowing the crown of Sicily to become merged with that of the Empire, but the guarantees he demanded were insufficient; Frederick rode over them roughshod, and so gained a greater power in Italy than any of his predecessors had managed to achieve.

The new Emperor was crowned in Rome in 1220 by Innocent's successor, Honorius III. It was perhaps the last favour he would ever receive from a Pope; the remaining thirty years of his life were to be taken up with a ceaseless struggle against the papacy. Honorius, who had been his tutor, was manageable enough; but his two successors Gregory IX (1227–41) and Innocent IV (1243–54) were to prove implacably hostile, excommunicating Frederick on no less than five separate occasions. Three of these were connected with his own sworn Crusade – the first for not leaving on it quickly enough, the second for leaving while still excommunicate and the third, for good measure, on his return – despite the fact that the Emperor had effectively negotiated the restoration of all the principal shrines to Christian hands before performing his own coronation as King of Jerusalem in the Church of the Holy Sepulchre. Nor did the Popes scruple to use the newly founded Mendicant Orders against their enemy. As a result, the majority of his subjects were persuaded to revile Frederick as a heretic or fear him as Antichrist; and Dante was later to relegate him to the sixth circle of Hell.

Back in Italy in 1229, for the next six years Frederick was able to devote most of his formidable energies to the development of his southern kingdom; but then a new Lombard revolt, championed as always by the Pope, called him north. At Cortenuova in 1237, with his Ghibelline allies, he smashed the revived League and avenged Legnano, thus earning for himself yet another excommunication. The accession of Innocent IV seemed to offer hopes for negotiation, but they were soon dashed; and in 1245, at the Council of Lyons, Innocent proclaimed Frederick once more excommunicate and deposed. This final ban, which St Louis of France and Henry III of England, the Emperor's father-in-law, both refused to recognize, made little immediate difference to Frederick's position; but in his last five years he lost much of the ground he had previously gained, and imperial power in Italy entered its final decline.

It is not, then, for his Italian achievements that Frederick is remembered as the most remarkable European ruler between Charlemagne and Napoleon; still less for his work in Germany, which he never visited when he could avoid it. What earned him the title of *Stupor Mundi*, the Wonder of the World, was the sheer force of his intellectual and physical personality. Not for nothing were Frederick I and Roger II his grandfathers. Both were themselves great men; but both, in their own fields, he surpassed. From Barbarossa he derived the immense energy, the military skill, the courage and the Augustan concept of Empire to which he devoted his life; to Roger and his Sicilian upbringing he owed the limitless breadth of his mind and interests, his familiarity with five European languages and cultures – to say nothing of the Arabic with which he had beguiled the Saracens of Jerusalem – and his passionate love of art and science. A poet among poets, his was the circle in which the sonnet was invented and Italian vernacular literature was born; his passionate curiosity over the nature of the physical and metaphysical worlds kept him in contact or correspondence with scientists, philosophers and theologians of every creed; while the surviving sculptures from the triumphal gate at Capua, which he designed himself, testify alike to his prowess as an architect and his munificence as a patron. He was the greatest of all Renaissance princes, two hundred years before his time.

On Frederick's death in 1250, the crown of the southern kingdom – the Regno, as it was now called – passed to his only legitimate son Conrad; but Conrad's life and interests lay in Germany, and the dying Emperor had therefore appointed, as Regent of both North Italy and the Regno, his bastard son Manfred. Italian history can boast few more romantic figures. Manfred possessed none of his father's Germanic qualities – his energy, thoroughness or passion for detail; son of an Italian mother, he was a man of the south, a scholar and a poet, outstandingly handsome, and with all the gentle sensitivity and charm of manner that his father had so conspicuously lacked. Yet he too had the Hohenstaufen steel. In 1258, without a shred of legal justification, he seized the Sicilian throne; two years later, after Ghibelline Siena had crushed Guelf Florence with his help, he became head of a great Lombard-Tuscan Ghibelline League. Meanwhile the people of Rome had elected him as sole Senator, to defend the Commune against papal power. By 1261 Manfred was the dominant figure of Italy.

Pope Urban IV (1261–4) was a Frenchman, and he chose a French solution. Legates were despatched to Charles, Count of Anjou, brother of St Louis, offering him the throne of Naples (which Manfred had made his capital) and Sicily. Charles accepted; his wife pawned her jewels to pay for the expedition; Louis gave his reluctant consent; and at Whitsun 1265 the new King arrived in Rome. It was typical of Charles's megalomania that he should at once have installed himself and his court at the Lateran. He was a natural autocrat, grim and ambitious, with an unshakable belief in himself as the chosen instrument of the Almighty.

Against his army of thirty thousand Crusaders – for Clement IV, Urban's successor, had by now declared the war a Crusade – Manfred stood little chance. In February 1266, outside Benevento, he went down fighting. Only after three days was his body discovered; then, denied by Charles a Christian burial, he was laid beneath the bridge of Benevento, with every soldier in the French army casting a stone on the cairn as he passed. Manfred's wife and three young children were imprisoned at Nocera. Of the four, three never emerged again; one son was still there forty-three years later. Charles, it appeared, was not a man to take chances.

In 1268 he proved it more conclusively still. Conradin, King Conrad's only son, marched south from Germany in a last desperate effort to save the Hohenstaufen inheritance. His army was shattered at Tagliacozzo; he himself was captured, tried, found guilty of treason and beheaded in the market square of Naples. He was just sixteen years old.

Tagliacozzo marked the supplanting of the Germans by the French as rulers of Italy. Now it was Charles and the Guelfs who were everywhere supreme, just as Manfred and the Ghibellines had been a decade before. All the new King needed was a subservient Pope. His influence was strong in the Curia, and for three years after Clement's death in 1268 he managed to keep the papal throne without a tenant; the succession was only forced when the authorities at Viterbo removed the roof from the palace in which the cardinals were assembled. Their hasty choice now fell on one of the Visconti from Vicenza, Gregory X. He proved distinctly stubborn, thwarting Charles's attempts to have his nephew Philip III of France elected Emperor, and allying himself with the Byzantines (against whom Charles had aggressive ambitions) to the extent of actually effecting, at the Council of Lyons in 1274, a temporary reunion of the Eastern and Western Churches. But in 1281, with the accession of another Frenchman, Martin IV, Charles got his way at last. Master of Italy, he was now free to march against Constantinople whose Emperor, Michael Palaeologus, Martin obligingly redeclared schismatic. It was only twenty years since the Greeks had recovered their capital from the Franks; as 1282 opened, their chances of keeping it looked slim indeed.

They were saved by the people of Palermo. The severity of their taxation and the arrogance of their conduct had made the French hated throughout the Regno; and when on Easter Monday a drunken sergeant began importuning a Sicilian woman outside the

An idealized portrait of St Thomas Aquinas (1225–74), 'the Angelic Doctor', who synthesized all the theological knowledge of the past. up to his own day. Last and greatest of the scholastics, his system is still taken as the basis of Roman Catholic philosophical teaching.

Right St Dominic (1180–1221) presiding over Gregory IX's diabolical invention, the Inquisition. This tight-lipped Castilian founded his order with the express purpose of crushing heresy underfoot. His followers, with the Franciscans, became the spiritual shock-troops of an increasingly corrupt and sybaritic Papacy.

Right In the constant struggle by successive Popes against their arch-enemy, Frederick II, they did not scruple to use a new and powerful weapon—the Mendicant Orders. This predella panel, of the school of Giotto, shows the forceful Pope Innocent III (1198–1216) giving his blessing to the Franciscan Order on its foundation.

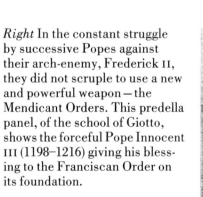

St Francis (1181–1226), a saint whose nature bore no trace of smugness, he would have been horrified to see his cherished ideal of poverty forgotten within a few years of his death, as well-fed friars spread hatred and slander against the Emperor across Europe.

Can Grande della Scala of Verona (1291–1329) was the first of the great northern prince-despots to create a splendid court in order to enhance his power and prestige. He gave shelter to Dante, and was rewarded by the dedication of the *Paradiso*.

Left Reminders of ancient Rome were ever present in medieval times. This stone container for the cinerary urn of Agrippa Senior was used in the Middle Ages as a grain measure. The SPQR inscription surmounted by a crown was the badge of the Roman Commune; below it are medieval coats of arms.

Pope Boniface VIII (1294–1303), corrupt heir to the tradition of Hildebrand and Innocent III, lacking both the godliness of the first and the breadth of vision of the second but, in his conception of the papal authority, more autocratic than either. A copper portrait statue by the Sienese goldsmith Manno (1301).

A fourteenth-century fresco by Jacopo di Cione with the famous Palazzo Vecchio and showing (far right) Walter de Brienne, titular Duke of Athens, being expelled from Florence in 1343. During a severe financial crisis in Florence, this soldier of fortune staged a *coup d'état* and seized power; but his despotism proved intolerable and he was soon driven out.

In the early fourteenth century the cities of Lombardy were ceaselessly at war. One of the many conflicts was that between Napo Torriani and the Visconti of Milan which ended in the Visconti triumph of 1311. An episode in this struggle, in which, as usual, the mendicant orders played an important part, is depicted in a contemporary fresco.

Church of Santo Spirito just as vespers were about to begin, it was more than her countrymen could stand. The sergeant was set upon by her husband and killed; the murder led to a riot and the riot to a massacre. Two thousand Frenchmen were dead by morning; Palermo, and soon afterwards Messina also, was in rebel hands. The rising was perfectly timed. Peter III of Aragon, Manfred's son-in-law, had already launched an expedition to recover Sicily. Charles's small punitive force hastily withdrew on the arrival of the Spaniards and Peter was crowned in Palermo. The French, however, would not relinquish their claims; and the War of the Sicilian Vespers continued intermittently for twenty years, while the Regno was split between the House of Anjou on the mainland and that of Aragon in Sicily, each determined to expel the other and reunify the country. At last, in 1302, after an abortive attempt to place Charles of Valois, brother of Philip the Fair of France, on the throne, Pope Boniface VIII was reluctantly compelled to recognize Peter's son Frederick as ruler of the island with the title of 'King of Trinacria' – a necessary, if somewhat precious, appellation since the Angevins at Naples still technically retained the crown of Sicily.

Pope Boniface had been elected in 1294, after the abdication of the saintly but wholly incapable hermit Celestine V, whose only qualification for the Papacy was that he had once, at the court of Gregory X, hung his cowl on a sunbeam. The new Pope was his antithesis in every respect. For him the great sanctions of the Church existed only to further his own temporal ends and to enrich his family, the Caetani. Foreign rulers he treated less as his subjects than as his menials, while the rival Ghibelline house of Colonna, of whom he was bitterly jealous and whose power he feared, was excommunicated *en masse*, its lands at Palestrina seized and devastated in the name of a Crusade. Such conduct brought the Papacy to a point of debasement from which it took centuries to recover; and it made Boniface hated and reviled throughout Europe. When the Colonna had all fled to France his principal enemies in Italy were the Fraticelli or Spiritual Franciscans, who had rebelled against the increasing worldliness of their Order to return to their founder's principles of asceticism and poverty. On their shoulders had fallen the mantle of the Patarines and of Arnold of Brescia, and to them the hapless, hopeless Celestine had represented the true papal ideal. Boniface they loathed, not only for his wealth and arrogance but because they

held him responsible – and not without good reason – for Celestine's abdication and his subsequent imprisonment and death.

Still more serious for Boniface was the hostility of Philip the Fair, whom he had excommunicated and threatened with deposition after the King had forbidden his French clergy to obey a papal summons to Rome. In the spring of 1303 Philip retaliated by calling a general council, at which he intended that the Pope himself should be arraigned. Guillaume de Nogaret, the ablest of his ministers, was despatched to Italy with Count Sciarra Colonna and an army 1600 strong, with orders to seize Boniface and to bring him, by force if necessary, to France. They found the Pope at his native Anagni, where he was putting the finishing touches to a Bull releasing Philip's subjects from their allegiance, and took him prisoner. Three days later a popular reaction in his favour forced them to withdraw; but their mission, though unsuccessful, had not been in vain. The old Pope's pride had suffered a mortal blow. His friends the Orsini escorted him back to Rome and there, a month later, he died.

The Fourteenth Century

Boniface and Philip were arch-enemies, but it was their combined efforts that finally broke the morale of the medieval papacy and destroyed what was left of its prestige in Italy. When in 1305 another Frenchman was elected as Clement V, he had himself crowned at Lyons. There he was joined by his Curia, and for the next seventy-two years there was no Pope in Rome. Petrarch's phrase 'the Babylonish Captivity' is arresting but misleading; the Popes were in no sense captive. Clement had gone to Lyons of his own free will and had no intention of becoming a catspaw of the French king – indeed it was only four years later, after a quarrel with Philip, that he moved his court over the frontier to Avignon, just inside the Provençal dominions of the Kingdom of Naples, where his independence could be more easily preserved. He and his successors never voluntarily loosened their hold on Italian affairs, nor ever looked on Avignon as anything but a temporary residence until such time as they could safely – and comfortably – return to Italy.

For Italy had become not only unpleasant but dangerous. There had been no crowned Emperor since the death of Frederick II in 1250 and the cities of Lombardy and Tuscany, untroubled by imperial incursions, had been left to develop in their own way. In most of them their hard-won communal government had given place to despotism, as one mighty family or another – the Visconti and Della Torre in Milan, the Montecchi (Shakespeare's Montagues) and later the Scaligeri in Verona, the Gonzaga in Mantua – asserted its domination. This mass of petty but absolute dictatorships, superimposed on a tradition of inter-communal strife within which the quarrel between Guelf and Ghibelline continued in full spate, undermined by the hostility of a commercially minded bourgeoisie, led to a deep unrest which permeated all aspects of North Italian life. Sometimes, admittedly, it provided a stimulus for the new spirit of artistic enquiry which was already heralding the Renaissance – Giotto was born in the year Manfred died – but more often the story is one of tyranny and unremitting bloodshed. Of the great northern sea-republics, Genoa and Pisa continued at each other's throats until Genoa's decisive victory off Meloria in 1284; only Venice remained relatively untouched by the prevailing chaos, thanks to her carefully preserved oligarchy, her freedom from faction and that delicate system of political checks and balances which was to make the government of the Most Serene Republic the wonder – and the terror – of Europe.

Another haven of comparative peace in the prevailing turmoil was Florence, the most artistically conscious of all the Italian city-states and still more remarkable in having evolved perhaps the only successful governments by artists and craftsmen the world has ever seen. Here the effective administrative control lay in the hands of six guild-masters, called Priors of the Arts; their powers were great, but held for only two months at a time. Florence could also look back on an entrenched Guelf tradition which might have preserved her from much of the feuding that so bedevilled less fortunate cities; but towards the end of the century a rift occurred among the Guelfs and in 1302, Boniface VIII having allied himself with the reactionary 'blacks', the leaders of the more moderate 'white' party were driven into exile.

Among them was Dante Alighieri (1265–1321) whose *Divine Comedy*, the greatest single achievement in the Italian language, is among other things a profound and bitter commentary in which the poet, purporting merely to meet the leading figures of his age as he progresses through the afterworld, in fact sits in awful judgment over them. The grandeur of the conception is as breathtaking as the technical mastery of a still developing vernacular; but the political ideas within it seem more redolent of the eleventh century than of the fourteenth. These ideas, which Dante develops more fully in his *De Monarchia*, are in essence a return to the old dream of a world-wide Christian Empire, governed in harmonious tandem by Emperor and Pope. Just how unworkable they had become was shown in 1310 when their most active exponent, Count Henry of Luxemburg, descended into Italy as Emperor-elect. Idealistic and painfully well-meaning, he received his first coronation in Milan with a replica of the Iron Crown (the real one was in pawn), still stressing his impartiality between Guelf and Ghibelline; but the Guelf cities of Lombardy and Tuscany left him in no doubt of their feelings towards an outmoded imperialism and he was Ghibelline enough by the time he reached Rome where, denied entry to St Peter's, he was forced to accept the Crown of Empire from papal legates at the Lateran. Meanwhile at Avignon Clement V, under pressure from Philip the Fair, had turned against Henry; and so had Charles of Anjou's reigning grandson King Robert of Naples. Reluctantly the new Emperor resorted to war, but it got him nowhere; and in 1313 he died of fever, having proved conclusively and incontravertibly the vanity of Dante's hopes.

Henry's successor, Lewis IV of Bavaria, applied a radically different technique when his turn came in 1327. This time there was no idealism, no pretence at impartiality, no nod in the direction of Avignon. Lewis arrived at the invitation of the Ghibellines of Italy, bringing with him the most formidable of all the anti-papalists of his time, Marsilius of Padua. Only two years previously this ex-Rector of the Sorbonne had published his *Defensor Pacis*, in which he argued that the whole edifice of papal domination and canon law was contrary to the basic principles of Christianity. Such company was unlikely to increase Lewis's popularity at Avignon, and long before he reached Rome he had incurred a double sentence of excommunication and deposition from Pope John XXII. But by this time the papal prestige in Italy had sunk even lower than the imperial, and the decree went largely unheeded. When Lewis was crowned by Sciarra Colonna, representing the People of Rome, at St Peter's in

difficilia emergunt circa negotia
huius artis. Rogauimus aut q̈
nusquam nobilem hoc exercere
et sola sui nobilitate iste debet
exercere. et ab auctoris instinc-
to ipsam legi fundata et exponi-
mus uno diuersis modis ... tam
cum ars ... sit a ... per
pria quadmodum ... et certe artem
et nos non inueniem̄ in grauia
... L. iunior uerba conuenientia
omnibus ... q̈ mag
... esse ... per quem
... possit intentio nostra. Est
...
...
...
...
que practica ... depū. Rursus
Ioann pars de generali descriptio-
ne tam eorum q̈ spectant ad
... ut in eos que spectant
ad practicam. ... uero de
special consideratione eorude in
Intentio uero nostra est manifestare
in hoc libro de uenatione auium
ea que sunt sicut sunt et ad artis certitudinem redigere quorum
nullus ... scientiam habuit
... Modus agendi est p̄ say
cius proemialis et exequtiuus exe-
quutiuus uero multiplex partim
nam ... diuisiuus partim descrip-
tiuus partim conuenientiam et

... ... uerā causarum
... ...
sequuntur ... nolo rege dauer̄
... inquisitor et ... amator
diuus augustalis Fredericus secun-
dus romanorum imperator ierlm
et sicilie rex. Vtilitas est magna et
enim nobiles et potentes solliciti erca
regimina mundanorum per huius
artis usum suis curis plerumq̈
gaudia ... Pauperes uero
et minus nobiles de hac arte nobili-
bus ... obtinebant ab ipsis
necessaria sue uite. Vnde uero per
hanc artem habent ... manifesta
tionem operato ... in ...
uir̄ ... ...
... natu ... ...
manifeste. Licet ille natura speri-
mento per hunc librum habita
alteram quodam modo uidebimtur
Libri titulus talis est. Liber diui
augusti Frederici secundi romanorum imperatoris ierlm et sicilie
regis de arte uenandi cum auibus
diuisiuus ... quibus ... ad ma
... nifestationem operationum natu
... in uenatione que ... res
... uacandi in singulis partibus
euidenter apparebit. Proemium
... ... uenationis ... In
... ... uero seu in ... uenatione
... ... et alia sunt ponuntur
... ... que secundum natu
ram priora sunt. ponuntur hiis q̈

January 1328 and when three months later, he formally pronounced the Pope heretic and deposed, it almost looked as though he might re-establish imperial control. But Robert of Naples proved his military match, and on returning to Rome he found that the pendulum had swung. The year 1330 saw him back in Germany. He too had learnt his lesson: Italy had outgrown imperialism, even if she was not yet ready for a unity of her own making.

Between the south and the north the difference was still immense, so deep that the effects of it can still be felt today. The Kingdom of Naples, under Robert and his flighty successor Joanna I, could boast an enlightened and cultivated court and two of the best universities in Italy – Frederick II's foundation in Naples itself and the world-famous school of medicine, already more than five centuries old, at Salerno. Outside these centres, however, the land was dominated, just as in Norman days, by an irresponsible and obstreperous baronage. Sicily under the Aragonese was less encumbered by feudalism and economically more coherent, but was permeated by much the same atmosphere of stagnation and inertia.

In the north, on the other hand, there is no escaping the sense of overpowering vitality. Gradually, as the fourteenth century progresses and the smaller city-states are drawn into the orbit of the larger, the great spheres of influence begin to appear: Venice, richer and more magnificent than ever, slowly outdistancing Genoa, her only remaining maritime rival, increasing her Italian dominions while still extending her influence beyond the Adriatic as one of the great powers of Europe; Milan under the superb house of Visconti, flooding like a great tide over Lombardy and Piedmont finally to engulf even Bologna, the centre of papal power in north Italy; and the Florence of Giotto, Orcagna and Andrea Pisano, her staunch republicanism foiling every attempt by a would-be despot, her great merchant bankers developing the art of international finance to undreamed-of levels of efficiency and sophistication. One of the advantages of Roman over Canon Law was that it made usury respectable; the way was now open for full economic growth and for the long-term credits which made possible the wealth and splendour that still dazzle down the centuries.

Across the centre of the peninsula and well beyond the effective control of their absentee landlord in Avignon, the States of the Church succumbed in their turn to the prevailing fashion for despotism. The Este of Ferrara, the Pepoli of Bologna, the Malatesta of Rimini and their like might call themselves Papal Vicars and punctiliously acknowledge the suzerainty of St Peter, but within their respective cities their power remained absolute. Only in Rome itself, despite the attempts of the Colonna and the Orsini, was popular republican feeling strong enough to hold its own; but Rome was by now perhaps the saddest place in Italy. Deserted by the Popes, its principal *raison d'être*, its population reduced by malaria, famine and factional strife to a pitiable twenty thousand, the capital of Western Christendom had sunk to a level of degradation such as it had never before known. More than any other city, it now needed a leader who would focus its aspirations and restore its self-respect; and, at the moment of its darkest despair, it found one.

Cola di Rienzo, son of a Roman washerwoman, was a visionary, a fanatic, a superb showman and a demagogue of genius. In 1344, when he was thirty-one, he launched his campaign against the aristocracy of Rome, inflaming the popular imagination with his evocations of the city's past greatness and his prophecies of its glorious rebirth. Such was his success that three years later, on the Capitol, he was invested with the title of Tribune and limitless dictatorial powers; then, summoning a 'national' parliament, he solemnly conferred Roman citizenship on all the cities of Italy and announced plans for the election of an Italian Emperor. But appeals for Italian unity, whether pronounced by a German prince or a Roman demagogue, were doomed to failure. By 1347 not only the other cities but the Roman mob itself had turned against Cola and forced him into exile. Seven years later he managed to return, but the old magic was gone: the mob, fickle as always, rose against him almost at once. In vain Cola showed himself on the balcony of the Capitol, clad in shining armour and bearing aloft the banner of Rome; they only jeered the louder. Disguising himself as a beggar, he tried to flee; but the gold bracelets glinting under his rags betrayed him. Minutes later his body was hanging by the feet in a public square – a similar fate to that which, in our own day, befell his closest and most successful imitator.

And yet, in his comet career, Cola had somehow managed to clear the minds of his fellow-citizens of much of the cumbersome detritus of the Middle Ages and to give them a new awareness of their classical past. What he had accomplished in the political sphere was paralleled in the world of letters by his friend and

Opposite The Marriage, a fourteenth-century fresco in San Gimignano. It may well be connected with one of the *Decameron* stories of Boccaccio, whose house still stands in the neighbouring village of Certaldo.

supporter, Francesco Petrarch (1304–74). It was only twenty years after Dante's death that Petrarch was crowned with a poet's laurels on the Capitol, but in those twenty years lay all the difference between the scholasticism of the later Middle Ages and the humanism of the Renaissance. Petrarch had none of Dante's gigantic vision; but his more slender genius led the way forward to a fresh, uncluttered outlook, based to some extent on the troubadour poets of Sicily and Provence, but drawing its chief inspiration from the Latin authors of antiquity.

The new conception of the classical past as a signpost to the future led to a similar revival of interest in the literature of ancient Greece, forgotten in the medieval west and even in the Byzantine Empire largely neglected. This was largely the achievement of Giovanni Boccaccio (1313–75), Petrarch's most gifted disciple, who kept for three years in his house an aged Calabrian Greek of revolting habits, preparing one of the first – and worst – translations of Homer into Latin. But it is not for his classical scholarship that Boccaccio is now remembered. His *Decameron* is a comparatively youthful work, but with it he did for Italian prose what Petrarch had done for poetry, simplifying it, refining it and forging it into a new literary instrument. The style which he developed, racy and astringent, gave the *Decameron* a European reputation, starting a revived narrative tradition that can be traced through Chaucer and Shakespeare to La Fontaine and beyond.

To the Popes at Avignon, the impact of Cola di Rienzo and the success of the *Decameron* must have sounded a new note of danger. If the fullness of papal power were not soon reasserted in Italy, it would be lost forever. Cola's return to Rome had coincided with the appointment of Cardinal Gil Albornoz as Legate, with the express task of bringing the States of the Church back into the papal fold. This terrifyingly able Spaniard succeeded to the point where, in 1367, Pope Urban v ventured to re-establish himself in the Lateran. He received a vociferous welcome from the people of Rome, and soon afterwards became the first and last Pope to receive visits from both the Eastern and Western Emperors. But he was an old man and he soon grew homesick; and in 1370 the attractions of Avignon became too strong for him. St Bridget of Sweden had warned him that a return to Provence would be fatal, and she was right. Within a few weeks he was dead.

Urban had shown with painful clarity why the papacy had been so long absent from its rightful home. All the Avignon Popes and most of their Curias had been Frenchmen – notoriously unwilling travellers at the best of times – to whom the ruins of Rome, insalubrious and smelly, must have constituted little enough temptation. It would take a serious crisis in Italy if, after seventy years, the papal conscience was to be re-awakened. But that crisis was not long in coming. Albornoz had been succeeded in the States of the Church by a horde of grasping French legates who made no secret of being out for what they could get and soon drove the unhappy cities to a state of open rebellion. In doing so, they did not hesitate to make use of the so-called 'Free Companies' – bands of foreign mercenaries who, when not otherwise employed, roamed the countryside supporting themselves on protection money, highway robbery and blackmail. In 1375 one of the worst of these, the 'English Company' of Sir John Hawkwood, was despatched by the Legate of Bologna to lay waste the Florentine harvests. To the Italian cities it seemed that papal iniquity could be carried no further. A wave of rabid anti-clericalism swept through Tuscany, Umbria and the Papal States, and by the end of the year no less than eighty towns had expelled their papal garrisons.

Away in Avignon, Gregory XI acted quickly and firmly. Florence, the leader of the rising, was placed under an interdict; all the Christian princes of Europe were commanded to seize Florentine goods wherever they might be found and to sell all local Florentine merchants into slavery. They were fearsome measures; but they had no effect. Gregory now saw that his only hope lay in an immediate return to Rome. Spurred on by the entreaties of St Catherine of Siena – carrying on where St Bridget had left off – he embarked with his reluctant Curia at the end of 1376 and, on 17 January 1377, made his formal entry into the city. It was a sad homecoming; in Florence and Rome simultaneously, his troops, under Cardinal Robert of Geneva, were taking hideous vengeance, while even in Rome his position was by no means secure. He was in fact, seriously contemplating a return to Avignon when, fortunately for Rome, he died in the following year. The Romans had not always treated their Popes with particular affection or respect, but they were determined not to let them go again. '*Romano lo volemo, o almeno Italiano!*' they shouted through the ensuing conclave, and they got what they wanted. The new Pope was an unmitigated disaster, but he was at least an Italian.

On 17 January 1377, the papacy returned from Avignon to Rome. In this fresco by Vasari, Pope Gregory IX, led by St Catherine of Siena is carried in procession to St Peter's.

DANTE · PETRARCHA

Transition

The period of the Avignon Popes marks the end of the Middle Ages. When Clement V left Italy the old order was dying, but little had yet appeared to take its place. Though the imperial throne was temporarily vacant, men still remembered the magnificent Frederick, and wept for Manfred and Conradin; while over the Alps in Germany Henry VII was still nursing his Ottonian illusions. Papal pride had been brought low, but a new Innocent III might at any time restore it to its former glory. Scholastic philosophy had reached, with St Thomas Aquinas, (1225–74) at once its highest pinnacle and its logical conclusion. It remained only for Dante to sum up, in the *Divine Comedy*, the achievements and the failures, the wisdom and the blindness, the ideals, the hopes and the fears of medieval Italy.

Gregory XI returned to a land which, though in some respects unchanged, in others could never be the same again. Unity was as remote a possibility as ever; Guelf and Ghibelline, their original differences long forgotten, still hammered on at each other and the blood continued to flow as it always had, copious and unavailing. But seventy years without a Pope or an effective Emperor had removed the old polarities; and in 1347–8 the Black Death, which within a few months wiped out some two-thirds of the Italian population, seemed to draw a further curtain across the past and expose the present yet more mercilessly to the winds of change. The secular, enquiring spirit which now spread over the land was not in itself new. Its roots went back to Roger of Sicily and his Greek and Arab sages, to Frederick and his falcons, to Manfred and his troubadours; to Arnold of Brescia and the Patarines; and to the doctors and lawyers of Salerno and Bologna. But the fourteenth century had given it a new momentum – in the political sphere with Cola di Rienzo and the despots of the north, in the cultural with Petrarch and the humanists, in the theological with Marsilius of Padua – and at the same time the papal barriers that had so long blocked its progress suddenly disappeared. The Renaissance was under way.

Opposite Dante and Petrarch. On these doors, decorated in intarsia in 1481 by Francione and Giuliano da Maiano, scholasticism is confronted with humanism, imperialism with republicanism, the Middle Ages with the Renaissance.

THE RENAISSANCE: ART, HUMANISM AND SOCIETY
1377 - 1559

Peter Burke

In the rebirth of secular civilization in fifteenth-century Italy, artists, humanists, scholars and literati became public figures who were in demand in the great centres of Florence, Rome, Naples, Venice, Milan, as well as at the courts of the minor despots. Florence under the Medicis, prosperous from its lucrative wool trade and international banking system, was a centre of talent and genius. Neo-Platonism in philosophy and an enthusiasm for classical antiquity made people seek the ideal which must lie behind all forms of reality, a search which led to systematic studies of anatomy and perspective, and an identity of science and the arts. A happy result was the universal man, like Da Vinci, Raphael or Michelangelo, who could express himself in any art. The Italian political situation, however, was uneasy, with the balance of power held by shifting alliances and the use of mercenary bands. After the sack of Rome by imperial troops in 1527, France and Spain contended for mastery of the country until the Treaty of Câteau-Cambrésis in 1559, by which France withdrew and Spain remained in control of Lombardy and the south. The Italian states, also buffeted by the Reformation, adopted the severely conformist Counter-Reformation codes of the Council of Trent. Soon it would no longer be true that whatever Italy did in one century, the rest of Europe would do in the next, for the Renaissance was at an end.

Renaissance intellectuals were convinced that they lived in a new age. Did they? There were more links with the past than they knew or than they were willing to admit, but there was also a serious change in the pattern of culture at this time, a break with the social heritage of techniques, habits, ideas and values.

In different periods, different human activities can claim pride of place. For the two centuries from the 1370s to the 1570s, this place belongs to the history of the arts, literature and ideas. But history is a seamless web and art and ideas have a social, political, and eco-nomic context, which in the pattern of Italian culture is not simple and is not fixed. The interplay of politics and ideas, religion and art in the seven generations of this two-hundred-year period does not constitute the history of a country, but the history of a number of states, each with a strongly differentiated character. Milan was not like Venice, nor Naples like Florence. But as the fifteenth century progressed Italy developed more of a common history, and the Italians grew more conscious of this. Two famous books bear witness to this increasing consciousness of unity: Biondo's

Opposite Maximilian Sforza, represented as the ideal young gentleman, riding through the streets of Milan. The son of Lodovico Sforza, he was installed as Duke of Milan by the Swiss in 1512, but three years later Francis I, who also claimed Milan, drove him out of the duchy.

Opposite The architect in his workshop, a fresco by the Florentine Bernardino Poccetti (1548–1612). The professional architect reappeared at the Renaissance; with him came the revival of the term 'architect', used in Roman times, but not in the Middle Ages, when architects were usually anonymous craftsmen.

Botticelli's painting of St Augustine (1480) is a reminder that Renaissance humanists studied the Fathers as well as the classics. Botticelli's acquaintance Ficino was a great admirer of Augustine, whose interest in Plato helps explain his attraction for them both.

Left and centre Cosimo de' Medici, who established his family's power, and his grandson Lorenzo, 'The Magnificent', whose adroit politics gave Italy an unwonted equilibrium during his lifetime. Although the Republic still existed in theory, in practice they both ruled Florence. Both were business men and patrons of the arts. These sixteenth-century portraits were ordered by Cosimo de' Medici, a descendant, to propagate the myth of Florence's golden age.

Right Politian with his pupil, Lorenzo the Magnificent's son, Giuliano, who was also painted by Raphael, sculpted by Michelangelo, and figured in Castiglione's *Courtier*.

Below A panel of a fifteenth-century *cassone* or wedding chest, appropriately portraying a wedding, with the Baptistry of Florence in the background. Painted by Francesco di Antonio for the Adimari family.

Italia Illustrata in the mid-fifteenth century, and Guicciardini's *Storia d'Italia* in the mid-sixteenth.

The Years of Preparation, 1370—1400

The end of the fourteenth century was a period of pause between the first and the second waves of the Renaissance. Of the first wave, Petrarch and Boccaccio died in the 1370s; Giotto and Simone Martini had already been dead for some time, and their successors, men like Agnolo Gaddi (d. 1396) and Lorenzo Monaco (c 1370–1425), were more traditional in style than they had been. The important works of architecture that were undertaken at this time, like the Cathedral of Milan and the Charterhouse of Pavia, continued the late Gothic tradition.

Economically, it was a period of recovery from the disaster of the Black Death; in religion, a period of crisis. There was a strong feeling that the plague had come as punishment for men's sins, and among the more obvious sins, there was the 'captivity' of the papacy in Avignon ('Babylon') for most of the fourteenth century. The latter part of the century was marked by attempts to reform the Church or to withdraw from it into heresy or mysticism. The Fraticelli formed a kind of 'left wing' of the Franciscan movement; and there was the mystic St Catherine of Siena, who influenced the reform of the Dominicans and received the stigmata, just as St Francis had done. She advocated a crusade against the Turks, and the return of the papacy from Avignon. The Swedish visionary, St Bridget, was also in Italy for a time. In keeping with these religious movements art became less worldly than it had been in Giotto's time. Art, in turn, affected religious experience, for St Bridget's vision of the Nativity of Christ faithfully reflected the depiction of this scene in Italian painting.

Possibly it was St Catherine of Siena who persuaded Pope Gregory XI to leave Avignon, but there were also good political reasons for him to return to Rome at this time. For one thing, it was now safe. The Spanish Cardinal Albornoz had restored order, reorganized and consolidated the Papal States, so that Rome was now one of the 'Big Five' – the five major powers in Italy – along with Florence, Milan, Naples, and Venice.

Another reason for returning was the war with Florence, called the War of the Eight Saints (after the eight Florentine officials who organized it), which had broken out in 1375, and ended in the year of the Pope's death, 1378. This war – like most wars of the Renaissance – was carried on by means of *condottieri*, men whose business was war and for whom war was a business. This was also the year of the Great Schism, when not one but two Popes were elected to succeed Gregory: Urban VI (1378–89) and Clement VII (1378–94). The split in Christendom over the question of recognizing contending Popes was to last thirty-nine years and add to the sense of crisis in Italy.

The crisis was most intense for Florence and its ruling class. The appearance of a powerful Papal State on her borders aroused fears which led to the War of the Eight Saints. During the War, Florence was laid under interdict, and when it ended, social conflict broke out within the city. Nominally, Florence had been ruled since the end of the thirteenth century by its twenty-one guilds; in practice, the seven greater guilds, including those of the bankers and wool merchants – two groups pre-eminent in creating Florence's economic greatness – controlled the city government. Not all workers, however, were guildsmen; the poorest, such as the wool carders, were not. In 1378, they demanded the right to form a guild, and so take part in the government. This was the famous Revolt of the *Ciompi*. Three new guilds were formed to include the wool carders, the dyers, and the shirt-makers; and a wool carder even became Gonfalonier of Justice (or Head of State), for two months. But the new guilds did not last long; they were first divided and then conquered. The wool carders' guild was abolished after a few months, the dyers' and shirt-makers' four years later, with the help of the English mercenary leader, Sir John Hawkwood. Having defeated the Pope and the common people, the oligarchy was back in power, but now they had to cope with Milan.

Giangaleazzo Visconti, the ruler of Pavia, seized Milan from his uncle in 1385. He was one of the most notorious Renaissance despots, and he has been called the creator of the first modern state. Utilising professional diplomats ('orators' they were called), soldiers, and civil servants, he rapidly built up an empire in north Italy. In the seventeen years before his sudden death from fever, Giangaleazzo vastly expanded his state by absorbing Verona, Vicenza, Padua, Pisa, Perugia, Siena, and Bologna. With Florence almost encircled, the Florentine government naturally saw him as a threat. The Florentines went to war with him twice, and were obviously marked out for conquest, when he suddenly fell ill and died.

Important for the political survival of Florence, these wars were also crucial in the development of Renaissance humanism, that is, of the twin Renaissance attitudes of enthusiasm for classical antiquity and faith in the dignity and powers of man. How this political situation and these attitudes might be connected can be seen most clearly in the career of one of the leading figures of the time, Coluccio Salutati (1331–1406), Chancellor of Florence. The Chancellor was virtually the Foreign Minister of the Republic. Salutati, a lawyer by profession, had taken this post in 1375, at the age of forty-four, after the War of the Eight Saints had begun. He might be regarded as counsel for Florence in the court of Italian public opinion. He defended his client, in his official letters, by presenting the war as a struggle for liberty against papal tyranny. Florence was the heir of Rome, founded by Sulla's veterans in the last years of the Republic; the papal armies he compared to the barbarians. In the wars with Milan, too, he put the Florentine case in the same way. 'Who does not see,' he wrote, 'that this city of Florence is the defender of the common cause of liberty in Italy?'

The potency of his rhetoric was something to reckon with; Giangaleazzo is said to have remarked that Salutati's letters did him more harm than a thousand Florentine horsemen. But its cultural importance was even greater than its political importance. These letters were a crucial event in the rise of humanism. Salutati was not the first humanist, nor the first Italian to try to write classical Latin, nor the first to try to revive classical ideals; Petrarch had preceded him here. And Salutati, a great admirer of Petrarch, shared his admiration for Virgil, Seneca, Cicero and Plato. Like Petrarch he tried to learn Greek, and like him did not succeed, though he brought a Greek, Chrysoloras, to Florence to give courses in the language. Again like Petrarch, he saw himself above all as a moralist. His slogan was *humanitas*, which he defined as 'moral erudition'. He defended poets in general and Virgil in particular because they praised virtue and censured vice. He attacked scholastic philosophers because they were sophists, who did not raise moral issues.

Salutati, however, was not simply a disciple of Petrarch. His humanism had a much greater 'civic' emphasis. Instead of escaping to the countryside and the pleasures of a solitary life, Salutati held public office. The way of life he defended was not just his own but that of Florence. He strengthened the Florentines' consciousness of what they stood for, by telling them and others what they were fighting for. In defending the values of a republic of lawyers, merchants and artisans, he suggested that true nobility depended on virtue and on achievement, not on blood. He argued that merchants were indispensable; he was critical of the clergy. Petrarch, the exile, the wanderer, the man without ties, was not the man to do this; it was Salutati's achievement. Thus, he helped turn humanism into a general movement, by associating it with civic patriotism: the Florentines learned to think of the Roman past as a part of their identity.

The Years of Discovery, 1400–30

In the early fifteenth century came the second wave of the Renaissance, particularly in Florence. Humanism became a general movement, and at the same time a revolution took place in painting, sculpture and architecture. All these activities have in common a new respect for the values of antiquity and the desire to discover its forms and techniques. The intellectual heirs of Salutati, who died early in the new century, in 1406, were Leonardo Bruni (1370–1444) and Poggio Bracciolini (1380–1459). Bruni carried on Salutati's civic humanism and political activities and he too became Chancellor of Florence. The aims of Florentine foreign policy remained much the same: to avoid being absorbed by bigger states and to try to swallow up smaller ones. The first threat to Florence came from Ladislas of Durazzo, King of Naples from 1386 to 1414, who was ambitious to extend his power to central Italy, and took advantage of the papal schism to assume the administration of the Papal States. When the death of Ladislas (in 1414) removed this danger, Florence was threatened once more by Milan, as Filippo Maria Visconti sought to reconstruct the empire which had disintegrated on Giangaleazzo's death. Meanwhile, the Florentines began to build up an empire themselves, first taking Arezzo, then

Francesco Sforza, a *condottiere*, or mercenary leader, who seized the duchy of Milan in 1450, was a typical example of the 'new prince' as described by Machiavelli. His family remained in power (with intervals) until 1515.

Sforza's wife, Bianca Maria Visconti, the illegitimate daughter of the previous Duke of Milan, who had married her to Sforza to ensure his support. Husband and wife are forcefully portrayed by the fifteenth-century Lombard painter Bonifazio Bembo.

Above Detail from the triumphal arch at Naples of Alfonso of Aragon and Sicily, who also became King of Naples in 1442. A great enthusiast for antiquity, he was called the Magnanimous for his lavish patronage of the humanists. Lorenzo Valla, scholar at his court, exposed the forged Donation of Constantine by which the papacy claimed temporal power.

Opposite, above Sixtus IV appoints the humanist Platina as Librarian of the Vatican (1478). Sixtus was active in politics and as a patron of the arts; the Sistine Chapel is named after him. Platina is best known for his biographies of the Popes.

Opposite, below Charles VIII of France entered Florence in 1494. Sixteenth-century Italians saw this date as the beginning of Italy's calamities, of the new barbarian invasions. Painting by Granacci, a friend of Michelangelo, *c* 1518.

Left Pius II, Aeneas Sylvius Piccolomini, was a famous humanist and diplomat before he became Pope in 1458, taking the name Pius as a pun on *pius Aeneas*. His works include a lucid and fascinating autobiography, a romance and a play. This detail from his funeral monument shows him with St Peter.

Columbus, a Genoese in Spanish service, is the most famous explorer in an age of world discovery. He made four voyages aimed at reaching India by sailing west. His first voyage discovered Cuba, his third the mainland of South America — but Columbus believed that he had found only islands.

Above The Florentine Amerigo Vespucci was sent to Spain by his employers, the Medici. He then made four voyages to the New World, including Brazil, and published accounts of them. His name was first applied to 'America' in 1507.

Pisa and Leghorn. Bruni defended Florence and what she stood for in his *Laudatio Florentinae Urbis* and his *Historia Florentini Populi*. He stressed the importance of liberty and its defence by a citizen army; at the same time, he suggested that by right of inheritance from Rome, Florence ought to rule the world.

Poggio Bracciolini had worked for Salutati, as a copier of manuscripts. Around 1400, he invented the 'humanistic' script, an attempt to revive the writing of the Romans which in fact was based on twelfth-century script. From copying manuscripts, Poggio went on to discover them. He toured the monasteries of Europe, turning up copies of Quintilian, Lucretius, Vitruvius and other lost classical writers, taking them from the 'dirt and filth' in which – so he said – he found them, and bringing them back in triumph to Florence. At the same time other enthusiasts were uncovering texts of Sophocles, Xenophon, Aristophanes.

It was no longer sufficient, as in the days of Petrarch and Salutati, to possess Greek manuscripts; it was necessary to learn to read them. After the death of Chrysoloras, there was nothing for it but to go and study in Constantinople; and Filelfo, who did this, returned to teach the Florentines the Greek he had learned there.

Florence was in these years not only the centre of humanism, but of the 'rebirth' of the arts. As Vasari pointed out four hundred years ago, in his *Lives of the Painters*, this was the second stage in the rise of the arts of painting, sculpture, and architecture. Antiquity was an inspiration not only to Bruni and Poggio, but to Brunelleschi and Donatello, who visited Rome to study its monuments. The beginning of modern sculpture is often dated from the first years of the fifteenth century, when Ghiberti (1378–1455), Brunelleschi (1377–1446), and above all, Donatello (1386–1466), were working, and when, as Vasari put it, 'statues began to look like living men'. He had in mind such works as Donatello's *St George*.

In architecture, the man who best represents the age is Filippo Brunelleschi. He was one of the first and one of the greatest of the Renaissance 'universal men', since he was goldsmith, sculptor, painter, engineer, and architect all in one. As a contemporary said, his importance was that he made the current style 'speak Latin', take on a classical form. For example, he revived the circular plan used in classical temples and carried on in Early Christian times, as in his unfinished *S. Maria degli Angeli*. He revived

classical proportions in the colonnades and pediments of the *Ospedale degli Innocenti* at Florence; and just as Poggio went back to twelfth-century script for inspiration, so Brunelleschi was inspired by the architecture of eleventh-century and twelfth-century Florence – the Baptistry, for example. He has been justly called 'the most creative scientist' of his age as well as one of its greatest artists. His scientific achievements include the study of perspective, by means of experiment, and the construction of the dome of the Cathedral of Florence, a dome of such a size that many contemporaries thought that it would be impossible to build.

In painting the greatest figure is that of Masaccio (b.1401), and his most famous works the frescoes in the Brancacci Chapel in the Carmelite church in Florence, Santa Maria del Carmine, which he painted in collaboration with Masolino (b.1383). Of the three visual arts, painting owed least to antiquity, and most to the fourteenth century – to Giotto. But Masaccio's achievement does echo that of his older friends. His paintings have a new degree of realism, like the sculpture of Donatello; they show a new sense of space, like the churches of Brunelleschi; and they adopt the latter's perspective. Paolo Uccello (1396/7–1475), also was active at this time, and his devotion to perspective became legendary. Why should so much have been accomplished so rapidly in one city? Why in Florence? It is perhaps presumptuous to attempt to explain genius, but it is at least plausible that a collective achievement like the early Florentine Renaissance should have a collective, social explanation. Of the other four major Italian states Milan and Naples had a less coherent cultural tradition than Florence (as they had achieved less in this respect in the Middle Ages, so they would achieve less throughout the Renaissance). But the same is not true of Rome or Venice.

In Rome one would have expected enthusiasm for antiquity to be at its greatest; if Florentines could identify themselves with the Roman past, how much more should Romans. But Rome during the schism was hardly the place for artists in search of a patron. During the schism the papacy went through a severe economic crisis; its income sank to a third of what it had been. Although the schism ended with the election of Martin V (1417–31), the new Pope's energies were taken up mainly with recovering what had been lost. When he entered Rome in 1420, it is said that he found it so dilapidated that it scarcely looked like a city at

Opposite This detail from an altarpiece depicts Lodovico Sforza, son of Francesco. He became ruler of Milan in 1479, displacing his nephew. He was Leonardo's and Bramante's patron, and encouraged Charles VIII's triumphant and disastrous intervention in Italy.

all. Like Albornoz long before him he based his policy on the reorganization of the Papal States, and relied for his revenues on this. He and his successors were engaged on two fronts: as spiritual rulers they were fighting the conciliar movement; as temporal rulers they were fighting their vassals and neighbours, men like the *condottiere* Braccio da Montone who had built himself an empire out of church lands. It is not surprising that Martin V, although interested in art and humanism, did not have the time or the money to do much for them beyond restoring Rome's dilapidated buildings.

As for Venice, she was rich enough, and possessed a large empire in Italy. At the end of the fourteenth century, Venice pulled ahead of her old rival, Genoa. She had kept out of war with Giangaleazzo: Milan was too good a customer. But on his death the Most Serene Republic had seized Vicenza, Verona and Padua. Doge Mocenigo halted expansion on the mainland at this point, wanting Venice to look East not West; but under his successor and opponent Doge Foscari, who ruled from 1423 to 1457, Venice acquired Brescia and Bergamo. Clearly Venice could have afforded the Renaissance if she had wished to have it. And in Venice there was a lively interest in antiquity. Guarino of Verona (1376–1460) went to Constantinople to study Greek, and then opened a school to teach it in Venice. Venetians were as interested as the Florentines in the natural sciences. About the time Padua came under Venetian control it began to take the lead in scientific studies away from Oxford and Paris, thanks largely to an Oxford man – Paul of Venice. Venetians were interested in art, but their art, more traditional than the Florentine, was still in the International Gothic style of conservative masters like Antonio Pisanello (*c* 1395–1455/6) and Gentile da Fabriano (*c* 1370–1427). The magnificent Gothic *Ca d'Oro* is contemporary with Brunelleschi's *Ospedale degli Innocenti*, a pioneer monument of the Renaissance. Venetian traditionalism may have reflected the fact that its ruling class was longer established and less open to new men, also that Venice did not engage in a long war with Milan and so was less likely to identify Republicanism and Rome.

The rulers of two small states, Ferrara and Mantua, began to take an interest in humanism at this time. Guarino of Verona was called to Ferrara as tutor to the Este children; and Guarino's friend and pupil Vittorino of Feltre received a similar summons to teach the Gonzaga children at Mantua. Accounts of Vittorino's teaching methods make him seem like the first modern schoolmaster. He believed that education consisted essentially in the training of character. He encouraged physical exercises, and made his pupils write in Greek and Latin and hold debates with one another.

The Years of Development, 1430–60

The second generation of the Renaissance abounds in pupils and successors of the great pioneer artists, humanists and patrons. Florence remained the centre, but the centre of an Italy which was becoming both politically and culturally more of a unity. It is possible to speak more realistically in this period of 'Italian' history, rather than the history of separate regions, thanks to two factors: the recovery of the papacy, and the advance of the Turks.

After initial reverses, the papacy under Eugenius IV (1431–47), Martin's successor, made considerable advances on both the temporal and the spiritual fronts. Eugenius, forced out of Rome by a republican government, spent his years of exile in Florence, but when he recovered Rome in 1443, he was stronger than before. While in exile, he called the Council of Florence, and invited the Greek schismatic bishops at his own expense. He persuaded them to agree that the Pope was the Vicar of Christ and the shepherd and teacher of all Christians. The Greeks repudiated this when they returned to Constantinople, but in the West the struggle for mastery between the Pope and the Councils had been won by the Pope.

The Greek Church only fifteen years later was faced with the catastrophe of the Turkish capture of Constantinople, in 1453. The new Pope, Nicholas V (1447–55), proclaimed a crusade, as did his successors, Calixtus III (1455–58) and Pius II (1458–64). The aim of these crusades was no longer the medieval one of recapturing the Holy Places; it was to drive the Turks out of Europe. Although the planned crusades failed, the Turkish menace and new threats of a French invasion stimulated the formation in 1455 of the Italian League of the five large states and their weaker allies.

Opposite **Woman Spinning**, fresco by Pinturicchio. A reminder that in the fifteenth century, the great Italian textile industry was organized partly on a home basis. Spinning was done by 'spinsters'. The capitalist 'woolman' provided the raw material and took away the finished product.

MIRABELLO CAVALORI

Bartolommeo Colleoni, a famous mercenary leader who served on both sides in the wars between Venice and Milan. He died in Venetian service, and the Republic called in the Florentine Verrocchio to make this equestrian monument.

Opposite Dyeing, unlike spinning, was carried out in factories, not in the home. This picture was painted *c* 1570 for Duke Cosimo de' Medici by Mirabello Cavolori. By that time, the Florentine cloth industry, once the basis of the city's prosperity, was in decline.

Right When Leonardo da Vinci recommended himself to Lodovico Sforza, he emphasised his military rather than his artistic skills, writing that he could supply 'an infinite number of different engines of attack and defence'. This chariot armed with scythes and the tortoise-shaped tank are among them.

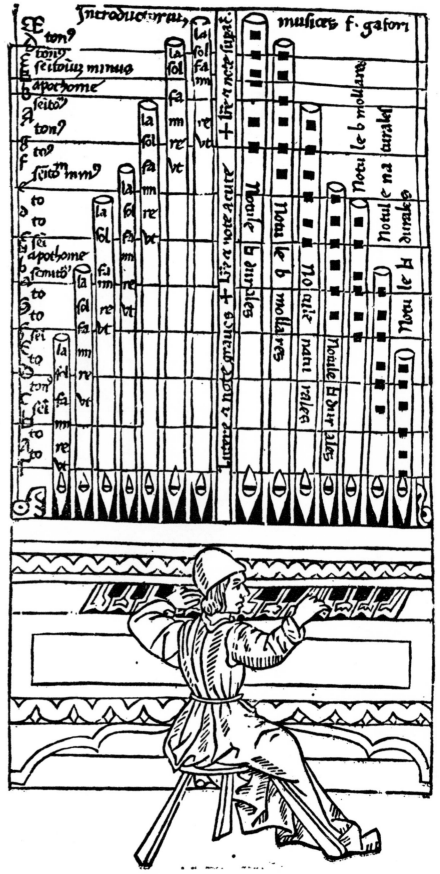

THEORICA MVSICE FRANCHINI GAFVRI LAVDENSIS.

Above top Rodrigo Borgia, Pope Alexander VI (1492–1503). The Pope helped his illegitimate son Cesare conquer the Romagna and build up a private empire.

Above One of the bulls in which Alexander VI gave the Spanish a virtual monopoly of navigation and settlement in the New World.

Frontispiece of the *Theory of Music* by Franchino Gafurio, 1492, who worked for Lodovico Sforza. The Renaissance saw a close analogy between audible and visual proportions, and so Gafurio was also asked to give advice on architectural matters.

Italy in 1454

Intermittently it is true, but for more than a generation the League was a force for keeping the peace in Italy, and was an important event both in the history of Italian unity and the history of the balance of power.

Rulers were proud of being cultivated. Ferrara was governed by Guarino's pupils, while Mantua and Urbino (where Federico of Montefeltro became Duke) were run by the pupils of Vittorino. Florence from 1434 to 1464 was ruled, in effect if not in name, by Cosimo de' Medici (1389–1464), whose riches, if not his power, were second-generation. Two professional humanists became Popes: Nicholas V, who created the Vatican library with his own collection of manuscripts as the nucleus, and Pius II, who wrote his memoirs in a form modelled on Caesar's commentaries.

In the traditional view, the fall of Constantinople, by driving Greek scholars to the West, had an important influence on the rise of humanism. It is probable, however, that the Council of Florence had a more striking effect, for it was at that time that Cosimo de' Medici met the Greek scholar Gemisthos Pletho, became interested in Plato and asked Ficino to translate Plato into Latin. It was as a result of the Council

that the Greek scholar Bessarion decided to remain in the West, and he gave an impetus to the study of Plato in Rome and Venice. Apart from these contacts with the Greeks, one would have expected humanism to develop at this time because men now adult had had the chance to study Greek and classical Latin from childhood, thanks to the pioneer efforts of an earlier generation. Now came the rise of an original neo-Latin literature. Poggio the copyist and discoverer of manuscripts had a third career as the writer of Latin works which included a dialogue on true nobility, a history of Florence, and an essay on the 'human condition' – a phrase that humanists were beginning to use. Lorenzo Valla, another pupil of Vittorino's who became important as a humanist was a kind of fifteenth-century Erasmus, and Erasmus was in fact to be a great admirer of his. Valla helped popularize the Renaissance by writing a Latin grammar. He criticized the monastic life and scholastic philosophy, and made important contributions to historical scholarship, for example by demonstrating the spuriousness of the so-called Donation of Constantine on which the Popes based their claim to temporal power. Another humanist, Flavio Biondo (c 1392–1465) virtually founded the study of archaeology by his book *Roma Instaurata*, which described the theatres, baths, gates and other monuments of Rome as they had been in classical times. The humanist Pope Pius II wrote a play and a novel (the *Tale of Two Lovers*) in Latin as well as his autobiography. A Florentine merchant, Gianozzo Manetti, wrote a treatise on the excellence and dignity of man.

Neo-Latin literature was centred on Rome: Poggio, Valla, and Biondo were all in papal service at some stage, and so was Pius before his own election. But in the visual arts, Florence retained her lead. In architecture, Brunelleschi's pupil Michelozzo Michelozzi (1396–1472) was now the major figure. He built for Cosimo the Palazzo Medici, among the first in the great series of Renaissance palaces, and rebuilt the monastery of S. Marco. Michelozzo, also a sculptor, worked with Donatello who was still active, and the first tombs in classical style came from their studio. It was now too that the classical bronze equestrian monument was revived, and one of the first, as well as one of the most famous, was by Donatello: the monument to the *condottiere* Gattamelata at Padua. The revival of the classical portrait bust also took place in mid-century Florence; the first known example, by

Mino of Fiesole (1429–84), is a portrait of a Medici—Cosimo's son Piero. In painting, there were fewer spectacular achievements: Masaccio had died young. But the profile portrait, a new *genre*, suddenly rose to popularity.

Elsewhere in Italy the Renaissance was still an innovation brought in from outside rather than a development from local tradition. In Milan, Francesco Sforza (1404–66), a *condottiere* who had succeeded Filippo Maria Visconti (after a short Republican interlude) in 1450, called in the Florentine architect Filarete to work first on a castle, then on a hospital in Renaissance style. The Renaissance was introduced to Naples by Alfonso I, a Spaniard, who was as interested as any Italian in humanism and the new architecture. After he had defeated the rival claimant to Naples, René of Anjou, he embellished the city with new streets and squares, and gathered a court of humanist writers and artists around him. In Rome, Nicholas V began the rebuilding of the Vatican, and commissioned the Florentine painters Fra Angelico (c 1387–1455) and Bennozzo Gozzoli (c 1421–97) to execute the frescoes in his own chapel. He planned a new choir and transept for St Peter's, but died when only the foundations had been laid. Pius II was also interested in architecture, but devoted his money and energies to reconstructing his birthplace (near Siena, and renamed 'Pienza' after him) as a model Renaissance town—again with a Florentine as architect. In Venice the architectural Renaissance did not arrive until the end of the period, with the building of the Arsenal, though Venice now had her own Renaissance painters—like Antonio Vivarini (c 1440–84), and Jacopo Bellini (c 1400–70/1).

Most of these cultural trends can be summed up in the career of Leone Battista Alberti (1404–72), another Renaissance 'universal man'. Of Florentine family, but living in Rome and elsewhere, he was an athlete, a musician, a distinguished architect, and a humanist. As architect he helped diffuse the Renaissance by the example of his churches of S. Francesco at Rimini, and of S. Andrea and S. Sebastiano at Mantua. His Latin treatises are important. His treatise on painting, dedicated to Brunelleschi, was a manifesto of the new wave in Florence, and at the same time the foundation of modern art criticism, whose vocabulary he created by taking over concepts used by Cicero to discuss oratory. An architectural treatise (presented to Pope Nicholas) advanced the new ideas in architecture, and

described a Renaissance Utopia, with plans for the social organization of the ideal city, including poorhouses. Finally, his book *Della Famiglia* is one of the first important prose works in the vernacular, the start of a movement which was to become important in the next generation.

The Age of Elegance, 1460–90

The years 1454–94 were four decades of relative peace in Italy, when a balance of power had been attained, with Venice, the most powerful state, usually counterbalanced by an alliance of Florence, Naples and Milan. It was a period seen in retrospect by the sixteenth century as a golden age, above all in Florence.

In Florence, Lorenzo de' Medici, 'the Magnificent', grandson of Cosimo, who was in power from 1469 to his death in 1492, surrounded himself with a group of artists and humanists. The artists included Sandro Botticelli (c 1445–1510), who painted his *Primavera* and his *Birth of Venus* for Lorenzo's cousin Lorenzo 'il Popolano'; the sculptor Bertoldo di Giovanni (c 1420–91), a pupil of Donatello's; and Antonio Pollaiuolo (c 1432–98), who was both painter and sculptor. The work of these men and other contemporaries is in great contrast to the work of Masaccio and Donatello at the beginning of the century. Force had been replaced by elegance. Works of art are often small; statuettes seemed to have the preference over statues. They are often esoteric: the meaning of Botticelli's mythological pictures is impossible to decipher completely now, and it can only have been understood by a few then.

Humanism changes in the same way: from public to private, from 'civic' to esoteric concerns. The old Florentine humanists, Salutati and Bruni, had put the active life before the contemplative, and Aristotle before Plato. The new circle of humanists and poets—Ficino, Politian, Landino, Pulci—reversed this. Their life was up at the villa—at such Medici villas as Careggi and Cafaggiolo—not down in the city. Lorenzo himself and Politian wrote pastoral poetry, escapist literature in praise of the simple country life. Lorenzo's own life was more like that of a medieval prince than like that of earlier Medici businessmen. He and his brother

Opposite Detail from the bathroom of Clement VII, painted by Giulio Romano, who began his career as one of Raphael's assistants. The decoration here is reminiscent of the Raphael of the Villa Madama; it derives from newly discovered imperial Roman wall paintings.

Above Plato, in a detail from Raphael's drawing for the fresco of *The School of Athens*, which was commissioned by Pope Julius II. Some critics believe that Raphael gave Plato the features of Leonardo. Plato's upward gesture symbolises his interest in a world beyond the terrestrial.

Right Clement VII, Lorenzo the Magnificent's nephew, in a portrait by the Medici court painter, Bronzino. Clement, the second Medici Pope, was renowned as a cardinal but despised as a Pope. After the terrible sack of Rome in 1527 he grew a beard, as seen here.

The battle of Pavia, 1525, depicted here in a Flemish tapestry, was a famous
episode in the wars between Francis I and the Emperor Charles V
for mastery over Italy. Francis was defeated and held prisoner in
Spain by imperial forces. Francis promised Charles French
Burgundy, was released, and then broke his word.

vom ab
las

Ius mai testi gra caues

ROM

O Sancta simplicitas

Verbrant werden die Blas
Dutch Caesar

Meemskerck Inuentor.

CAPTA VRBE, ADRIANI PRAECELSA IN MOLE TENETVR
OBSESSVS CLEMENS, MVLTO TANDEM AERE REDEMPTVS.

1527

Giuliano took part in tournaments, a pastime in which their grandfather Cosimo had not engaged. Pulci wrote a tale of chivalry for Lorenzo – the *Morgante*, and Politian, a poem on *The Joust*.

This esoteric Florentine humanism often referred to as 'neo-Platonism' is perhaps best represented by Marsilio Ficino (1433–99), 'the platonic philosopher, theologian, and doctor', as he called himself, 'the priest of the muses'. The high priest of the platonic mysteries, we might say. Ficino founded a Platonic academy. He used to celebrate the supposed date of Plato's birth by a solemn reading of the *Symposium*, and he was accused of lighting a lamp before Plato's bust as if Plato were a saint. In his book, *Theologia Platonica*, he tried to reconcile Plato and Christianity, as Aquinas had tried to reconcile Aristotle and Christianity. A student of still more occult knowledge, he delved into astrology, magic and the 'wisdom of the East', more particularly that of the ancient Egyptian sage (as Ficino thought him) Hermes Trismegistus, who was an Egyptian Moses, just as Plato was a Greek Moses.

Esoteric humanism and a mixture of antiquity and chivalry also flourished elsewhere. At Ferrara, Borso d'Este was the patron of those elegant painters of mythologies, Cosmè Tura (before 1431–95) and Francesco del Cossa (1435/6 – probably 77). Borso was extremely interested in astrology, an interest reflected in the frescoes in his Palazzo Schifanoia, which represent the signs and the gods of the zodiac as well as scenes from classical mythology. He was also a great lover of 'The Story of the Round Table', and confessed that it gave him more pleasure than the capture of a city. Under Borso's successor Ercole, Boiardo wrote a famous poem on this subject, *Orlando in Love*. Another small court where the arts flourished was Urbino, whose duke, Federigo da Montefeltro, employed such notable artists as the painter Piero della Francesca and the architect Luciano Laurana (d.1479).

An unexpected fruit of esoteric humanism is the Renaissance novel. The second-century *The Golden Ass* of Apuleius had become fashionable; Boiardo translated it into Italian, and its devotees included the Duke of Ferrara, Ercole d'Este (who read it every day, he claimed) and the Marquis of Mantua. A reading public for novels now existed, so it is not surprising to find novels being written. The most famous novelists are Jacopo Sannazzaro (1455–1530) who wrote *Arcadia* and Francesco Colonna (1432–1527) who wrote *Poliphilus*. *Arcadia* was written at the Court of Naples by a member of its 'academy', the equivalent of the Platonic Academy in Florence. It is a sort of fictionalized autobiography in a pastoral setting, written in Italian in a mixture of verse and prose – the mood and setting are similar to those of Politian's play *Orpheus*, which was performed at the court of Mantua; the hero retires to the woods and lives among shepherds to forget an unhappy love affair. *Poliphilus* is a Latin novel by a Venetian monk, which tells of the wanderings of Poliphilus in search of his beloved, through a fantasy-landscape of Greek, Roman and Egyptian ruins. Both books were to become famous, and the *Arcadia* influential, thanks to the invention which was to popularize humanism – the printing press.

Italy was the first country to which the Germans took their new invention. Between 1465 and 1471, presses were established at Rome, Venice, Florence, Milan, and Naples. Among the first books printed in Italy, which give some idea of the current interests of educated men, were Cicero's *Orator*, Augustine's *City of God*, and Bessarion's defence of Plato. Some people despised the production of books by mechanical means; Duke Federigo of Urbino refused to have printed books in his library. Early books were in fact clumsy things, but they soon improved and manuscripts very rapidly became obsolete. Printing was also a shock to humanist values, because it was a new invention. One humanist, Pomponio Leto, refused to believe that the Greeks and Romans did not possess the printing press.

With the failure of the crusades, the Turkish threat was a very real one for Venice, whose first war against the Turks took place from 1463 to 1479. The Venetians sought help where they could and even sent three missions to Persia, to make an alliance with the Shah against the Sultan. At home Venice saw the construction of the city's first Renaissance Church, S. Michele all' Isola; and the creation of the first important Renaissance sculptures. In painting it was the age of the Bellini brothers, Giovanni (c 1430–1516) and Gentile (c 1429–1507) who were sons of the painter Jacopo Bellini, and their brother-in-law Andrea Mantegna (c 1431–1506), who became court painter at Mantua.

In Rome, the most outstanding figure was Sixtus IV, Pope from 1471 to 1484. He was more concerned with asserting his power inside Italy than abroad. On the temporal front this brought him into conflict with Lorenzo de' Medici, over Imola, a town on the borders of the Papal and Florentine States; Florence was laid

Opposite, above The lion stands for the Medici Pope, Leo X, who was trying to raise money by means of indulgences for the rebuilding of the ancient Basilica of St Peter's in contemporary style. Luther's attack on indulgences may thus be seen as an attack on the Renaissance.

Opposite, below The sack of Rome by Charles V's troops (1527) followed the alliance of Clement VII with Francis I. This engraving (after a drawing by van Heemskerck) shows the siege of Castello S. Angelo where the Pope, seen in the loggia, had fled. Cellini, as he relates in his autobiography, helped fire the guns.

under interdict, as it had been a hundred years before, and the Pope was party to the unsuccessful attempt to assassinate Lorenzo. Sixtus was also an important patron of the arts, and the Sistine Chapel was built at his command and decorated (mainly by Florentine artists) with paintings which may be read as a manifesto of papal primacy.

Milan was now ruled by Lodovico Sforza, the most cultured member of his house, who came to power in 1480. When Leonardo left Florence shortly afterwards, it was to Lodovico Sforza's court that he came, ready to build bridges or make machines for attack and defence as well as to paint or sculpt or make designs for court festivals.

Lorenzo de' Medici and Pico della Mirandola were the most notable 'Renaissance men' of the day. Pico was only twenty-seven in 1490, but he was a prodigy who died young. A friend of Ficino, but more of an orientalist, he tried to learn Hebrew and Arabic. At the age of twenty-three he announced that he would defend by disputation nine hundred theses on such subjects as magic, astrology, and the Cabala. His most famous work, the *Oration on the Dignity of Man*, was only the introduction to this disputation, which never took place. Its theme is the same as Manetti's, some thirty years before; the principal difference is the esoteric Eastern material which supplements the Greek and Roman writers. In this respect the *Oration* is typical of the generation in which it was written.

The Age of Crisis, 1490–1520

If political events were very much in the background in the previous period, in this one they were inescapable. An age of almost permanent crisis, it was also the age of the High Renaissance in the arts. Politically and culturally, the two factors helped make Italy more of a unity than before.

In 1494 the French invaded Italy. Looking back on this event, sixteenth-century Italians saw it as the beginning of Italy's calamities. If Italy was the new Rome, these were the new barbarian invaders who were to destroy her. The historian Guicciardini, writing in the 1530s, perhaps over-stated the extent to which

the years before 1490 were a 'golden age', but he hardly exaggerated the disasters that had happened since.

The first of three French invasions was that of Charles VIII, who claimed the Kingdom of Naples as descendant of Alfonso I's unsuccessful rival, René of Anjou. Louis XII then claimed Milan, and also attacked Naples and Venice. Francis I, the third invader, concentrated on winning Milan. Invasions of Italy were also mounted by the King of Spain, (Ferdinand the Catholic) and the Emperors Maximilian I and Charles V.

Italy thus became the theatre of operations for a European struggle for mastery, as well as the prize of the victors. After a period of small-scale battles, a succession of major ones followed: Fornovo, Novara, Cerignola, Agnadello, Ravenna, Marignano. Many Italians were killed, whether serving with the French or the Spanish or against them. To add to the crisis there was the impact of these invasions on the domestic politics of the Italian states. Piero de' Medici was driven from Florence; Lodovico Sforza was driven from Milan. Italian princes made war on one another with the help of foreign armies, as in the case of Julius II who conquered Perugia and Bologna and attacked Venice with the assistance of Louis XII and his troops. The Medici returned to Florence in the baggage of the Spanish army.

Italians reacted to this crisis in different ways, many of them sensing a spiritual crisis behind the political ills, and seeking salvation in reform. This attitude was typified in the Dominican friar Savonarola, who began to see visions and make prophecies some years before 1494. He saw the sword of God hanging over the earth, and declared that there would be a flood of foreign invaders, but a mystical ark would appear in which the Florentines could take refuge. After the invasion had taken place and Piero de' Medici was driven out, Savonarola had Christ declared King of Florence. His policy was moral reform. Charles VIII, he said, was God's instrument to reform the Church, and had been able to conquer Italy so easily because of her sins. Savonarola attacked dice, cards, blasphemy, drunkenness, and low-cut dresses. He was particularly scathing on the sins of the Borgia Pope, Alexander VI, who not only continued to keep mistresses after his election but held parties in the Vatican over which they presided. He also opposed the Renaissance: painters who depicted pagan goddesses, humanists who thought only of poetry and rhetoric, and tried

Opposite The smaller the Italian Renaissance court, the greater the patronage. One of the fresco cycles commissioned around 1470 by the Duke of Ferrara for the Palazzo Schifonoia was Francesco del Cossa's *The Months*, in which the signs of the zodiac are combined with scenes from classical mythology.

Overleaf Piero della Francesca portrayed in these two allegorical compositions (c 1465) his patrons, the Duke of Urbino, Federigo da Montefeltro, and his wife, Battista, niece of Francesco Sforza. Derived from descriptions of Roman triumphs, the scenes retain a medieval flavour by such details as the presence of unicorns.

CLARVS INSIGNI VEHITVR TRIVMPHO ·
QVEM PAREM SVMMIS DVCIBVS PERHENNIS ·
FAMA VIRTVTVM CELEBRAT DECENTER ·
SCEPTRA TENENTEM

QVE MODVM REBVS TENVIT SECVNDIS ·
CONIVGIS MAGNI DECORATA RERVM ·
LAVDE GESTARVM VOLITAT PER ORA ·
CVNCTA VIRORVM ·

to find out about the cure of souls from Virgil and from Cicero. He must have been persuasive, for his followers included Botticelli, Michelangelo, and Pico della Mirandola.

Savonarola did not last long. Charles VIII's invasion had made his reputation; Charles's withdrawal destroyed him. He was excommunicated by Pope Alexander VI and accused of heresy. In 1498, the year of Charles's death, he was burned at the stake in the main piazza of Florence. His supporters in the Florentine government were purged, and among the replacements was Machiavelli, now appointed Second Chancellor.

Niccolò Machiavelli was twenty-five in 1494, so the crisis came at a time when his opinions were forming. For him as for Savonarola, Charles VIII's easy conquest of Italy was a lesson; but what it taught him was very different from what Savonarola learned. He learned that mercenaries cannot be trusted; republics, to survive, need citizen armies – a point Leonardo Bruni had made one hundred years before. It also became clear to him (and here we see his generation reacting against its predecessors, as a result of the new experiences) that men are not godlike but 'ungrateful, fickle, liars and deceivers'. For him, then, the invasion caused an intellectual crisis, a crisis in the assumptions recently made about human nature in general and the nature of politics in particular. When the Medici returned to Florence and Machiavelli was removed from office, he wrote down his new ideas in his *Discourses* and his *Prince*. A man who tried hard to be without illusions, he still suggested in the *Prince* that Cesare Borgia, Alexander VI's son, could have saved Italy had fortune been willing.

Another reaction to the crisis was escapism. It was now that Sannazzaro's *Arcadia* and Colonna's *Poliphilus* were published, and Ludovico Ariosto (1474–1533) wrote his *Orlando Furioso*, which ignored the present and plunged into a world of chivalry and love. Written in Ferrara, the poem is a development from Boiardo and the culmination of the local tradition. The real world breaks in only in prophecy, when it is foretold that artillery will destroy chivalry and its virtues. Ariosto's patron, Alfonso d'Este, ironically enough, was an expert on artillery, and had himself painted by Titian with his hand on a cannon. At the same time, Ariosto revived the comedy by his adaptations and imitations of Terence and Plautus. The Venetian Pietro Bembo (1470–1547) evoked

Arcadia in his *Asolani*, a dialogue set in the grounds of a castle near Venice, where three men and three girls discuss the nature of love. Bembo's friend Baldassare Castiglione (1478–1529) wrote a similar work, the *Courtier*, which defines the attributes of the perfect courtier. It also includes a discussion of the virtues of the court lady, and its setting, the Court of Urbino, can almost be described as a *salon*, since the Duke went to bed early and the Duchess, Elisabetta Gonzaga, presided. In fact women did have a relatively high place in Italian aristocratic society – yet another sign of its 'meritocratic' nature. Outstanding women of the Renaissance include Lucrezia Borgia and Isabella d'Este, one of the most famous of Renaissance patrons.

Another way of escape from the world was taken by Paolo Giustiniani and some other Venetian noblemen: they became hermits, Camaldolese monks. Like them, Leonardo da Vinci (1452–1519) seemed to have ignored the crisis altogether. He was still in Milan when Charles VIII invaded, working on an equestrian monument to Francesco Sforza, for which he had prepared a full-scale model. Then the invasion began and the bronze was taken away to be made into cannon. Leonardo went on working in Milan, and his *Last Supper* dates from this time, as do his earliest surviving anatomical drawings – Leonardo and his contemporary Luca Signorelli were among the first artists to make a study of anatomy. Subsequently, he left and wandered about Italy without identifying himself with any side in the conflict. He worked for the French in Milan, as well as for the Duke they had driven out, for the Medici in exile, as well as for the Florentine Republic. Finally, he went to France with Francis I, and spent the rest of his life there.

Leonardo's *Last Supper*, one of the great works of the High Renaissance, belongs to a tradition; not the tradition that the apprentice Leonardo had learned from his master Verrocchio during the age of elegance, but the older tradition of the 'Grand Manner' created by Masaccio seventy years before. Similarly, Michelangelo in sculpture continued where Donatello had left off.

The High Renaissance, developing out of a Florentine tradition, is above all the work of two great Florentines – Leonardo and Michelangelo Buonarotti (1475–1564). But two men who were not Florentines, Donato Bramante (1444–1514) and Raphael (Raffaello Sanzio) (1483–1520), who both came from Urbino, also made important contributions to High Renaissance art, and some of their most significant works were produced in Rome. The explanation is probably that Florence was not a good place for artists at this moment, whereas in Rome this was the age of two art-loving Popes, Julius II (1503–13) and Leo X (1513–21).

Julius II, the nephew of Sixtus IV, carried on his uncle's programme for the Sistine Chapel as well as his policy in the Papal States. Julius was as impetuous and aggressive a patron as he was a statesman. He forced Michelangelo to paint the frescoes of the Sistine ceiling when Michelangelo wanted to sculpt, not paint. They had an affinity, nevertheless; both loved the grandiose in scale and they shared a quality called *terribiltà* by their contemporaries. It was also Julius who commissioned Bramante to rebuild St Peter's, a project that strongly influenced subsequent plans for the basilica, and it was for Julius that Raphael began to decorate the Vatican.

The climax of the High Renaissance came in Rome during the reign of Leo X, a Medici, who was a much less aggressive man; Raphael seems the artistic expression of his personality, as Michelangelo was of Julius's. Raphael did in fact become the chief of the Pope's artists. At the Papal Court, he continued to decorate the Vatican and he was made architect of St Peter's, as well as Superintendent of Roman antiquities. To cope with all his commissions, he was obliged to build up a 'shop' of assistants, an important stage in the development of academic classicism.

Venice had its own position in all these developments, political and cultural. Venetians kept out of the crisis as they had kept out of war with Giangaleazzo Visconti a hundred years before. In 1509, Louis XII, Julius II and the Emperor Maximilian combined to attack Venice, and she lost all her mainland possessions, but not for long. The Venetians, however, had other problems, such as the war with the Turks, which was going badly. There was also a slump in trade, following the Portuguese discovery of a new route to the Indies; the English and Flemings stopped coming to Venice, since they could now buy spices more cheaply from the Portuguese.

In art and humanism too, Venice stood on the margin of Italian developments. The Venetian High Renaissance had a distinct character of its own, which synthesized the work of Giovanni Bellini, of Carpaccio, of Giorgione, of the young Titian. Where the Florentines emphasised line, the Venetians traditionally dwelt on colour and atmosphere. One of the most famous

contemporary humanists lectured in Venetian territory Pietro Pomponazzi (1462–1525), the author of *The Immortality of the Soul*, which caused a sensation because it declared that Aristotle had taught that the soul was mortal. Although denying the immortality of the soul philosophically, he accepted it as a Christian thus following the 'double truth' line of reasoning which stemmed from the Middle Ages. Pomponazzi in fact sprang from a local tradition, the Aristotelian and Averroist tradition of the University of Padua. Aldus Manutius (1449–1515), the printer, was another Venetian personality of the time who not only made classical texts much more easily available than before, but was a distinguished humanist himself.

During the Renaissance, Italians played an important part in world discoveries. The Genoese Columbus made four voyages to the New World for Ferdinand and Isabella of Spain; the Venetian Cabot explored the North Atlantic for Henry VII of England; and the Florentine Amerigo Vespucci, who took part in Spanish and Portuguese expeditions to the New World, had his name given to 'America' in the first years of the sixteenth century. Here, too, Italian traditions may have been important. The mathematician Toscanelli, a friend of Brunelleschi's, had already in the 1470s considered the possibility of reaching the Indies by the Atlantic route, and it is likely that his idea was known to Columbus.

The Disintegration of the Renaissance, 1520–50

The years of political crisis, 1494–1520, do not seem to have had any obvious direct effect on the arts. Between 1520 and 1550 the political crisis continued, but there was a religious and artistic crisis as well. The reaction of some men was to make more rules for behaviour, for belief and for the arts; the reaction of others was to rebel against such rules. While some men broke with the values of humanism, others continued to accept them, and many were torn by conflicting impulses. It may therefore be useful to speak of the 'disintegration' of the Renaissance.

In 1520 Michelangelo was forty-five; he was the master of *David*, of the Sistine ceiling, of *Moses*, but his most remarkable achievements were still ahead of

Above France and Spain fought to dominate Italy until the latter's victory was sealed in the Treaty of Câteau-Cambrésis (1559). This fresco illustrating an episode in the conflict, the Truce of Nice (1538), shows Pope Paul III (Farnese) who acted as mediator, between Francis I (on his right) and Charles V (on his left). Part of a cycle celebrating the glories of the Farnese family.

Left Platonism was so popular during the Renaissance as to affect household objects. The Venetian ceramic jar shown here has been decorated with a clearly labelled portrait of Plato. As was usual for philosophers he is represented as venerable-looking.

Right A medal struck during the pontificate of Paul III (1534–49) shows Rome as still a relatively small city, huddled round its famous ancient monuments, such as the Colosseum and the Pantheon. Its population was about 50,000, a third the size of Venice.

Left Michelangelo amidst his most famous works. His hand is on the *Belvedere Torso*, fragment of an ancient masterpiece signed by Apollonius of Athens. A work Michelangelo never ceased to admire, it was executed in Rome in late Republican times.

Opposite, far right Pope Paul III and the English Cardinal Pole, by Jacopino del Conte. The Pope did a great deal for his family, the Farnese, and for Church reform.

Opposite, right The design and construction of St Peter's and its great dome have a complicated history from the mid-fifteenth century until the completion of the new fabric in the seventeenth century. The dome, one of the most impressive architectural works ever executed, was designed by Michelangelo, 1558–60, and inspired a great number of famous cupolas from that of St Paul's, London, to the Capitol, Washington.

Opposite, below Michelangelo was consulted in 1537 about the redesigning of the palaces on the Capitol. The print shows an early phase of the project, when the celebrated equestrian statue of Marcus Aurelius had already been moved from the Lateran to its present position, but before the reconstruction of the palace façades.

Below A tournament held in the Vatican in 1565. In the background Michelangelo's dome and the nave of St Peter's are seen still in construction.

Capitolij, et adiacentium sibi aedificiorum dextra, sinistraq, nuper instauratorum, si-
mulq, equestris Mar. Aurel. in media area, quae occidentem prospi-
cit, aenea Statuae imago Romae.

Above, left At the height of the Renaissance papacy's nepotism, Giulia Farnese became a mistress of Alexander VI. To show his favour the Borgia Pope made a cardinal of her brother Alessandro, who later was elected Supreme Pontiff himself, as Paul III. Luca Longhi's portrait of Giulia Farnese shows her with the mythical unicorn, a symbol meaning that she is intended to personify Chastity.

Above, right Isabella, daughter of Ercole d'Este, Duke of Ferrara, wife of Francesco Gonzaga, Marquis of Mantua, and one of the most celebrated women of her time. She was an excellent Latinist and an important, though dictatorial, patroness of the arts. This portrait, by Titian, painted when she was sixty (1536) is based on an earlier one.

Left An engraving after a design by Giulio Romano, the famous Mannerist painter and architect. Among his patrons were Leo X, Clement VII, Isabella d'Este and Federigo Gonzaga.

him. In the 1520s, he worked on the Medici Chapel and the Laurentian Library in Florence, and as his great admirer Vasari pointed out, astonished everyone by deliberately breaking the accepted 'rules' of architecture, such as using massive columns and brackets which are not required to support any great weight. In the 1530s, he caused equal astonishment with his painting of the *Last Judgement*, in the Sistine Chapel, which breaks sharply with Renaissance symmetry and realism. His paintings of the 1540s, the *Conversion of St Paul* and the *Crucifixion of St Peter* continue the new approach which was to affect the main current of art for the rest of the century.

Among the important contemporaries who were immediately influenced by this art of discord and shock was Giulio Romano, (d. 1546), for years Raphael's chief assistant. His fresco *The Fall of the Giants* painted at Mantua in the 1530s, where the illusion of crashing columns is meant to overwhelm the spectator, made spectacular use of the foreshortened nudes in difficult poses that are a hallmark of Michelangelo's late style. This art is not, however, simply the 'school of Michelangelo'; the Florentines Jacopo Pontormo (1494–1556) and Giovanni Battista Rosso (1495–1540) broke with the Renaissance in painting, before he did, as did many others later on, including Domenico Beccafumi (1485–1551) and Francesco Parmigianino (1503–40). Humanist proportions and 'natural' postures are replaced by elongations of the human figure and contorted expressions and poses. At the same time there is a revival of the more medieval themes of judgement and hell.

Too widespread and popular to derive from the personality of one man, the movement seems to reflect a change in the Italian sensibility. The new atmosphere was not apparent everywhere, for this is the great central period of Titian's long life, when he painted for the city of Venice, for Pope Paul III and for the Emperor Charles V. The stability and assurance of Venice, again, gave it a special position in the Italian world. Paul Klee has suggested that the more fearful a place the world is, the less realistic art becomes; the new art of Mannerism seems to be the expression of a crisis, spiritual as well as political. A similar explanation might be offered for the preoccupation with death shown by the eccentric Florentine artist, Piero di Cosimo (c 1462–1521) in his designs for pageants.

The political crisis was even more serious than in the previous period. Milan ceased to be an independent state and was 'ruled' by the last of the Sforzas, the puppet of Charles V; Charles and Francis I then fought to possess it, and finally it was ruled by a Spanish viceroy. For the Milanese it was a time of wars, plagues, famines, and a decline in population, trade and industry. Naples too was governed by a Spanish viceroy, who drained the kingdom of money to send to other parts of Charles V's empire, mercilessly repressing opposition to the regime and condemning 18,000 people to death. After Pope Clement VII had made an alliance with Francis I, Rome was sacked by imperial troops – Germans and Spaniards – in 1527, probably the greatest disaster to happen to the city since its sack by Alaric and the Visigoths over eleven hundred years before. The Florentines took advantage of the plight of the Pope, besieged in Castel S. Angelo, to rebel against Medici rule; Christ was again declared King of Florence. But after the Pope and the Emperor were reconciled, imperial troops besieged Florence, which was forced to surrender in 1530. The only great Italian city which escaped disaster was Venice, where industry was expanding and war did not penetrate. Titian painted Venuses as if no crisis existed.

On the whole the spiritual crisis was perhaps even more severe than the political. Luther, at the beginning of the period, criticised the papacy more radically, and also more successfully, than Savonarola had done in his time. The occasion of his famous protest was the indulgence intended to raise money to rebuild St Peter's. Luther's action may be taken to symbolise the reaction against the Renaissance, since the project for the new basilica was the greatest single undertaking in the arts of the Renaissance. Luther's works and those of Erasmus, Melancthon and Calvin had a considerable Italian public. Groups of 'Lutherans' (as heretics were usually called, irrespective of their precise beliefs) were discovered more and more frequently in Italy. In Ferrara, the Duke's wife, Renée of France, protected heretics and had Calvin to stay. Anabaptists were numerous in Venice and in Vicenza, and another stronghold of heresy was Lucca. In Naples, the Spaniard Juan de Valdés (d. 1541) who believed that sacraments and ceremonies were matters of no importance, had a circle of followers, some influential, including the noblewomen Vittoria Colonna, the friend of Michelangelo, and Giulia Gonzaga.

The idea of reforming the Church from within attracted many Italians. New religious orders were founded, like the Theatines, the Barnabites, the Somaschi and the Capuchins. The Jesuits were founded by a Basque, Ignatius Loyola (1491–1556), but were highly influential in Italy from the first. In Rome in the 1520s, a group of priests and laymen who called themselves the Oratory of Divine Love, met on Sunday afternoons to discuss theology and practise spiritual exercises. Another group, of cardinals, proposed a set of reforms to the Pope in the 1530s, including the recommendation that holders of benefices should reside in them, and that indulgences should not be allowed in any place more than once a year. It was sometimes difficult to distinguish the reformers from the heretics, since both emphasised a more 'interior' religion. A famous example of a man who moved from one group to the other was that of the popular preacher, the Sienese Bernardino Ochino, a member of the Valdés circle, who became general of the Capuchins, then went to Geneva, left the Catholic Church and married.

Both reforming groups, the relatively orthodox and the relatively unorthodox, had in common their opposition to humanist values – the exaltation and appreciation of antiquity, of this world, and of man.

Rome itself, however, provided some continuity for the humanists as a social group, during the reigns of two Popes, Clement VII (1521–34) and Paul III (1534–49) Clement VII was, like Leo X, a Medici, and like him, a patron of the arts and of humanism. Carrying on the Renaissance tradition as if no reform or reaction had taken place, he was the patron of Machiavelli, commissioning his *History of Florence*; of Giovio, a historical writer whom he made a bishop; of Marco Girolamo Vida (*c* 1490–1566) a neo-Latin poet who wrote the *Christiad*, a Virgilian epic on the life of Christ, and whom he also made a bishop; and he had the humanist Piero Carnesecchi as his secretary. However, two of the most famous humanists, Pietro Bembo and Jacopo Sadoleto, who had been domestic secretaries to Leo X, left Rome at this time; Bembo to go into scholarly retirement, Sadoleto to devote himself to his duties as a bishop. In general there was a gradual move away from Renaissance secularism and into the Church, which became still more marked during the reign of Paul III. Paul III was of the same generation as the Medici Popes, Ariosto, and Michelangelo. His early life was that of a Renaissance prince, and even when he was a cardinal he kept a mistress and he built the

magnificent Farnese Palace. Although Renaissance cardinals were often in minor orders only, his conversion in 1513 to a less worldly life led him to ordination as a priest, and he became one of the reformers. Yet he did not reject his past altogether. One side of him is the traditional 'Renaissance Pope'. He made Bembo a cardinal, and offered the red hat to Erasmus; he was interested in astronomy (Copernicus dedicated his *De Revolutionibus* to him); and he used his power to advance his family, giving his son the Duchy of Parma and Piacenza, and making his grandsons cardinals when they were still boys. The other side of him is the reforming Pope, responsible for calling the first assembly of the Council of Trent (1545–7), for reorganizing the Inquisition (1542) and using it to suppress heresy at Lucca.

Thus some humanists turned into churchmen; others moved into mathematics and the sciences. One of the most typical 'Renaissance men' in this period was Pomponazzi's pupil Girolamo Fracastoro (1483–1553), who was interested in mathematics, astronomy, botany, medicine, poetry, music. The first of the Renaissance nature philosophers, (who now began to replace the 'philosophers of man') he produced a corpuscular theory to explain action at a distance, wrote a treatise on contagion, and the celebrated Latin poem on the shepherd *Syphilis* who was afflicted with the disease which takes its name from him. The 'Bologna school' of mathematicians included the famous rivals Niccolò Tartaglia (1500–57) and Girolamo Cardano (1501–76); they discovered how to solve cubic equations, and Cardano the 'gambling scholar' wrote a book on dice playing which was the beginning, a century before Pascal and Fermat, of the theory of probability. Tartaglia's 'new science' – as he called it – of ballistics was also important for the future.

In literature, Pietro Aretino (1492–1555), one of the first professional writers, produced a mixture of pornography and piety (both probably what his public wanted), which represents the cross-currents of the age. The popularity of the horror-plays, imitating Seneca, like those of Sperone Speroni and Giambattista Giraldi (Cinthio), was what might be expected from an age of crisis. No great tragedies were produced, but a tragic vision informs Francesco Guicciardini's *History of Italy* (1494–1534), a work notable for its realistic, objective observation and its attempt, for the first time, to give a history of the whole peninsula. In one important respect literary trends ran counter to artistic ones:

Opposite Leonardo Loredan, Doge of Venice 1501–31, by the Venetian painter Carpaccio. Loredan was Doge during a critical period in Venetian history. In 1509, the Pope, the Emperor and the King of France combined to attack Venice and strip her of her mainland possessions. Most were recovered by 1515. Carpaccio, follower of Gentile Bellini, was famous for his pageant-like paintings and scenes of Venice.

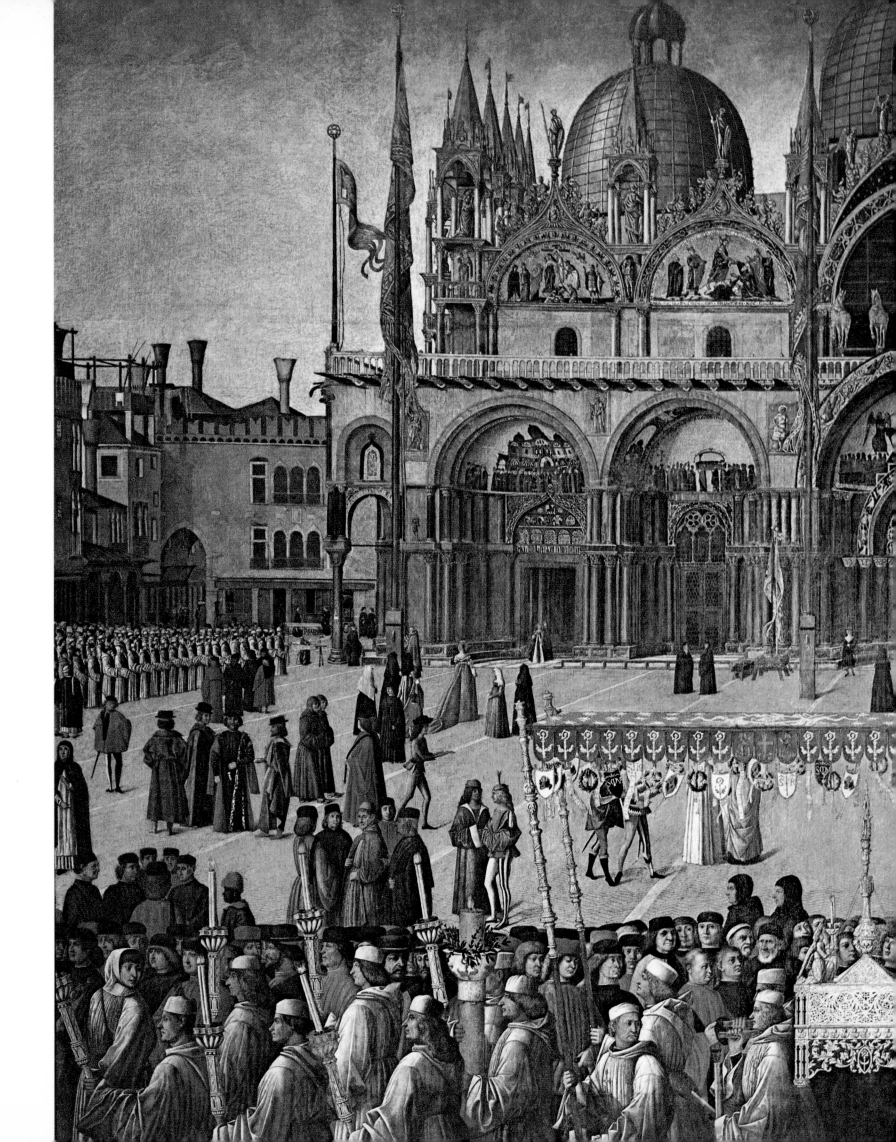

Opposite A detail from Gentile Bellini's picture of the Corpus Christi procession in St Mark's Square at Venice, painted in 1496. The festivals of Corpus Christi, Easter Sunday, and particularly the Ascension—the day of the wedding of the sea—were celebrated with great pomp and civic enthusiasm at Venice.

Below The seasons and their activities, from a sixteenth-century wedding chest. This brilliant example of Renaissance craftsmanship depicts autumn occupations

Above Villa Medici, the French Academy in Rome since Napoleon's day, was built by Annibale Lippi in 1544. Typical of Roman Renaissance buildings, the garden façade seen here has been richly decorated with ancient and contemporary marble and stucco reliefs, friezes, busts and garlands. The Medici coat of arms of five pills (or perhaps pawnbroker's balls) appears above the central arch.

Above Ignatius Loyola, the Basque nobleman, ex-soldier and finally saint, who persuaded Pope Paul III to let him found the Jesuit order in 1540. The Society of Jesus played a vital role in the Counter-Reformation and has remained one of the most important orders of the Catholic Church.

Above, left Titian's portrait of Eleonora Gonzaga, the daughter of Francesco Gonzaga and his wife Isabella. She married Francesco Maria della Rovere, a nephew of Pope Julius II, who became Duke of Urbino in 1508.

Left Andrea Doria, Genoese nobleman and naval commander. In the Hapsburg–Valois wars he fought first for Francis I, then for Charles V. He also led several expeditions against the Turks. Bronzino has painted him as Neptune; a typical conceit of Renaissance art.

Below Bronze medal struck by Pius V to celebrate the naval victory of Lepanto (1571). The Turks, who had just taken Cyprus from Venice, were defeated by a combined Spanish, Venetian, and papal fleet, led by Don John of Austria. But Cyprus was not recaptured.

in literature making rules was the main aim, not breaking them. Vida wrote an *Art of Poetry*. Giraldi produced rules for the composition of comedies, tragedies, and epics. Bembo laid down rules for writing 'classical' Italian; it was necessary to write Tuscan, and it must be the Tuscan of Petrarch and Boccaccio. Michelangelo, however, wrote poetry which is the literary equivalent of his sculpture and painting; harsh, discordant, powerful religious sonnets which strike the ear like the sonnets of Hopkins and of Donne.

The Triumph of the Church, 1550—80

In the previous period, the humanists and their opponents were evenly matched, and it would have been difficult to say which group was more likely to become preponderant, just as it would have been difficult to classify some people as either. The issues now became more sharply defined, and the Counter-Reformation, militant before, was now clearly triumphant. The Jesuits, for example, were firmly established in Italy by the end of the 1550s, with a university at Messina, the famous Collegium Romanum in Rome, and other colleges at Bologna, Ferrara, Florence, Loreto, Modena, Naples and Perugia. They educated laymen at their colleges, and so helped determine the values that would be held by generations to come. More able men were attracted to the Church, or at least went into it as an end in itself rather than as a means to a secular end. A shift of creativity into religion appears to have taken place, and missionaries were more common than discoverers. In 1580 the Jesuit Alessandro Valignano was forty-two years old, and had been eight years in the Far East. He had most of his missionary career ahead of him, years during which the Jesuit Matteo Ricci would turn mandarin in order to convert the Chinese, and the Jesuit Roberto de Nobili turn Brahmin to convert the South Indians. As political opportunity dwindled in Italy, men entered the church who earlier might have become civic and humanist leaders; as it was the church absorbed the energies of exceptional personalities like Possevino, Baronio, Bellarmine, Acquaviva, Borromeo. As the triumph of the Church become more certain, and its persecution of dissent more efficient, the heretics left Italy, or were executed. Many fled to Switzerland, and in 1559–60 there was a mass migration from Lucca to Geneva. Some went to England, like the Florentine Protestant, Pietro Martire Vermigli, who was for a time Regius Professor of Divinity at Oxford; or Michel Angelo Florio, the father of the translator of Montaigne, who made a living teaching Italian in London. Others sought refuge in eastern Europe, like the Unitarian Lelio Sozzini, who was in Poland in the 1550s, or Ochino, who died in Moravia.

There was all the more reason for heretics to leave Italy after 1555, when Paul IV (Carafa) was elected Pope. In the 1520s, Paul had been a reformer, a member of the Oratory of Divine Love and a founder of the Theatines. Since then he had moved from reforming the Church from within to defending it against reform from without. He saw heresy everywhere, and was obsessed with the idea that a heretic might succeed him as Pope. Paul had the aggressive spirit of a Julius II, but his energies went into the expansion of the spiritual power of the papacy, not the temporal. The result was that Paul IV's reign was a reign of terror (a phrase which even a cautious Catholic historian like Pastor finds himself compelled to use). The Pope gave the Inquisition precedence over other tribunals. He never missed its weekly sessions, and enlarged its numbers and powers. Men in high places were not safe. (A sign that in the previous period the issues were not sharply defined was that so many of the unorthodox were in high places). The reforming Cardinal Morone was arrested on suspicion of heresy, and remained in prison until Paul's death. Morone's friend Cardinal Pole was also suspected of heresy by the Pope, but he was safe in England and Queen Mary would not extradite him. Unorthodox humanists who had survived into this period – Castelvetro, Carnesecchi, Aconcio – now fled to Switzerland. Paul attacked books as well as men, and his Index of Prohibited Books of 1559 shows clearly his opposition to the Renaissance as well as the Reformation, for it includes the works of four of the most celebrated Renaissance writers – Erasmus, Rabelais, Machiavelli, and Aretino. He also had breeches painted on some of the nudes in Michelangelo's *Last Judgement*.

One fierce old man does not make an age. Paul's successor, Pius IV (1559–65), restricted the powers of the Inquisition and released Cardinal Morone; but he did not reverse Paul's policy, he simply moderated it. Pius might be described as a Counter-Reformation

Pope in spite of himself. He began his reign in the old style by summoning his nephews to Rome, including the Borromeo brothers, Federigo and Carlo. Carlo, the younger, whom he made cardinal and Secretary of State was a hard-working young man, a great huntsman and a lover of magnificence. When Federigo died suddenly in 1562, Carlo was expected to leave the Church to take his place, for in any case he was only a sub-deacon. But this reminder of mortality brought about his conversion. He became a priest, took Loyola's spiritual exercises, studied theology, reduced his household; and when he was made Archbishop of Milan, he asked permission to visit his see. The Pope never quite approved of this conversion; he wanted to see Carlo more jovial and less strict. Carlo, however, had a considerable influence over him; he persuaded Pius to call the third assembly of the Council of Trent (1562–3) and helped draw up the catechism which it adopted. Subsequently he retired to his archbishopric where he spent his life carrying out the Tridentine reforms. Carlo Borromeo is as representative of this new age as Alberti had been of the Renaissance.

Among the things Borromeo condemned were paintings of nudes and circular churches, which he thought were pagan. The Counter-Reformation was beginning to have an impact on the arts. In the year of Michelangelo's death, 1564, Gilio da Fabriano published a book called *Degli Errori de' Pittori*, in which he criticised Michelangelo for such 'errors' as representing angels without wings, and showing Christ at the Last Judgement as standing instead of sitting. In the 1570s, Veronese found himself in trouble with the Venetian Inquisition for painting a Last Supper which included 'buffoons, drunkards, Germans, dwarfs and similar vulgarities'; it was thought these profane elements brought discredit on the Church. Tasso, whose choice of subject for his epic, *Jerusalem Delivered*, reflects the current preoccupations, feared that it would be prohibited as offensive to religion. His worries about his own orthodoxy caused a nervous breakdown; such was the effect of the Counter-Reformation on an already unstable personality. There were also attacks on polyphonic music, on the grounds that it prevented the words of the liturgy from being properly heard and understood, that it made use of secular themes, and was 'lascivious'; but it was strongly defended and in a somewhat pruned down form managed to survive.

Changing religious attitudes did not only affect the arts in a negative way, by prohibition and correction; in the course of time they began to have a more positive influence. When the artist Jacopino del Conte was converted he changed his style. El Greco's years in Venice and Rome, about 1566–76, had a decisive effect on his painting. The art of Tintoretto seems to be the expression of the new religious sensibility; it is significant that he did not (like Titian) paint for courts, but for religious institutions—churches and confraternities. Palestrina was a friend of Philip Neri and the austerity of his music corresponds to internal need as well as external pressures.

In its effect on economic life the Counter-Reformation was bad for industry and trade. Not only religious leaders left Italy, but many entrepreneurs and workers as well, taking their capital and their skills to Italy's economic rivals, to Lyons or to Switzerland. The silk merchants of Lucca emigrated as did the cloth-workers of Como and Milan. The consequences for Italy were, in the long run, like the consequences of the expulsion of the Moriscos for Spain and the expulsion of the Huguenots for France—economic decline. To make matters worse, competition from the Netherlands and from England was markedly increasing. Decline, however, was not rapid, and in 1600 north and central Italy was still one of the economically advanced parts of Europe, with a relatively high standard of living.

The period saw not only the triumph of the Church, but the triumph of absolute monarchy, in some parts of Italy at least. By the treaty of Câteau-Cambrésis in 1559, the French were obliged to withdraw from Italy, leaving the Spanish to consolidate their rule in Sicily, Naples, and Milan. In Florence Cosimo de' Medici, who ruled from 1537 to 1574, ably built up his despotism. He utilized the arts to glorify his reign, and organised artists into an Academy under the command of Vasari. In the Papal States, too, there was increasing centralisation and the growth of a bureaucracy, whether this is to be seen as the successful conclusion of the policy of Albornoz or part of the general sixteenth-century trend towards absolutism.

In many respects the Renaissance was over; it was only necessary to describe it, as Vasari now did in his *Lives*. But pockets of Renaissance still remained, above all in Venice, where neither the Church nor absolutism had triumphed and industry still flourished. There Veronese continued to paint in the

Opposite Felix Peretti, Pope Sixtus V (1585–90), established the main arteries of the present town plan of Rome, linking the major basilicas. He was particularly fond of erecting obelisks to punctuate the townscape vistas. His numerous building projects, including waterworks and fountains, for which Domenico Fontana was chief architect, were commemorated in this print.

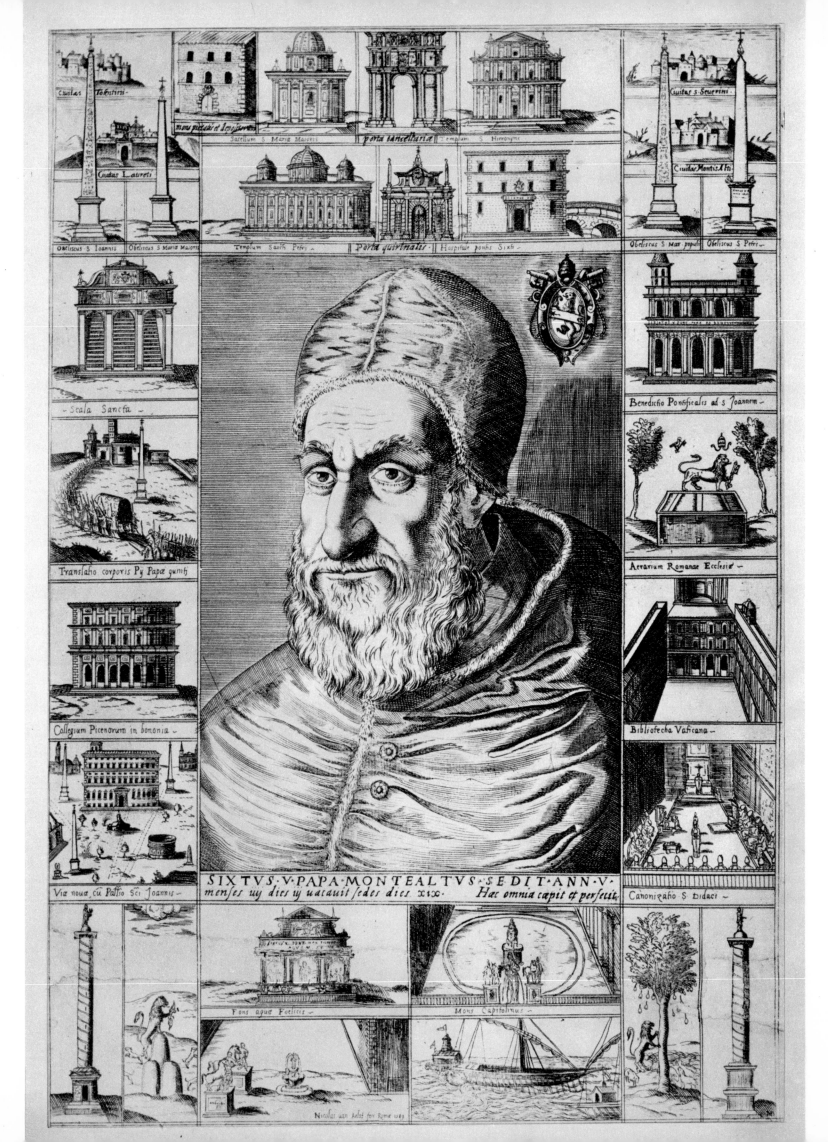

Ciuitas Tolentini · | mons pietatis et Seminarium · | Sacellum S. Mariæ Maioris · | Porta cancellariæ · | Templum S. Hieronymi · | Ciuitas S. Seuerini ·

Ciuitas Laureti · | Ciuitas Montis Alti ·

Obeliscus S. Ioannis · | Obeliscus S. Mariæ Maioris · | Templum Sancti Petri · | Porta quirinalis · | Hospitale pontis Sixti · | Obeliscus S. Mar. populi · | Obeliscus S. Petri ·

Scala Sancta · | Benedictio Pontificalis ad S. Joannem ·

Translatio corporis Pÿ Papæ quinti · | Ærarium Romanæ Ecclesiæ ·

Collegium Picenorum in bononia · | Bibliotheca Vaticana ·

Via noua cū Pallio Sci Joannis · | Canonizatio S. Didaci ·

SIXTVS · V · PAPA · MONTEALTVS · SEDIT · ANN · V ·
menses uÿ dies ij uacauit fedes dies · xix · Hæc omnia cæpit et perfecit.

Fons aquæ Fœlicis · | Mons Capitolinus ·

Nicolas van Aelst for. Rome 1589

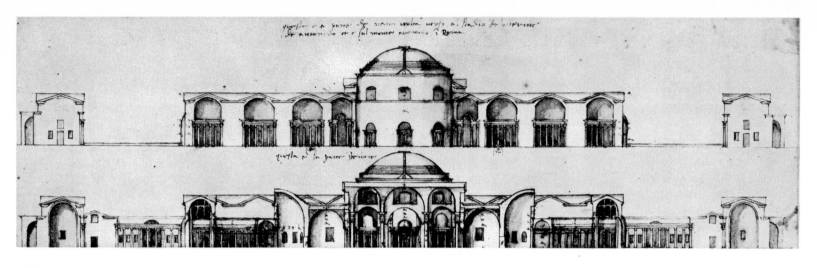

Above The Baths of Caracalla, drawn by Palladio, one of the greatest Renaissance architects. His town houses and country villas in Venetia, particularly in and around Vicenza and along the Brenta, creatively utilised his careful studies of ancient buildings. His work had considerable European influence, especially in England.

Left Outstanding in an age of fountains and a Roman landmark today, the Fountain of the Tortoises was conceived by Giacomo della Porta and carried out (1581–4) in bronze and marble by Taddeo Landini.

Opposite The Council of Trent was held between 1545 and 1563. As it established the anti-humanistic principles and the thought control of the Counter-Reformation, it marked the end of the Renaissance in Italy. Here the bishops are shown in session; in the foreground is the Church, triumphant.

Below Sixteenth-century street vendors, from a contemporary engraving. They sell from left to right: rice; chairs; horn combs; bellows and mousetraps; and coal.

tradition established by Bellini, Giorgione and Titian, and Palladio continued to build in Renaissance style. Among other things his *Four Books of Architecture* praised circular churches at the same time as Borromeo was condemning them. Cellini, in the 1560s, wrote his autobiography, which has become a sort of symbol of the Renaissance for many people from Goethe's day to ours.

These exceptions apart, what happened to Renaissance art and humanism? Some men willingly abandoned Renaissance values, others had this renunciation forced upon them. Equally important is the fact that Italian creativity did not so much decline as shift – slowly – from art to music, from the philosophy of man to the philosophy of nature. The beginning of a glorious period in Italian music starts now, with Palestrina, the Gabrielis and Merulo. The important scientists include Telesio (whom Bacon called 'the first of the moderns') and Colombo, one of the discoverers of pulmonary circulation. Botanic gardens, collections of dried plants, and museums of natural history were Italian innovations introduced at this time; and of course the next generation was to be that of Bruno and Galileo.

Opposite Michelangelo's influence on successive generations of artists was overwhelming. His fresco in the Sistine Chapel of the Last Judgement, the greatest work of Mannerism, is seen here in a faithful, reduced replica by his follower Marcello Venusti (1512/15–79). The composition includes incidents from the Inferno of Dante, whom Michelangelo greatly admired.

Aldo Garosci

The Spanish Empire dominated Italy from the mid-sixteenth to the beginning of the eighteenth century through control of Lombardy and the Kingdom of Naples, with the Genoese Republic as satellite. Rome, the universal city, held the most prosperous part of the country. Venice after Lepanto was on the defensive, having lost Cyprus and Candia, but Savoy and Tuscany were building up strong state organizations. For the country as a whole loss of independence in politics was accompanied by a decline in trade, and capital left industry for investment in the land. But music, theatre and the arts flourished on an unparalleled scale, and entire cities, like Rome transformed by Bernini and Borromini, became baroque masterpieces. All Europe continued to imitate Italian painting, whether following the conservative traditions of Pietro da Cortona or the Bolognese eclectics, or the revolutionary theatrical realism of Caravaggio. At the same time the ideological conflict of Church versus humanism resulted in such atrocities as the burning at the stake of Giordano Bruno as an unrepentant heretic, and the condemnation of Galileo's scientific investigations. Not until the later eighteenth century was Italy strongly influenced by European rationalism, although enlightened despotism became the norm with Austria's entry on to the Italian scene. The reforms of the new regimes stirred revolutionary fervour, and Napoleon easily conquered and republicanized northern Italy. National aspirations were crushed, however, by an Austro-Russian army, and Italian intellectuals and heroes went into exile as the absolute monarchs returned.

The seventeenth century is generally regarded as a period of decline in Italy. From the political standpoint, some of its most important regions had lost their independence towards the middle of the sixteenth century, coming under the rule of the Emperor and later of the King of Spain. Now Spanish rule itself was in danger from the revival of power in other countries.

Such intellectual life as still remained in Italy was struggling against the bonds of religious and political oppression. Vigorous thought was being stifled, uncertain whether to carry humanism to its logical extreme or revert to a convenient acceptance of the old medieval ideas. The country's economy was in a sounder state; despite the loss of many trade routes industry was still fairly flourishing, and indeed the second half of the sixteenth century has been called the economy's 'St Martin's summer'.

Nevertheless the beginnings of an economic decline were also apparent in the seventeenth century; capital was being gradually withdrawn from industry and put into landed property, which was burdened almost everywhere by complicated obligations and privileges; and as a result of wars, epidemics and natural disasters the population was actually declining. Yet for some time still Italy retained her traditional primacy in the technical skills that she also passed on to other

Opposite Galileo Galilei (1546–1642), was prosecuted by the Inquisition on publishing *Dialogo sopra i due massimi sistemi* (*Dialogue on the Great Systems*, 1632) in which he persisted in embracing the heliocentric system of Copernicus, and the hypothesis that the earth revolves around the sun, a notion that had been declared heretical. The book is dedicated to Ferdinand of Tuscany who, though a patron of science, later failed to defend him. The frontispiece shows Galileo in imaginary discussion with Copernicus and Ptolemy.

DIALOGO
di
GALILEO GALILEI LINCEO
AL SER.mo FERD. II. GRAN. DVCA DI
TOSC   ANA

Stefan. Della Bella. F.

The Counter-Reformation, in defending the Church against other political and religious systems, was substantially aided by Italians with a call to piety and public service who created new religious orders. Filippo Neri founded the Oratorians in 1564; Carlo Borromeo the Oblates in 1578; and Camillo Lellis the Camillans in 1582. Camillo Lellis—represented here in a detail from a painting by Pierre Subleyras showing him rescuing the patients of the Ospedale di S. Spirito, Rome, from a flood—was the last to be canonized, in 1746.

Cosimo II, Grand Duke of Tuscany from 1609–21, was the last of the Medicis to head both the State and the family's international bank. Cosimo summoned Galileo to Florence as Court Mathematician and sought the territorial expansion of the Grand Duchy. The spirited drawing is by Jacques Callot (1592–1635), a French artist who spent many years in Florence.

advancing countries; there were still occasional flashes of artistic genius, and the feeling for magnificence in shows and social display persisted.

But the centre of historical development had moved away from Italy – to the Reformation countries, where new moral habits were being fostered by a vital religious experience; to the big states which were developing and changing the whole face of economy and communications; to the oceans, where the peoples of western Europe were discovering an extension of their civilization; and to a complex moral strife in which the medieval demands for freedom were finding a new application in conditions containing the germ of modern civilization. Lastly, that centre now lay too among the educated classes of western and northern Europe, where the first intimations of rationalism and experimental science were gradually developing, a course on which Italy in the early seventeenth century had barely begun to embark.

True, the idea of decline is not positive but negative; it suggests a failing, not a development; it depends to a great extent on our conception of life. As Croce has said of this period in Italian history, if we were still to regard asceticism and chivalrous honour as the highest ideals we should see this era with its monasteries and its duels not as an age of decline but as a culminating point.

The differing emphasis we may attach to the various aspects of life will also cause us to assign differing dates to the onset and advance of the decline. If we set store by things of the intellect and regard a rich and varied participation in political life as an essential element for progress we shall follow eighteenth-century and later historians in dating the onset of the decline from the fall of Florence in 1530, or the congress of Bologna in 1529, or the treaty of Câteau-Cambrésis (1559) which established unrivalled Spanish domination in the peninsula. If we greatly value freedom in matters of religion we shall certainly assign an important place in the origins of the decline to the conclusion of the Council of Trent (1564). If, on the other hand, we are thinking more in terms of authority, organization, order and the economy we shall discern signs of vigour and progress even after the decline of the Renaissance: for instance, in the achievements of the Grand Duke of Tuscany, Cosimo I, who made Tuscany into a self-reliant, orderly state, or of Emmanuel Filibert of Savoy, who recreated Piedmont within the framework of the Italian states, and more especially in the work of

Italy after the Treaty of Câteau-Cambrésis, 1559

organization, inspiration, and social and moral aid carried out by the Counter-Reformation Church. This last was, it is true, international, but it had its centre in the heart of Italy, in Rome, and was directed by Italians, supported by Italian forces, and operated in Italian territory. It defended the Church against attacks from other political and religious systems, creating religious orders of which the founders were Italians (Filippo Neri, of the Oratorians, 1564; Carlo Borromeo, of the Oblates, 1578; Camillo Lellis, of the Camillans, 1582) or which later came under the control of Italians, as with the Jesuits under the generalship of Fathers Mercuriano and Acquaviva; and it inspired the coalition which, under Spanish leadership but with a considerable contribution from Italy, won the battle of Lepanto against the Turks in 1571. Moreover the economic activity of the second half of the sixteenth century, when much new building was going on and towns were expanding, marked an era of prosperous advance, which came to an end with the period with which we are now concerned.

By the end of the century, however, when our story begins, the decline in every aspect of life had set in.

Opposite In the climate of the Counter-Reformation, sculpture, as well as architecture and painting, embodied the drama of resurgent Catholicism. Italian baroque sculpture, dominated by Bernini, also found individual expression in the work of masters such as Francesco Aprile and Ercole Ferrata who respectively began and completed this statue of S. Anastasia for the church of S. Anastasia, Rome.

The Spanish armies turned their attention towards the north of Europe and the Atlantic, towards the Low Countries and Britain. France between 1590 and 1600 was emerging from civil war. The Spanish system had begun to crumble and the Italian states were once again, as towards the end of the Renaissance, dragged into the struggle for balance of power. On the eve of the great offensive against the Reformation in Germany, the Church in Italy increased its vigilance and pressure against intellectual speculation and the new trend towards scientific experiment. Around the middle of the century the Po valley again became a theatre of war; Venice, which had already lost Cyprus, struggled to preserve herself by permanent neutrality. Former flourishing centres of humanistic culture disappeared: first Ferrara and Urbino, both absorbed by the Papal State, and then Mantua, still an independent principality but sorely stricken by the sack of 1630 and the change in her ruling dynasty. The south was subjected to severe taxation on behalf of the Spanish empire, and a revolt against it broke out in Naples.

The Peace of Westphalia (1648) and the Peace of the Pyrenees (1659) marked the end of the active and reconquering phase of the Counter-Reformation and the Spanish domination. Italy, which had shared in it, also felt its effects. The conscious sensation of decline was now resented by the educated classes, who were interested in the new ideas emerging in Europe but could find no means of expressing them in the existing political system. That system, however, was to enter on a more pronounced period of crisis, releasing fresh energies, with the beginning of the eighteenth century.

The Spanish Domination and its Crisis

Very great social differences existed between Milan and the Kingdom of Naples at the time when both came under Spanish rule. In the state of Milan, the *signoria*, or rule of an overlord, had extended over a whole network of close-lying industrial communes connected by good communications; the privileged position of the ruling classes was linked with wealth and activity within an urban type of life. The Kingdom of Naples, on the contrary, was a fundamentally baronial state where only the capital city and the educated class it had produced afforded constant loyal support to the

dynasties; elsewhere, towns were few and far apart, communications bad, and feudal anarchy reigned. Persisting feudalism had been unwilling to bend to the wishes of the dynasties and had therefore been repressed by the Spaniards, who inculcated loyalty by force under the long rule of the Viceroy Pedro de Toledo, appointed in 1532; but a state of moral and material chaos existed among the population. Spanish rule had brought some benefits to Naples and Milan; but in neither state had it thought fit to base the government and its policy on the indigenous leading class, as had been done in Spain and initially in the Low Countries. It had taken some of the local leaders into the King's service in the army or government administration, leaving the rest their local privileges, exercised, however, under the strict authority of the representative of the central government, whose power was quite independent of them.

This represented both a forward and a backward step in the technique of government. It was a forward step as regards co-ordination and the establishment of an independent bureaucracy; but it was a step backward in reverting to medieval ideas and methods of arbitrary government, which also involved administrative inefficiency. The Spaniards brought with them a general inability to deal with legal or fiscal problems, and by the time Spanish domination ended both Milan and Naples were in the throes of a deep economic depression whose consequences marked the subsequent history of the southern Kingdom.

But it should not be forgotten that restrictive economic measures, such as monopolies and heavy unevenly distributed taxation, were not peculiar to the Spanish domains in Italy, nor even to Spain itself, but were a common feature of seventeenth century government. They were not an immediate cause of the economic decline in Italy under Spain, nor did they prevent other states from prospering in spite of them. A more deep-rooted demoralization existed for which later generations, and some contemporaries too, blamed the Spanish regime, and which did undoubtedly develop under it. This demoralization really had its roots in the values and ideals which, under the Counter-Reformation and in particular under the Spanish domination, permeated the whole of Italian life. They were the values of a medieval and backward society which regarded as the supreme good the service of the King, of God, and of His priests, exalted privilege and hierarchy, and debased work, at any rate as viewed

Opposite In contrast to the idealization of the Bolognese and Roman masters, the painting of Michelangelo Merisi da Caravaggio (1573–1610) was vividly realistic, as in his early *Boy with Basket of Fruit*. Ostensibly conforming to Counter-Reformation ideas of simplicity, his religious and genre subjects, theatrically lighted, conveyed a sense of tension and drama. European art owes much to Caravaggio who influenced other masters like Rubens and Rembrandt.

from the standpoint of the aristocracies; the art of politics was the prerogative of the court and the principality, and culture was just an ornament and a technical accomplishment.

The rigorous exclusion of the leading classes from government, the regime of hierarchies, exceptions, and privileges, had quite different effects in Milan and in Naples. In Milan, it increased the power of the city's patricians, whose activities, restricted in the spheres of economics and politics, expanded in charitable works and in their organization throughout the vast archdiocese of Milan (and even to some extent in the Po valley) under Carlo Borromeo and later, during the more difficult period of economic and social crisis in the Duchy, under his nephew Federico, Archbishop of Milan from 1595 to 1631. Around these socially prominent churchmen there developed the organization not only of charity but also of culture (Federico, for example, founded the Ambrosian Library in Milan) and even, thanks to the extensive immunity of the clergy, of a social police. Only they, the Governor and the Senate, are remembered in this period, not the administrators or artists or businessmen.

For Milan the decisive crisis of Spanish power arose during the period of the Olivares ministry and the conflict with France, from the local wars of Monserat and Valtellina (1612) until the Peace of the Pyrenees at mid-century. During this time the prosperous development of the Milanese territory was disrupted by a serious crisis in the wool industry and another, if less grave, in the silk industry which particularly affected the small towns and the countryside. Lombardy's economy in the future was to be based on the export of raw and woven silk. But for the present, the very fact of Milan's position as a centre of communications and entrepôt trade, a link between the Spanish dominions in the north and the south, which had achieved relative prosperity in times of peace, intensified the virtual collapse of the state machine that now occurred through the effects on business of the wars. It was not until 1662, when peace was restored, that the so-called *rimpiazzo* was introduced, a tax on the communities 'replacing' the arbitrary levies exacted from them for the maintenance of military garrisons. But the greater number of economic and religious 'immunities' of certain classes, the reduction of productive activities, and the increase in arbitrary methods all tended to produce a more 'personalized', less public-spirited society in Milan, although economic exploitation

of the country to serve the aims of Spanish policy was a good deal less severe than in Naples.

For in Naples the overall picture was dark indeed. True, the Viceroy Toledo won praise for his repression of the insolent barons – with what were undoubtedly good effects as regards their relations with the crown of Spain, but not as regards society in general. These same barons, deprived of arms as a menace to the state, squandering their fortunes in luxury and litigation to the profit of the lawyers, nevertheless continued to be regarded as the models of society, and to prevail over the *università* or communities, overriding the intentions and even the decrees of state tribunals. Naples, the capital, had already expanded to an unwarranted extent for a town without an industry, and its population now represented some 10 or 12 per cent of the whole kingdom.

As its political life weakened, it became unable to deal with its unemployed proletariat – a common enough occurrence in all cities, but here reaching beyond all bounds of political or social control.

In Naples, too, the crisis coincided with the wars, though a little later than in Milan. In 1616 the Viceroy, Lemos, had good hopes of restoring the Kingdom's finances; but his successor, the Duke of Osuna, an enterprising man but no statesman, abandoned the effort. The situation became worse in the following years when, under the Viceroys Monterrey and Medina de las Torres, between 1630 and 1643, the tax burden increased fourfold. At the same time, abuses like 'pretaxing' merchants and misuse of funds beggared the Kingdom's economic capacity.

All this led in 1647–8 to a revolt of the Neapolitan populace, led by a fisherman, Masaniello, against the then Viceroy, the Duke of Arcos, which achieved immense notoriety. It had been instigated behind the scenes by French agents and by Osuna's former adviser, Genoino, who aimed at a revival of the political power of the Neapolitan populace and patricians. It turned into a popular rising in which various different elements became involved, with varying fortunes; but the feudal nobles after some uncertainty sided with Spain in order to crush the active discontent of the peasant communes. Masaniello was assassinated and under a new leader, Gennaro Annese, the rebels proclaimed a Neapolitan Republic and sought an alliance with Henry of Guise. But the popular forces were in fact too isolated to attempt successfully any alliance with the great Powers, or to produce any lasting unrest

Opposite Limited in politics and economics under Spanish rule, Milanese patricians like Carlo Borromeo devoted themselves to charity and social work. *S. Carlo Borromeo Distributing the Wealth of the Principality of Oria to the Poor* by Cerano (1567–1633) and the other great narrative canvases in Milan Cathedral celebrating Borromeo's exemplary life, were intended to help the cause of his canonisation.

and aspiration for autonomy such as developed in Catalonia or Messina.

The first half of the seventeenth century saw the total disruption of the Spanish system both economically and politically, in the domains directly under it. To complete the picture of 'Spanish' Italy however, some mention must be made of the Republic of Genoa. As a result of close co-operation with Spain, Genoa enjoyed a period of prosperity, and in the service of the Spanish empire throughout the Mediterranean found splendid opportunities to expand her own trade. She served as a port of embarkation for the Spanish troops going over-land to the Low Countries or the Austrian states. From 1580 gold coming from America and later silver, destined for central Europe, was landed there; she practically controlled the exchanges at the annual trade fair in Piacenza; and she held a virtual monopoly of the profits of trade from the southern Kingdom during its period of prosperity when it exported silk and raw materials. Thus Genoa found in her functions within the Spanish system compensation for the loss of her last possessions in the eastern Mediterranean; and her alliance with Spain protected her against the French, thus enabling her to retain her colony of Corsica. When Spanish rule weakened, she did not hesitate to insure her position by loans to rival states such as Venice, while at the same time remaining linked politically with the fate of Milan and checking attempts by the Duke of Savoy to stir up unrest within her own territory.

Although circumstances at this time served to increase Genoa's economic prosperity and to implant in her citizens a patriotic love of independence (of which they later gave striking proof when the city was bombarded by the French in 1684, and later still in the revolt of 1746 against the Austrians), all this could not suffice to restore her old political vigour and capacity to dominate the rich oligarchy of merchants in the interests of the community; with all the strength of her old institutions Genoa still remained fundamentally a mercantile community, lacking the inner capacity for reform and development.

Rome and Tuscany and Lesser Principalities

When the territorial divisions in Italy became stabilized in the middle of the sixteenth century the Roman state was a considerable power, despite Machiavelli's invective ('*Costoro hanno stati, e non li governano*'–'They have states but don't govern them'). Its capital was a universal city, the seat of a flourishing culture; it controlled much of the most industrious and prosperous part of Italy including Ravenna, Bologna, and Ancona, as well as that part of the Apennines which supplied the main strength of the Italian militias. It had made Rome itself the spectacular capital of a supra-national organization; the papacy had freed itself from the pressure of the rural feudal nobility; and Ancona was becoming an important port for overseas trade. The papacy at that time represented the headquarters of an international organization rather than a local principality. It drew its forces, and often its leaders, from the state itself, but it used its resources to carry out its international function; and this was logical, for as the vitality of the Renaissance waned the state had been preserved and strengthened largely by the prestige and international solidarity attached to the Holy See.

This prestige and strength still survived at the end of the sixteenth century and were reflected in the expansion of the state. In 1598 Pope Clement VIII, Ippolito Aldobrandini, succeeded in annexing Ferrara and the nearby territories of Cento and Comacchio to the Papal State, thus taking its frontiers across the Po to the borders of the Venetian Republic. A great centre of humanistic culture, as well as the outlet of the river Po, thus came into the hands of the Holy See.

A similar capacity for expansion was shown by the Barberini Pope, Urban VIII, in the annexation of the Duchy of Urbino in 1631 following the death of the last Duke of the Rovere line, Federico Maria. Such annexations were possible because the princes or the heirs concerned, whether Este or Della Rovere, had come to regard themselves more as landowners than as rulers.

But the process of 'personalization' mentioned in connection with Milan and Naples, also threatened and eroded the Papal State. In 1606–7 Pope Paul V failed to quell Venice in the dispute over his Interdict. In 1641, when Urban VIII attempted to confiscate the Duchy of Castro from Odoardo Farnese, Duke of Parma and Piacenza, because of Odoardo's heavy indebtedness to the Holy See, he encountered setbacks, a defeat in Emilia, the invasion of his own state as far as Acquapendente, and at the end a truce amounting to a victory for Farnese in 1644. True, a few years later, under the next Pope, Innocent X, the tables were turned and Castro was destroyed and a column set up there with

The Spanish Jesuit Miguel Molinos (1628–96) was arrested by the Inquisition in Rome when his mystical ideas were at the height of their popularity. The quietism he represented, close in spirit to Protestant pietist mysticism, was one of many controversial theories that arose within the Church during the seventeenth century. Molinos publicly recanted his views in S. Maria Sopra Minerva, Rome, in 1687, as shown in the engraving, and was sentenced to life imprisonment.

Left Charles Emmanuel I, Duke of Savoy from 1580–1630. Restless and adventurous, he involved the Duchy in many wars but at his death left little to show for it. Like the other Italian princes, the Dukes of Savoy sought a place in the sun for their principality. Savoy avoided the general decline largely through the merits of Charles Emanuel's descendant Victor Amadeus II (1671–1730).

CAROLVS EMANVEL D. G. DVX SABAVDIÆ P.P.

ALIA NON EST ARBORE PALMA

HVNC ANIMO INTREPIDVM VIRTVS INVICTA TVETVR, ET, QVAM PROTEXIT, PROTEGIT ALMA FIDES.

Right Johannes Gross of Lucerne, a member of the Swiss Guard, the foreign mercenary bodyguard established by Pope Julius II. As the inscription states, Gross also served as a guide to the tourists in Rome, and he is shown, with his finger pointing, against a background of Roman monuments, including Trajan's Column, the Pantheon and the medieval Torre delle Milizie.

La uera Guida de' gl Oltramontani
Hò qui retratto al natural sembiante

Mostra l' antiche, e le moderne piante,
É le fabriche eccelse de Roma.

Each savant belonging to the Accademia della Crusca had a paddle with his motto and device as an emblem of membership. Dedicated to the study of the Italian language, the academy's main purpose was the compilation of a definitive dictionary. The first appeared in 1612, and was followed at long intervals by three more complete versions until the fourth edition appeared in six volumes in 1738.

A detail of a contemporary engraving of a cholera epidemic in seventeenth-century Rome shows the municipally organized fumigation of infected houses and the disposal of the dead.

The rebuilding of St Peter's, begun in 1452, was finally completed under the patronage of Alexander VII (1655–67). The magnificent elliptical piazza with its two hemicycles of columns was the work of Gian Lorenzo Bernini (1598–1680), official architect of the Vatican, whose creations in painting, sculpture and architecture are among the major monuments of baroque Rome. The background of the scene has remained unchanged. The imaginary construction at the left was never built, but a pavement was subsequently laid and visitors have always been numerous.

the inscription 'Here was Castro'; but such boasting over an insignificant victory was in itself a sign of weakness. And the same weakness was shown later on, in 1687–9, when Innocent XI had to suffer the arrogant demands of Louis XIV on a question of diplomatic immunity in Rome itself.

In fact, the loss of power of the aristocracy, already noted in other states, was further complicated in Rome itself by the ambition of members of the great families to enter the service of the Church as a career. The papacy practised what was known as 'petty nepotism', by comparison with the 'great nepotism' that had prevailed in the Renaissance states. Now the Pope's relations, and in particular the 'Cardinal nephews', became his ministers and the founders of princely dynasties. Roman and Tuscan families – the Borghese, Pamphili, Barberini, and Chigi families – 'personalized' the Counter-Reformation Church, if not in its general direction, which continued on the lines laid down by the Jesuits, at any rate in the government of the state.

During the Renaissance the Church of Rome's relationship with Tuscan civilization and power had acquired great significance. The two Medici Renaissance Popes, Leo X and Clement VII, were Tuscans; immediately after their time Rome had also experienced a veritable colonization by Tuscans – outstanding examples are the great artists such as Michelangelo and the Florentine bankers who furthered the development of Rome by organizing the public debt. In Tuscany, the Medici dynasty itself was linked with the papacy through the installation, with imperial approval, first of Alessandro, then of Cosimo I, and later, when the Counter-Reformation was already well advanced, through Pius V's grant – without imperial approval – of the title of Grand Duke, which gave Cosimo the primacy of rank among the Italian princes. But in later times Tuscany, though its story was still linked to some extent with that of Rome, gradually lost its function of an intellectual nursery and reserve of talent for Rome.

Nevertheless under Ferdinand I, the former Cardinal who in 1587 became the third Grand Duke, Tuscany still retained much of its Renaissance splendour and prosperity. He encouraged trade and shipping through the new port of Leghorn, as well as the dynasty's traditional banking activities; contracted alliances with the great European dynasties (his niece, Maria de' Medici, became Queen of France, his own wife was Christina of Lorraine, and his son Cosimo II married Maria Maddalena of Hapsburg); and maintained a balance between France and Spain. But even in this flourishing period it was plainly not easy for a former free seigneurial republic to turn itself into a principality; its once enterprising character altered and under Cosimo II (1609–21), the last of the Medicis to combine control of the state with control of the international bank, passiveness prevailed, a readiness to accept traditional policies, though Cosimo was still sufficiently open-minded to summon the astronomer Galileo to Florence and he also aspired, if unsuccessfully, to expand the frontiers of the Grand Duchy.

It was under the succeeding regency (which capitulated to the Barberinis in Rome and did nothing to protect Galileo) and under Ferdinand II with his family nepotism that many signs presaged the dynasty's decline. Though in Ferdinand's last years and in the early years of Cosimo III's long reign (1670–1732) scientific research was still encouraged, especially by Cosimo's brother, Cardinal Leopold (with the foundation, in 1657, of the Accademia del Cimento), the former breadth of view and courage was lacking, especially after the humiliation of Galileo. The dynasty's break with the intellectual traditions of the state, the withdrawal of capital from industry for investment in landed property, the end of the state's own militia, the general atmosphere of bigotry, all formed part of the particular way in which the decline showed itself in Tuscany, making it, as it entered the new era, a very different state from the others.

The Po valley principalities of the Farnese, Este and Gonzaga families whose dynasties were swept away at the end of the seventeenth century, are often compared unfavourably by historians with the little state of Savoy, which throughout a series of military conflicts seemed to be preparing itself for its future role as a native Italian force in the peninsula. It is certainly true that the Duchy of Savoy, continuing the shrewd policy laid down by its restored leader, Emmanuel Filibert (1559–80), and favoured by the international situation, played an active part in the wars at the beginning of the seventeenth century. But the Farnese, the Gonzaga and the Este were also active at that time, within their more restricted domains, in warlike enterprise and in contracting alliances. If the Duchy of Savoy contrived to avoid the general decline, this was due largely to the gifted leadership of Victor Amadeus II (1675–1730) and to the different mentality of the Savoyard élite.

Opposite With numerous important commissions under six successive Popes, Bernini transformed the face of Rome. He expressed his genius in such baroque masterpieces as the Four Rivers Fountain in the Piazza Navona which was commissioned by Innocent X (1644–55) and executed by Bernini's workshop between 1648 and 1651. A detail, the River Ganges, is shown in the photograph.

Emmanuel Filibert's son, the adventurous Charles Emmanuel I (1580–1630), took an active part in the civil and religious wars of France, campaigned for many years against Spain, but finally fought as an ally of Spain against French and imperial forces in Italy. On the death of his son Victor Amadeus I the history of Savoy becomes confused with dynastic struggles, not unlike the French *Fronde*, until it was restored to French influence by Mazarin in 1642.

In all their campaigns the Dukes of Savoy demonstrated military ability and the drive to make a place in the sun for Savoy, but in these features they did not differ notably from the other princes, who also aimed to secure and expand their states by means of wars and alliances. There was no great difference in this respect between Emmanuel Filibert and Duke Alessandro Farnese of Parma, who attained great military distinction in the service of Spain, dying in 1592.

The same can be said of the Este family, who, though deprived of their true centre of power, Ferrara, nevertheless under the third Duke, Francis I, rebuilt the principality's strength around the new capital, Modena.

In other words, not only the remote little Alpine principality of Savoy but also the two principalities in the Apennines, hemmed in between Lombardy and the Papal State, gave proof of their vitality in the seventeenth century. It was not till the wars of the eighteenth century that their real decline began.

The same cannot be said, however, of the Duchy of Mantua and Monferrat. Here the problem was created by geography. The Gonzaga family ruled over two separate buffer states, one of them, Mantua, lying between Spanish territory and Venice, and the other, Monferrat, between Spanish territory and Piedmont; they proved unable to preserve either of them, or to secure that consolidation of the state achieved in the other regional principalities. Forced to guard two fortresses simultaneously, their ownership of Casale, capital of Monferrat, accelerated the decline of the Gonzagas' cultural capital, Mantua, which was further weakened by the inability of the neighbouring and largely maritime Venetian Republic to pursue an active policy on land. The sack of Mantua in 1630 and the sale of its art collections signified the end of a great centre of Renaissance culture. Like Ferrara and Urbino, Mantua became one of the 'dead cities' of Italy, regaining its true place and vitality only in modern times.

Venice

Venice is the last piece in the balance of power among the Italian states that prevailed from the end of the Renaissance throughout the seventeenth century and, with much remodelling, into the 1800s. It was to all appearances a model state, jealous of its independence and ready to make serious economic sacrifices to preserve it, and therefore determined to remain outside Spanish influence and to find in its own resources the strength to maintain the trade, shipping, and colonial possessions to which the state owed its prosperity.

But Venice encountered serious practical problems in the seventeenth century which it proved unable to solve. The chief of these was the dilemma of having to confront the Turks in the Mediterranean and at the same time to remain the chief port for the shipping lines trading with the Turkish Levant. The impossibility of meeting her adversary on an equal footing caused Venice to adopt a policy in which energetic defence alternated with long periods of compromise.

Despite the Christian victory of Lepanto over the Turks, Venice had had to cede Cyprus, a source of cotton and sugar, to them in 1573. The first half of the seventeenth century saw the spread of piracy in the Mediterranean, partly under the auspices of Powers trading with Venice (the Empire, in whose territory lay the Gulf of Quarnaro, base of the Slav pirates, the *Uskoki*, and the English, who prolonged to the North Sea the Mediterranean routes of which Venice was the terminal). Unable to beat the *Uskoki* at sea, she managed early in the century to secure a compromise with the Empire whereby their bases were taken from them. But this compromise caused Venice to play an increasingly passive role in Italy which cut her off from possible sources for revival of her power. In the second half of the century, after the Turkish attack on her other possession in the Levant, Candia (1645), Venice sided increasingly with the Hapsburg Empire in resistance against the last great offensives of the Turks. But though the Austrians' new military techniques eventually secured them victory, Venice lost Candia in 1669.

Earlier on, Venice had nevertheless afforded a last example, in 1606–7, of the oneness of the state and her intellectual élite. Rome's claim to jurisdiction over certain internal church affairs in Venice was disputed by the Venetians and in reprisal Pope Paul V pronounced an Interdict forbidding religious services

Opposite The baroque has been called the Jesuit Style after the Society of Jesus, perhaps its most enthusiastic patron. Suitably spectacular for the church of the Jesuits' founder, S. Ignazio, in Rome, the 'cupola' was the work of Andrea Pozzo (1642–1709), mathematician, painter, architect and Jesuit lay brother. Fifty-six feet across, it is one of the largest *trompe-l'oeil* compositions ever painted.

to be held there, to which Venice replied by disregarding the Interdict and expelling the Jesuits. The Republic was advised by the Servite friar, Paolo Sarpi, who fostered the idea of a wholly spiritual Church living in observance of the sovereign ruler's commands and exercising wide tolerance in discussion, thus to some extent presaging the churches of the eighteenth century, controlled and reformed by the states' rulers. This episode was perhaps the last moment of European significance in the history of the Venetian Republic; nor can it be separated from the intellectual development that accompanied it, from the *History of the Council of Trent* that Sarpi wrote, and from Venice's contacts with the scholars then propounding the new doctrines of state in Europe. The dispute partly reproduced the circumstances of earlier medieval conflicts, partly anticipated the ideas which were to influence the state and society in modern times. Venice's last great idealistic moment ended in a compromise with the Vatican. A few years later the last attempts to assert herself as a military power in Italy also failed, and the conservative oligarchy that presided over the fate of this great mercantile community provided no idealistic impetus. Venice henceforth concentrated on preserving her independence; with it she preserved for modern times a high degree of civilization but, despite some recovery in the eighteenth century, she could achieve no genuine revival of her former vitality.

Counter-Reformation, Thought and Literature

On 17 February 1600, Giordano Bruno, of Nola near Naples, was burned at the stake as an unrepentant heretic in the Campo de'Fiori in Rome.

This was by no means the first punishment meted out by the Roman Inquisition, for humanist heretics such as Carnesecchi and Paleario had also paid for their religious convictions with their lives. Under such a Pope as Paul IV people had come to realise that these punishments were not only horrible in themselves but also struck a blow against the whole exercise of thought as well as against religious opinions. '*E ragionate poco, che contro la ragione esiste il foco*' – 'Reason as little as you can, for against reason there is fire' – said Pasquino in one of his famous lampoons. But in Bruno's trial there was something more. The philosopher of

Nola, one of the first intellects to conceive of the coincidence of opposites in an infinite cosmos, who in the midst of myths and religious frenzies spoke up for natural religion and the creative nature of art and politics, when arrested in Venice after a long sojourn in Protestant countries asked to be tried in Rome. As a rationalist who also appreciated the value of the mystical and social functions of religions, he probably imagined that his acceptance of the need for the popular religion that the Catholic Church maintained, and his hostility to the transcendental but more rigid Christianity of the Protestants, would earn him some honourable compromise with the Inquisition. When he saw that the Church, far from confining itself to its disciplinary function, not only condemned him but aimed also to destroy his whole philosophy, he refused to retract, and went to the stake, as it seemed to his executioners, blaspheming.

Bruno's attitude is less unreasonable than it might seem at first sight. It was based on the conviction that the Counter-Reformation Church had absorbed something of the rationalism of the Renaissance; but the burning of Bruno proved that an ideological conflict had opened not only between the Reformation and the Church but also between the Church and humanism.

A further proof of this conflict can be seen in the different fate of another no less energetic southern philosopher, the friar Tommaso Campanella. His driving idea was of a natural, universal and egalitarian religion; and this conviction was so strong in him that it not only brought him several times before the Inquisition but also caused him to plot from his Calabrian monastery against the Spanish Government with the aim of bringing about a communist type of society adhering to natural religion. For this Campanella was imprisoned and tortured in the Viceroy's prisons and then, after feigning madness and asking to be sent to Rome, was condemned to 'perpetual' imprisonment for heresy. The sentence lasted for twenty-seven years, during which he continued to expound in messages to the outer world his ideas of a universal, papal monarchy. There is a certain ambiguity in Campanella's ideas in relation to Christianity, but what saved the monk's life and, which is more important, his work and books, was the ecclesiastical and authoritarian turn that his heretical ideas took. Campanella managed to end his days in Paris, now placing his hopes for the establishment of a universal and natural monarchy in the King of France rather

Opposite The Carnival of Venice became a European institution and helped establish the city, otherwise a great power in decline, as an international resort. A detail from a painting by Giuseppe Heintz the Younger (c 1600–78) shows masked revellers, side shows and bull baiting in St Mark's Square. Heintz was a forerunner of the painters of Venetian views of the eighteenth century.

than in the Powers that had brought about the Counter-Reformation – Spain and the Pope.

Campanella and Bruno had nothing behind them but their own intelligence and the vigour of their religious speculations. Behind Sarpi and his rejection of papal supremacy within the State there stood Venice, which continued to protect him even after an unsuccessful attempt on his life.

Someone should also have protected the Tuscan Galileo, whose trial and condemnation, although not resulting in his death, represented another important stage in the Counter-Reformation. Galileo, by education and inclination an experimental mathematician, made sensational discoveries in astronomy, using the new instrument that he constructed, if he did not actually invent it – the telescope. But his researches led Galileo not only to accept but also to give a deeper meaning to the heliocentric system of the Polish astronomer Copernicus. This meant putting science and methodical research on a par with the Scriptures as a source of truth ('the latter as a dictate of the Holy Spirit, the former as the rigidly observant executor of the orders of God') and claiming that the critical method in science was in fact the living instrument of truth. Though a mathematician at the court of the Grand Duke of Tuscany, Cosimo II, who was also his pupil, Galileo had to submit to the rigours of ecclesiastical persecution in a first trial in Rome in 1616, which formally proclaimed as heretical the proposition that 'the sun is the centre of the world and is therefore immovable'. An outcome of his research was thus transformed into a heretical dogma, even if he personally was spared.

With the coming of the new Pope, Urban VIII, Maffeo Barberini, a Florentine and protector of savants who had already supported him in an earlier scientific dispute, Galileo thought he could safely resume, in his *Dialogo sopra i due massimi sistemi* (*Dialogue on the Great Systems*), his discussion of the Copernican system, if only as a hypothesis. The *Dialogue* had immense success in the scientific world but produced violent reactions from the Pope and the Holy Office (the Inquisition). Galileo was tried in Rome and in June 1633 was forced to abjure. Condemned to prison and under strict surveillance to prevent him from spreading his views even in conversation, he spent his last years until his death in 1641 in resuming his old scientific experiments. Viviani, Torricelli, and Bellini were his pupils in this last stage of his life, and passed on the Galilean method to the Accademia del Cimento.

The condemnation of Galileo marks one of the culminating points in the Counter-Reformation and a decisive stage in the progress of thought in Italy. This was not a question of a purely religious or even philosophical-religious heresy, but the condemnation of a scientific method which was to spread and permeate the life and development of the most advanced nations in Europe. A Pope who professed to be the protector of savants, who himself wrote poetry, had let the judgment take its course; a prudent and practical theologian, Bellarmino, today a Saint, had taken part in the condemnation of both Galileo and Bruno; priestly intrigue had undoubtedly contributed, and perhaps even, or so at least Galileo thought, the jealousy of the Jesuit mathematicians, proud to bring to the Church the ornament of science so long as it carried no consequences in other spheres of life. But even such rulers as the Medici, protectors of science, accepted the consequences; so the splendid school of Galileo which developed in their state remained without influence on general ideas and was reduced by wish of the rulers to something of a technical curiosity.

Can the persecutions be regarded as the 'cause' of the stifling of intellectual vigour in Italy and the onset of the decline? The obvious answer is no; in periods of progress thought is not quenched by punishments and prohibitions. But it is equally obvious that these things played their part, were indeed part and parcel of the process of decline itself and signs of a general trend, an indication of the difficulties that stimulating thought had to face in seventeenth-century Italy.

For it is no coincidence that these few 'heroes' – Bruno, Campanella, Sarpi and Galileo – were also the greatest Italian writers of the seventeenth century; that one of them, Campanella, sounded the sole note of poetry, mingled with prophetic exaltation, to be heard in Italy since Tasso; and that at the same time the literary scene was dominated by the cold and artificial style of baroque writers such as Marino, by vulgar provincial heroic-comic poets like Tassoni, and by theatrical preachers like Segneri.

Baroque was now the fashion in literature, a fashion that, far from arousing repugnance, seemed the only way in which it was possible to write. It was based on the theory of using astonishment to secure artistic effect, arousing that astonishment by means of 'conceits', or the bringing together of curious and unexpected images and associations of ideas, woven into a plot of little or no importance. Not intended to express

Above, right S. Carlo alle Quattro Fontane, dedicated to S. Carlo Borromeo, was the first independent work of Borromini (1599–1667). Unlike the other two great baroque masters working in Rome, Bernini and Pietro da Cortona, he was almost exclusively an architect. The furthest from classicism, his architecture is the most original and shows a nervous compression of forms, as in the oval cupola of S. Carlo.

Above, left The baroque façade of S. Lorenzo in Miranda emerges from the remains of the second-century Temple of Antoninus and Faustina in the Roman Forum. In the Renaissance spirit, for a visit of Charles V, the medieval church previously occupying the body of the temple was cleared away to reveal the Roman construction. Counter-Reformation piety led to the church's rebuilding and the erection of the façade, by Orazio Torriani in 1602.

Left Alexander VII (1655–67), a Chigi of the Sienese banking family, was the last of the Popes whose patronage made Rome the outstanding artistic centre of Europe. The drawing is a design for his exuberant baroque tomb in St Peter's which was executed in coloured marbles and bronze by Bernini and his workshop between 1672 and 1678.

Left Cardinal Scipione Borghese, an outstanding art connoisseur and a patron of Caravaggio and Bernini, exploited his position as nephew of Paul V to build the Villa Borghese. This allegory of his death, by J. Stella, marshals the wealth of emotional detail and literary symbolism typical of the baroque.

Right Dutch and Flemish painters in Rome produced *genre* representations of everyday and low life which appealed especially to the middle class. This print shows a street vendor offering caricature figures representing subjects such as *commedia dell' arte* characters.

Below The grandiose entry into Rome in 1655 of Queen Christina of Sweden befitted such an important convert to Catholicism. Her interest in arts and letters helped create an intellectual circle that was not completely dominated by the Vatican. She spent the latter part of her life in Rome, and is buried in St Peter's.

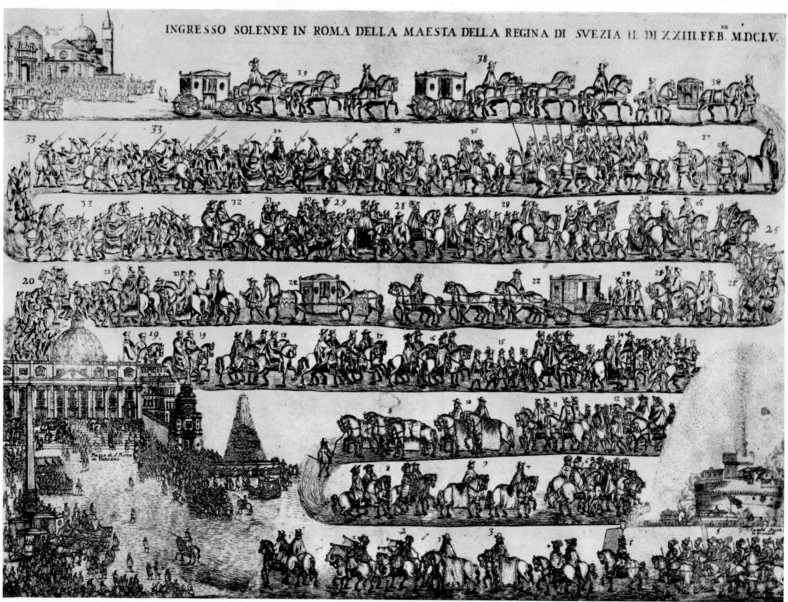

Cesare Beccaria's *Dei delitti e delle pene (Of Crimes and Punishments)*, one of the most influential books ever written on criminal law, approached the problem of crime in the rational spirit of the Enlightenment. As the frontispiece indicates, Beccaria (1738–94) denounced the use of torture and the death penalty. Subsequently an Italian state, Tuscany, had the distinction of being the first country to abolish capital punishment.

Below Torture, a regular and universal tool of justice in criminal cases, was also utilized by the Inquisition to force heretics to confess and implicate others. The whole proceedings of the Holy Office from arrest on suspicion to secret trial were arbitrary but carried out in the interests, it was considered, of the individual's soul and the spiritual health of the Catholic community.

DEI DELITTI
E
DELLE PENE

EDIZIONE SESTA
Di nuovo corretta ed accreſciuta.

In rebus quibuscumque difficilioribus non expectandum, ut quis ſimul, & ſerat, & metat, ſed praeparatione opus eſt, ut per gradus matureſcant. Bacon. Serm. fidel. nu. XLV.

HARLEM,
Et ſe vend'
A PARIS,
Chez Molini Libraire, Quai des Auguſtins.

MDCCLXVI.

Gian Battista Piranesi (1720–78) etched hundreds of views of ancient and contemporary Rome that stamped the image of the city on the minds of generations. No longer among the greatest metropolises of Europe, Piranesi's Rome was its antiquarian capital.

Below The eighteenth-century papacy could no longer afford to build on the scale of the past. One of the few great rococo monuments of the period, the Porto di Ripetta, designed by Alessandro Specchi, was one of the two river ports that served the leisurely commerce of Rome. It was destroyed during the construction of the Tiber embankments at the end of the nineteenth century. A Piranesi print.

feelings, it was a style meant to seize the attention.

This style makes it difficult to read today such serious literature as many seventeenth-century writers produced; but at the time they maintained Italy's reputation abroad, as well as continuing along the paths of research initiated under the Renaissance in politics, the art of poetry, travel, geography and history. Serious writers such as Zuccolo, Botero, Nani, Davila and Bentivoglio emerged in this type of literary endeavour, utilizing baroque forms but seeking the truth.

It remains to be considered how far the figurative arts, especially architecture, to which the term was first applied, and music, can be regarded as 'baroque', and how an authentic new art emerged in these particular fields despite its disparaging name. As far as the figurative arts are concerned, the term 'baroque' would seem to be a quite inadequate definition for painting. In architecture, the word brings out the spectacular element that the new feeling for official magnificence imposed on the great palaces and churches, but it was first employed to censure as bizarre the uncanonical use of classical forms. As to sculpture, it refers to its extensive use as a decorative element. In music, the baroque aspects can be regarded as little more than the inevitable reflection of contemporary tastes. Except as a matter of convenience, therefore, the creative output of the seventeenth century apart from literature cannot be referred to simply as 'baroque'.

It is not difficult to explain why in the figurative or musical field personalities of genius emerged more readily than in the literary or poetic during baroque times. Architects found obvious stimulation in the demand for grandiose public buildings and whole capital cities that required an eclectic mastery combining new visual excitements and the different elements of local tradition in a generally accepted style. And Italy had in Rome, first and foremost, Bernini and Borromini: the former an untypically Neapolitan artist, who took infinite trouble to achieve the purity and simplicity of his results and fused sculpture and architecture into a single visual whole; the latter poised to represent in the novelty of his forms the uttermost tensions that the mind can control, overcoming all theatricality by the power of his conception. Borromini treated architecture as a form of liberation from the material aspect of the buildings he was commissioned to create, bringing lightness, colour and landscape into the grey grind of their execution. There were of course instances of spectacle and bravura for

their own sake, but if this was true of, for instance, Father Pozzi, it was not so with Juvara or the late baroque architects like Vanvitelli who created the splendid settings required by the absolute princes.

Not much that is 'baroque' can be said truly to exist in painting. The Mannerism of Michelangelo's Florentine followers is largely a Renaissance phenomenon. The portraits by the great Mannerists such as Pontormo, Bronzino, and other Medicean painters combine the abstract qualities of Michelangelo's later period with the psychological observation that the simplest and most popular earlier artists had practised naturally. The achievements of the Carracci school, eclectic rather than baroque, were mainly technical. The genius of Italian seventeenth-century painting is Caravaggio; and in him we find a temperament that stood apart from the fashionable world, elaborating his own ideas with little regard for the demands of the society in which he lived and for which he was ill-suited.

The masterpieces of painting, architecture and sculpture were made possible in part by the absence from the figurative arts, if not of ecclesiastical pressure, at least of the precise criteria through which that pressure was exercised on literature, and the very nature of the workmanship involved in those arts, enabled them to produce the great flowering of baroque art.

As for music, the seventeenth century saw its rise from its—and its performers'—earlier status of social inferiority to that of a recognized art. In this field, which was also less subject to ideological pressures, a sort of delayed Renaissance occurred. The austere Florentine *Camerata del Bardi* anteceded the music-drama of Rinuccini and of Peri who began by setting some of Dante's cantos to music (and, when he later passed on to pastoral tales, kept to a very simple and clear form of words accompanied by music); the sacred music of Palestrina, who pursued classicism and antique modes, is also marked by severity; while the music of Monteverdi combines that element with a tragic vein.

From the Arcadia to Vico

In the last decades of the seventeenth century modes changed and the search for luxurious spectacle and contrived surprise gave way to the ideal of simplicity in fashion and a life ruled by reason, research and work, concepts already elaborated abroad by the philosophers of rationalism, Descartes and Gassendi. The Counter-Reformation, its virulence played out in the Wars of Religion and the Thirty Years' War, declined both in vigilance and prestige. Italy at that time was, in Croce's opinion, 'resurgent', and among the first signs of this resurgence was the Academy of Arcadia, standing for a 'literary and stylistic revolution' distinguished by the 'need to write simply and modestly'. It may at first sight seem paradoxical to attach such importance to what was really just a literary society game of feigning a pastoral and idyllic simplicity. But almost a century later even a man of practical modern outlook, Pietro Verri, was to say of it: 'The Academy of Arcadia, which came into being to free literature from barbarity, collapsed together with it . . .'. So it fulfilled its task.

The general movement of minds that initiated the Enlightenment found different forms of expression in the different types of society existing in the various regions of Italy. In Naples it gave rise to a movement started by Tommaso Cornelio who, after returning from Rome where he had studied Galileo and Descartes, gathered round him a group of intellectuals of various professions. They all regarded philosophy as the basis of their activities; among them were Leonardo da Capua, Francesco Argento, Aulisio and, in the next generation, Doria and Celestino Galiani. This group fostered the import of foreign books and the revival of interest in studies, especially in the university. At the same time one of the last Spanish Viceroys, Bernardo del Carpio, effected reforms in education and public security. The new mood aroused the hostility of the Jesuits, the chosen political corps of the Counter-Reformation. One of the Neapolitan opponents of the Jesuits, the lawyer and literary critic, Giovan Vincenzo Gravina, around 1690 became one of the founders of the Academy of Arcadia in Rome, acting as its legal adviser and enthusiastic supporter until 1711.

It is no accident that the foundation of the Academy of Arcadia was linked with the last adventure of Queen Christina of Sweden, who had abdicated, and spent the latter part of her life in Rome. Her conversion was a triumph for Catholic propaganda. In fact, however, she reflected the changing nuances of fashion; she had been a protector of Descartes, and now in Rome – quite apart from any other intrigues or scandals – she was founding not a religious order, but a literary circle in the capital of the Counter-Reformation itself! The importance of the Arcadian Academy lay, however,

in its bringing together a group which, though simply social and literary, was still something quite apart from the recognized hierarchies and authorities to which it nevertheless professed devoted regard.

Arcadian taste dominated poetry though it had its opponents both because of the prosaic quality of its poetry and also because it made poetry seem a futile amusement. Though detached from the baroque tradition, it developed from a literary convention, the pastoral allegory, which was somehow associated with baroque taste, and it also had other related traits, if in more refined form, such as conventional worldliness. It gradually came to seem less serious and important as the new style prevailed over 'barbarity', but its influence lasted throughout the whole period of progress in the eighteenth century.

In Tuscany the new ideas from beyond the Alps readily mixed with the tradition of Galileo's followers, and Florence and its rationalism, the 'Studio' in Pisa and its lawyers, became the vehicle for the passage of new ideas to Naples and Milan.

One of the lesser principalities of Italy that seemed to have received its death-blow with the end of the Renaissance, Modena, was the centre of activity of the historian Ludovico Antonio Muratori, whose great work of medieval research still lives today in his *Annali d'Italia* and *Antiquitates*. But Muratori was also an active citizen who defended his prince against the Holy See in the dispute over Comacchio, counselled public health measures in his *Governo della peste*, opposed the spread of monasticism, and believed that 'the man who invented a machine for weaving stockings must be a great philosopher'. Muratori had a sincere and spontaneous reverence for religion; but he had moved beyond the Counter-Reformation. He was not alone: other scholars were appearing, such as Maffei in Verona, who loved their native lands but also lived in an international atmosphere. Their historical researches, going back to before the Renaissance, revaluating the contribution of the Italic peoples as opposed to Rome, enlarged the perspective of both past and present.

These intellectual stirrings were not to culminate in the Enlightenment until after the wars of the first half of the eighteenth century had produced political changes throughout the peninsula. Society needed new rulers before rationalism could spread. But in the meantime there emerged a man whose thought, virtually overstepping the Enlightenment, acts as a

Opposite Unemployment and heavy taxation by the Spanish government of Naples provoked the celebrated insurrection in 1647 called the Revolt of Masaniello, after the young fisherman who led it. The insurgents obtained a constitution, Masaniello was assassinated, and under his successor a republic was declared, which however survived only briefly. The painting is the masterpiece of Michelangelo Cerquozzi (1602–60).

link between humanistic speculation and modern historicism: this was Giovan Battista Vico (1668–1744).

Early influenced by the Cartesian spirit of the Neapolitan group, Vico was led to reconsider the history of politics, art and law as revealed by humanistic research. He based the essential idea of his *Scienza nuova*, according to which human history is made by men and can therefore be understood and reconstructed through critical thought, on reason and experience. Religious conceptions and myths, such as that of Providence made immanent and incorporated in human history, and humanistic conceptions and myths, such as that of the cycle, are brought together in Vico's philosophy. Human development is rational and comprehensible even if it does not correspond to an abstract or mathematical pattern. Vico excluded religious sacred history, the history of the Jews, from this theory, professing adherence in this respect to the traditional legend—whether from conviction, or prompted by caution, is not known. In Vico's philosophy, the idea of progress in human intelligence throughout history was lacking. He retained the Renaissance idea of cyclical rhythms, the *ricorsi*, but elevated the conception to such a powerful idea as the periodic recurrence of barbarism. The logical conclusion of his theory would have led him, despite his respect for history, not to the kind of reform sought by the rationalists but to something much more radical from the religious standpoint, and to a conflict of no lesser dimensions than that which cost Bruno his life. Yet some of Vico's concepts or rather the myths and symbols attached to them, filtered through even into the rationalists' interpretation of history.

From the Peace of Utrecht to the Peace of Aix-la-Chapelle (1713–48)

While the stimulus from the modern world, and especially from France under Louis XIV, influenced the educated classes in Italy, it had little immediate effect on the states' policy. Piedmont alone strove to imitate France, if in a spirit of political rivalry. Her proximity to France caused her to be more aware of the changing character of the monarchy under Louis XIV and its increasing authoritarianism. France had come almost to take the place of Spain as a bulwark of the

Counter-Reformation, as witness, for instance, the revocation of the Edict of Nantes and the attitude adopted towards Jansenism. Though ready to imitate France, Victor Amadeus II was irked by his great neighbour and aspired to make Piedmont a state with clearly defined frontiers, self-sufficient in economic and military resources; but he realised that to do this he must risk everything and join the great European coalitions. In 1690 he joined the Grand Alliance in the war which the allies waged against Louis XIV from 1686 till the Peace of Ryswick in 1697. But after suffering defeats he went over to Louis in 1696, securing from him territories which included the key position of Pinerolo. In the subsequent War of the Spanish Succession (1700–14), which ended with the treaties of Utrecht and Rastadt, he went even further. He began the war as a general at the head of the French army; but in 1703 he went over to the Grand Alliance, leaving his little army to be captured by the French. He held out with troops mustered at random until in the struggle for Turin, the imperial army under a prince of his own House, Eugene of Savoy, came to his aid. The subsequent victory brought him Monferrat and Lomellina, thus giving him a frontier in Lombardy and also Sicily, with the title of King. He subsequently lost Sicily, exchanging it for Sardinia under the Peace of Cambrai in 1720.

The Wars of the Polish and Austrian Successions, ending in the Peace of Aix-la-Chapelle in 1748, brought Piedmont, then under Charles Emmanuel III, Novara, Tortona, and the Novarese territory west of the Ticino. A significant aspect of these wars was the way the Piedmontese intellectual class showed itself ready to accept the consequences of the revival of political will in the state. Victor Amadeus, exalted to the rank of King, found his policy supported not only by prudent statesmen and diplomats but by men with the daring ideas of the earlier rationalist reformers, such as Carlo Alberto Radicati, who, forced into exile in England, became an advanced deist and forerunner of the Enlightenment.

Though he turned out Radicati, Victor Amadeus was nevertheless ready to foster innovations. He reorganized the University, abolished teaching by the Jesuits, curtailed the nobles' feudal privileges, and started a land register and codification of the law. In the disputes between Jansenists and Jesuits (the former had been condemned by the Papal Bull 'Unigenitus' in 1713) he drew on Jansenist ideas but forbade any discussion of the Bull. He was, in fact, a reformer, a forerunner of the Enlightened Despots; in the interests of policy

Opposite Italy retained its European primacy in music, opera and theatre during the eighteenth century. *Concert in the Teatro Argentina*, by the major painter of the Roman scene, Gian Paolo Panini (c 1692–1765/8), depicts a fête given by the French Ambassador and attended by notables such as the English Pretender. Seated on clouds are singers representing Amor, Jupiter, Minerva and Mars.

he chose his ministers for their devotion to the state rather than to his own person.

He thus created a tradition of sound administration, but he failed to produce an enlightened ruling class. Under his successor the intellectuals who had come to the fore in the new political atmosphere had to find employment abroad, or study in the seclusion of academies where an atmosphere of suspicion reigned between themselves and the throne. But this orderly country, which under Victor Amadeus' successors was to become known for its extreme bigotry, nevertheless produced constitutional revolutionary noblemen such as Vasco and even freedom-loving pre-romantics like Alfieri. During this period Piedmont, despite successive crises, established its candidature for the part it was to play in Italy's history. It was a relatively strong state (though in no sense comparable with Prussia); but it was also a state in which there was an increasing separation between the government and those with wider ideas.

By the middle of the eighteenth century Piedmont had achieved a position of greater balance and power. The second half of the century witnessed the rise of Enlightened Despotism in the other states of Italy. This development was produced by both domestic and European causes. Following the Wars of Succession, Spanish rule in Italy came to an end and there were changes among practically all the dynasties in the peninsula. After 1748 the position in the various territorial divisions was as follows. Lombardy, and Mantua, now united, were under Austrian rule. Naples and Sicily constituted an independent Southern kingdom, though under a Bourbon ruler. Tuscany was governed by a younger branch of the Lorraine family; and Parma and Piacenza, the Farnese family having died out, was ruled by a younger branch of the Bourbons. The only states to remain unchanged were the Venetian Republic, the Duchy of Modena, the Papal State, and the little Republic of Lucca. In other words, apart from the vital presence of Austrian rule in the north and from remains of Spanish and French influence in the states under Bourbon rulers, a considerable part of Italy now enjoyed autonomy, though her fate still remained linked with the overall policy of balance of power in Europe. Moreover, all these new regimes, even if they had come to power through outside rather than purely Italian forces, were now administered, after two centuries of exclusion from the public administration of their own states, by Italians themselves.

Enlightenment and Reform

At the end of the seventeenth century – even before the great political change – the movement known as the Enlightenment began to take shape in Italy. It was illustrated first by the work of such people as Pietro Giannone. Giannone was born in Naples in 1676, and in the early 1700s before Spanish rule had ended there, began to write his history of the Kingdom of Naples, *Storia civile del regno di Napoli*, which was symptomatic of the Enlightenment for two reasons: firstly, it was essentially a civil rather than a military or dynastic history, and secondly it was anti-clerical. Like his contemporary in Piedmont, Radicati, who was also engaged in a defence of civil power, Giannone was forced to escape to avoid imprisonment for his views; and in Vienna he came in contact with Protestant thought. He was trapped into returning to Savoy from Geneva and there held prisoner until his death in 1748. In spite of this he managed to finish his book *Il Triregno*, an attack on the papacy from the standpoint of primitive Christianity.

Giannone is the forerunner of many reformers, among them a man who is often regarded as the initiator of civil revival in the south, Bernardo Tanucci, a Tuscan minister of the Bourbon King Charles III, who for many years guided the Kingdom of Naples, especially in his defence of state prerogative against the entrenched or acquired rights of the clergy. Tanucci did not really belong to the Enlightenment; he had studied law at the University of Pisa and was primarily an administrator of the old type, a convinced Christian and monarchist; and his relations with the rising innovators in Naples were not always cordial. But the effect of his work was to encourage the innovators and theorists, who quickly made the Neapolitan cultured aristocracy aware of the problems of their own state and society. The originator of this movement, which was both religious and cultural, was Antonio Genovesi, who in his devotion to the social problems of his own generation has been compared to Diderot. Genovesi inspired a group, not of Encyclopaedists, but of humanitarian reformers who aimed to restore work and society to their true place; he educated a political élite which began really to know their own country and, though entertaining no illusions about its situation, believed it could be reformed. The vital problem of the abolition of feudalism was radically tackled by followers of Genovesi such as Grimaldi, Filangeri, and Pagano, and by others, Galanti, Delfiro, Palmieri, who investigated

Opposite, above In the eighteenth century the Pantheon was painted and engraved innumerable times to satisfy the antiquarian fervour of tourists. As much a symbol of Rome as the Colosseum, the Pantheon has always excited the enthusiasm of visitors.

Opposite, below Rome of the seventeenth- and eighteenth-century Papal State centred on the Tiber, which like the rest of the city alternated squalid views of dilapidated houses and ruins of past grandeur. Vanvitelli's (1653–1736) landscape conveys the golden nostalgic atmosphere of the city, which fascinated visitors.

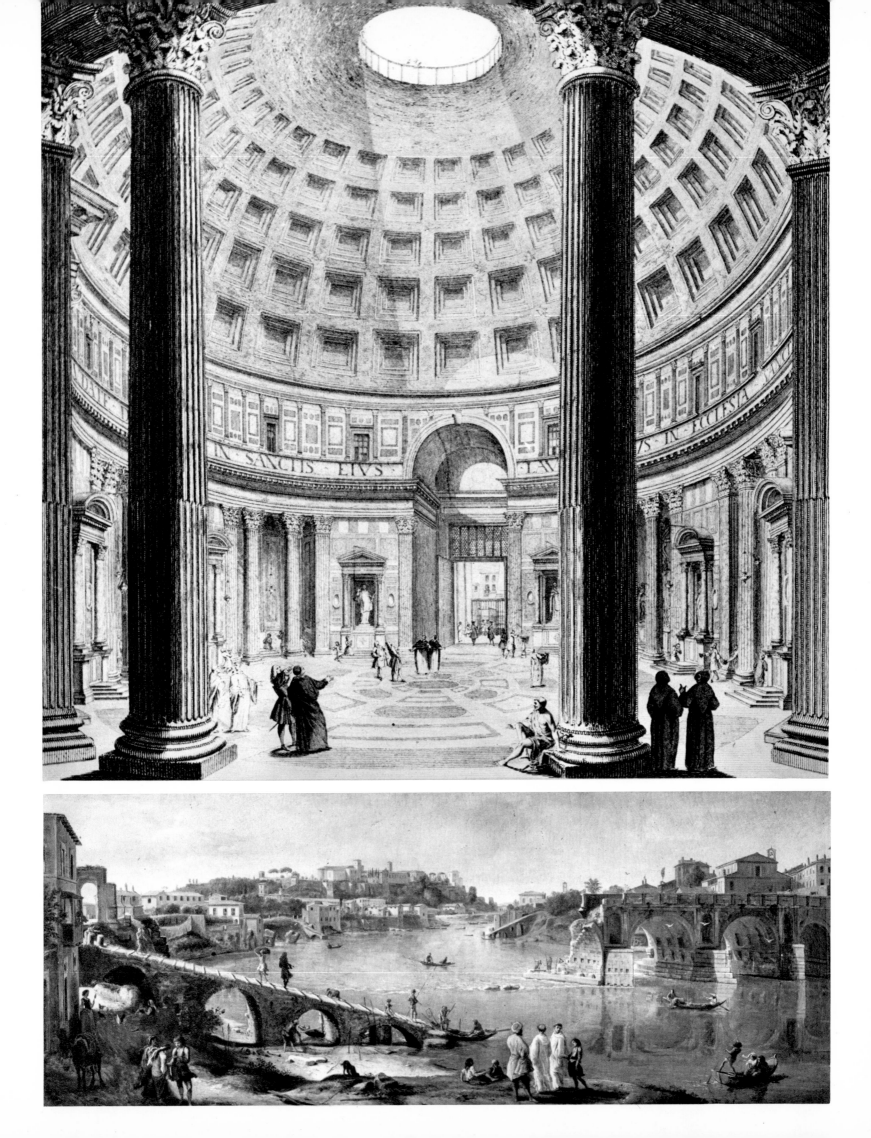

the kingdom's economic conditions in the provinces and the countryside. In Sicily, Tanucci's representative Caracciolo, and Prince Caramanico attacked the privileges of the barons. And while a politically conscious class was thus developing the kingdom was gradually acquiring a much-needed state structure.

Another Tuscan besides Tanucci figures in Genovesi's life: this was Bartolomeo Intieri, who managed to establish for Genovesi the chair of political economy at Naples University from which, it has been said, that great teacher made his fellow-citizens into a 'new nation'. Yet another Tuscan, Pompeo Neri, a fellow law-student of Tanucci's at Pisa, son of a minister under the Medici and himself a Tuscan official, initiated the first liberal reforms of the economy in Tuscany under the Austrian regency of Ribecourt (before Leopold I came to reign there) and later instituted a land register which was the basis of agrarian and fiscal reform in Lombardy. Though the Tuscan tradition had, as we have seen, fallen into decline, the heirs of humanistic thought nevertheless continued to give proof of their capability in the new atmosphere of rationalism. Not only in Neri but also in Bandini of Siena before him, and later in Gianni, the Tuscan official class, with its capacity for lucid calculation in dealing with economic and agricultural problems (under the stimulus, in particular, of the terrible famine of 1733–4), showed that it was much more than a mere instrument of government, even though it lacked the power to act on its own.

The change of regime in Lombardy from Spanish to Austrian rule brought with it considerable reforms, carried out under the Empress Maria Theresa and her son Joseph II by enlightened ministers such as Kaunitz and Haugwitz who transformed the Hapsburg monarchy. Hapsburg military prestige had already been revived by such leaders as Prince Eugene of Savoy, who became the first Austrian Governor of Milan.

The Austrian reforms may perhaps have had such great importance in Lombardy because the Hapsburgs had shown in their own hereditary domains how, when faced with new and complex European responsibilities, a state could adapt itself which had owed its earlier existence to its rôle as a bulwark of the Catholic faith against the Turk and against Protestant Germany. Confronted now with a European situation in which the power of Austria might otherwise have been swamped by more modern states, Maria Theresa and her ministers sought to utilize to the best advantage a patrimony in

which elements of feudal aristocracy and bourgeois Renaissance civilization converged. And in so doing they awakened forces that they themselves could not have foreseen. This was in fact the change that came about under Joseph II, who regarded himself not only as the owner of a land to be made prosperous but also as the servant of the state and its people.

Thus in Lombardy, too, the first reforms were concerned with taxation and the stimulation of production: reform of the *diaria*, or the customary military contribution, and the abolition of internal customs duties, which hampered the transport of silk, the chief Milanese export product. Next came the land register, carried out, as we said, by the Tuscan Pompeo Neri on the model of a similar earlier undertaking of Victor Amadeus in Piedmont and concluded within ten years. This register not only established an improved system of taxation but also gave a new direction to the activities of the patricians and raised the problem of the relationship between traditional privilege and the new needs.

Capital in Lombardy in the preceding century had been increasingly transferred from industry, which was suffering from the competition of the new centres of production, to agriculture. The new measures recognized this fact, and went on from there to encourage the revival of capital accumulation and civil development which old-fashioned industry could not ensure. It was easier in Lombardy than in Tuscany or the south to take advantage of the extensive network of agricultural production which hitherto had to serve the uneconomic needs of the privileged class. This meant both social and legal changes, and a change in the attitude of the nobility towards the state.

It is not surprising that the new climate in Lombardy under Maria Theresa and Joseph II stirred up forces which in the next generation provided the stimulus for intellectual revival. Cesare Beccaria, the author of *Dei delitti e delle pene (Of Crimes and Punishments)*, was one of a group of young intellectuals centring on the paper *Il Caffè*, among them Pietro Verri and his brother, Gianrinaldo Carli, and Paolo Frisi; and they, together with the southerners Genovesi and Filangeri, were the reformers of European stature produced by the Enlightenment in Italy. True, in Europe itself the only writer to achieve a reputation comparable to that of Voltaire or Rousseau was Beccaria, with his simple and moving rejection of the use of death, torture and violence as weapons of the law. It was only natural that the main effort of the Italian Enlightenment should be directed towards the resurrection of Italy itself rather than to European society in general. Eighteenth-century Europe still looked to Italy for the same sort of services in the sphere of the arts that she had provided in the preceding century; but now there was a new social inspiration behind them.

Along with the economic revival and social reforms in Lombardy the Hapsburgs were bringing changes to Tuscany, especially under Maria Theresa's second son, the Grand Duke Leopold (later on the Emperor Leopold II). Under his stimulus the men of the Enlightenment in Tuscany—who, as we have seen, had their own deep roots in local culture and administrative experience—came to co-operate in the government. They instituted a liberal policy which enabled agriculture to become more than the mere instrument of a subsistence economy; they overcame the old barriers between one city and another, inherited from the days of the communes and the *signorie*; and they also introduced humane and progressive legislation, being the first to apply Beccaria's principles in abolishing capital punishment and torture. The Tuscan state, advanced though it was, still lacked any intense political life, as can be seen from the relative ease with which it submitted to Leopold's wishes. It remained almost an example of a Utopia brought to realization (as indeed could also be said of the little state of Parma after the change of dynasty under Du Tillot's ministry). Nevertheless it is the great merit of the Enlightenment that it revived and gave new direction to traditions that seemed to have become sterile, reawakened the relationship between philosophy and politics, and linked up what had been the leading civilization in the sixteenth century with the rhythm of the younger European civilization of two centuries later.

Consciousness of this link with the past caused people to begin to speak of this period as a *risorgimento*, or resurgence, thus making use of a word and an idea that were synonymous with another word, used by the humanists in relation to ancient civilization – *rinascimento*, or renaissance. This reflected the conception, still held valid, that life moved in a cycle rather than by linear progression, and it was also prompted by the historical consciousness underlying even the most radical forms of Enlightenment. It was, in fact, this awareness of a process of decline and revival that was to assist in forming the Italian nation at an educated rather than a popular level.

European influence was a necessary factor in awakening in Italy the latent energies that had been stifled during the period of decline. But that influence would not have sufficed without another vital factor, namely, the strength of feeling in the new states against the Church of Rome. We need only to recall the fate of those who, from Bruno to Radicati and Giannone, fought against the Church on their own account to understand why this was so. True, the Church on occasion exercised repression in other countries as well as in Italy, for instance against Jansenism in France under Louis XIV; but in those other countries it found itself up against traditions and independent institutions still remaining within the framework of Christianity, such as could hardly exist in Italy. There was virtually no real Jansenism in Italy until after 1713 and the Papal Bull 'Unigenitus'; regalism, or the doctrine of royal supremacy in ecclesiastical matters, had, as we have seen, its martyrs and heroes, but it had no centre of organization comparable with that in Vienna under Joseph II. Thus Jansenism ended by fusing almost completely with rationalist reformism in Italy, where its most notable expression was in Tuscany under the Bishop of Pistoia, Scipione de' Ricci.

The Church of Rome in Italy relied on its own policy and on the strength of vested interests and of the two forces which it had welded into one weapon, the superstitious religion of the people and modern political technique. The latter was now beginning to escape its grasp, but not entirely; and it was therefore fighting a defensive battle more against outside than against Italian forces. The outside forces, which appeared to have gained a complete victory with the suppression of the Jesuits in 1773, derived their main impetus from the monarchies first of Portugal and later of France and Spain, together with the Bourbon courts in Italy. Thus Italy had some share in the struggle against the Church, but the original stimulus was international.

The Church organization put up an effective resistance on its own plane, fighting a long rearguard action by means of compromise and attempts to make use of its adversaries' weapons (it was in eighteenth-century Italy that Spedalieri put 'the rights of man' to the service of the Church, and that Lantieri strove to copy the Enlightenment's methods of organization). The only innovating concessions that the papacy made to the educated class were in the cult for classical archaeology and the use of neo-classical art in Rome. From then dates the ill repute of the Roman state to which Alfieri gave expression in a famous sonnet:

Opposite, left A visit to Rome was the main goal of the Grand Tour which became so popular during the eighteenth century that tourists provided a major source of patronage for artists. This drawing of English tourists was done in 1792 by Archibald Skirving (1749–1819).

Opposite, right A painter's studio in Rome with representations of his works 'skyed', as paintings were in all collections. On the lower right is a portrait of Benedict XIV, the most enlightened of the eighteenth-century Popes. Pierre Subleyras, the artist, was internationally known for portraiture and religious subjects.

Venice's greatness was in the past. Neutral and frivolous, the ancient Republic had become the playground of Europe. The galley that stood for Venice's maritime glory was a gold and red rococo fantasy, which Francesco Guardi (1712–93) painted against a background of the Grand Canal and as many landmarks as he could include.

The Colosseum was used as a quarry for building material until the eighteenth-century Popes made a great effort to preserve the ruins and control the export of antiquities. To stop the devastation, Benedict XIV (1740–58) consecrated the Colosseum as a church.

Above The romantic nostalgia that accompanied systematic archaeological investigation in neo-classical Rome is epitomized in *The Artist Moved by the Greatness of Ancient Ruins* by Fuseli (1741–1825). The hand and foot represented are fragments of a colossal statue of Constantine on the Capitol. Fuseli was a friend of Winckelmann, Mengs and David.

Below Alessandro Volta (1745–1827), who gave his name to the volt, continued the experiments of Luigi Galvani. His studies on current electricity, published in 1800, made him a world celebrity.

ALESSANDRO VOLTA

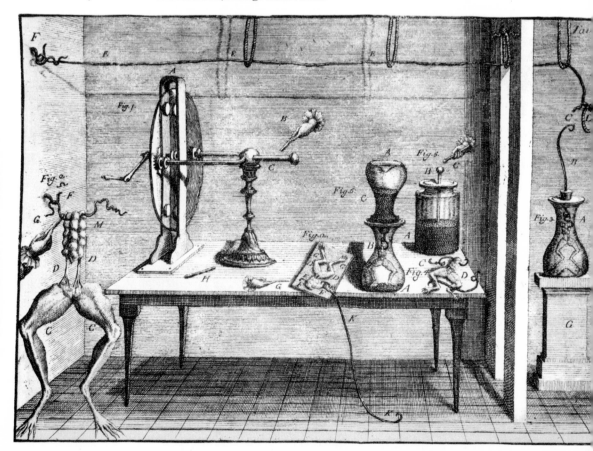

Vuota, insalubre region, che Stato
ti vai nomando; aridi campi incolti...
città, non cittadini; augusti templi,
religion non già...

(Empty, insalubrious site that is called a State; arid untilled fields...a city without citizens; august temples void of religion...).

It was Alfieri, too, who indicated the directions in which the Church's psychological sense would prompt it to frame its appeal as against the counter-appeals of reason:

Grato alla vista, all'ascoltar soave...
è il nostro culto...

(Pleasing to the sight, sweet to the eas...is our Church...)

Thus Italy at the end of the eighteenth century appeared to be actively sharing in European trends; but except for Beccaria the protagonists of this intellectual revival remained relatively obscure. Outside the fraternity of the Enlightenment, in European society influenced by the new ideas the Italians' reputation still rested mainly, as in the past, on their proficiency in the 'politer' arts, in the theatre, music (especially opera), science in its more accessible manifestations, and great spectacles. Metastasio, a pupil of Gravina, was writing for the theatre in Vienna, and one of his successors, Da Ponte, wrote librettos used by Mozart; Italian was still the language of songs throughout Europe. The Venetian Goldoni strove to replace the outworn *commedia dell'arte* by plays more nearly reflecting current manners and good taste. The 'grand tour' through Italy customarily undertaken by the European élite in the sixteenth and seventeenth centuries had by now become a nostalgic search for escape into the past (this can be seen both from the works of foreign writers such as Goethe and from the fascination exercised by Venice which, though politically a dying city, still provided the stimulus for the art of Guardi, Canaletto, and Tiepolo, steeped in nostalgia for the great Venetian past). The music of Paisiello, Cimarosa, and Pergolesi, though unable to rival its great competitors further north, still maintained its own traditional charm. Scientists such as Lagrange and Galvani, Malpighi and Volta still belonged in part to the international Republic of Letters as well as to the new sanctified élite of scientific research. Even that curious phenomenon, the adventurers into occultism and the like, combined the decadence of the past with the civilizing influence of the new manners and customs. The lives or memoirs of Casanova, Da Ponte, or Cagliostro all demonstrate

how in them the old and the new converge.

These signs of intellectual activity on the borderline between two epochs have caused some historians to believe that the era of enlightened despotism and reforms represented a great indigenous movement towards social advance which was later interrupted and destroyed by the French invasion and the Revolution. Others maintain instead that this movement was merely the result of foreign influences and counted for little in itself, and that the true resurgence begins with the changes brought in by Napoleon's armies. Neither of these theories is quite true. Both manifestations really form part of a single movement in which Italian forces shared, if with varying degrees of control and responsibility. It was a movement that destroyed in its advance no less than it created (it destroyed, for instance, the last states with republican origins, Venice, Genoa and Lucca); and the period of enthusiasm, hopes, and development which, seen in perspective, appears as one of regular advance – even if to contemporaries it seemed slow-moving and tortured, as if the reforms would never be attained – came to be regarded by generations more aware of the sharp break with the past as the *belle époque*, the 'St Martin's summer' of an era gone beyond recall.

The Revolutionaries and the Revolution

Towards the end of the eighteenth century, even before the storm of the French Revolution broke, there were already signs that the influence on governments of the Enlightenment was waning. In Tuscany, Bishop Ricci's efforts for Church reform were opposed by the majority of the Tuscan bishops; Du Tillot's enlightened government in Parma was succeeded by the rule of an obtuse and bigoted prince; in 1787 that same Caracciolo who had shown himself a courageous reforming minister and Viceroy in Sicily concluded a Concordat with the Pope; the rigid attitude of the government in Piedmont towards any cultural innovation has already been described; and the old republics clung to their traditions in opposing any change. The outbreak of the French Revolution was welcomed with joy by all the more thoughtful elements in Italy, but it naturally alarmed the governments; in any case, it brought matters to a head. Those who had been instrumental in carrying out reforms under the absolute monarchies became suspect; but even more the governments feared the young unknown elements whom they characteristically,

Opposite Luigi Galvani (1737–98), after whom galvanism was named, studied the reaction of muscles to electrical currents and published his treatise *De viribus electricitatis in motu musculari* on the subject. His experiments provided the basis for the more advanced work of Alessandro Volta.

and with some justification, believed to be 'plotting' against them. So repressive measures were set afoot, and in Naples, De Deo, Giuliani and Vitaliani were executed; Di Biasi in Sicily and De Robertis in Bologna suffered the same fate; while in Piedmont the reformer Vasco finished his life in prison.

Such elements were not in a position to overthrow the instruments of absolute government on their own. They were the product of a humanistic revival and as such had little influence on the peasants; at the same time the extent of their support in the towns varied considerably. For in the capitals the court and state still carried much weight, while at the other end of the scale little support beyond sporadic agitation was to be expected from the impoverished masses. Nor were the older men of the Enlightenment who had enjoyed some power in a position to use it to further the struggle. The task thus fell largely to the younger generation, in collaboration either with the intellectuals, in places where the Enlightenment had an enthusiastic following, or, in places where the state exercised tight control, with humbler people from the local bourgeoisie.

How widespread the influence of the Enlightenment was, is shown by the fact that, when abruptly deprived of support from the public authorities, the movement, far from capitulating, provided itself with an organization, spread news, both through the official press and by clandestine propaganda, of what was going on in Europe, and wherever possible took the side of the revolution. Meanwhile the reactionary states and powers drew closer together. When, in 1795, the first European coalition against revolutionary France was formed, the Italian states, reformist and reactionary alike, joined it: Turin and Naples, Florence and Rome, all bowed to the logic of absolutism, while Venice and Genoa remained neutral.

The war at first developed mainly in northern Europe; and indeed the only state in Italy to put up any effective resistance to the French Republican troops was Piedmont, in alliance with Austria. But the campaign went badly, and the French secured not only Savoy but also Nice and Saorgio, on the direct route of communications to Piedmont. Meanwhile in Italy repression intensified, and at the same time political conspiracy and emigration developed. Among the emigrants was Filippo Buonarrotti, who went to France and later took part in Babeuf's communistic conspiracy.

Between 1796 and 1799 the whole Italian state system of the past two hundred years was overthrown by the French armies. Napoleon cut the link between the Piedmontese and Austrian armies and on 28 April 1796, concluded the Armistice of Cherasco with the King of Sardinia, whereby Piedmont withdrew from the Austrian alliance and ceded Nice and Savoy to France; he then advanced into Lombardy, forcing the Austrians back on to Mantua, which succumbed only after a six months' siege.

Napoleon thus became master of northern Italy and favoured the establishment of republican governments there. In October 1796 the Cispadane Republic, consisting of the Papal Legations of Bologna and Ferrara and the Duchies of Modena and Reggio, was proclaimed south of the Po, and in the following month Lombardy became the Transpadane Republic. In February 1797 he concluded the Peace of Tolentino with the Pope, who thereby recognized the new frontiers; and after the surrender of Mantua he resumed the campaign against Austria, signing the Armistice of Leoben in April. Venice's neutrality was violated, and in October 1797, under the Peace of Campoformio, Venetia was ceded to Austria in exchange for recognition of the conquests in Italy. The conquered Italian territories were then united under French control as the Cisalpine Republic.

During 1798, while Napoleon was absent on his Egyptian campaign, France imposed her hegemony over the weak and discredited Italian sovereigns. Typical of her methods were the events in Piedmont, where Jacobin risings were first encouraged by the French then abandoned to the forces of repression, and then encouraged again; eventually the King had to take refuge in Sardinia. The Papal State was proclaimed the Roman Republic. The attempt of King Ferdinand of Naples to rise to the Pope's defence was quelled by a punitive expedition, which led to the royal family's flight to Sicily and to the establishment by the French of a republican regime in Naples, known as the Parthenopean Republic.

In 1799 a second anti-French coalition was formed and an Austro–Russian army under Suvarov crossed the Adige in March and swept the French out of northern Italy. The Italian republics were abolished and republican leaders went into exile. Many of those prominent in the Enlightenment paid with their lives, especially in the south, and a rapid change of ideas came about, causing, in particular, the more radical among the Italian Jacobins, mindful of the pattern the French had imposed in Italy, to visualize a united Italy as the solution to be hoped for.

Opposite, above A counter-revolutionary Italian cartoon caricatures Democracy as an unstable French acrobatic act poorly balanced on the backs of Freemasons. The baleful glare of Military Genius will bring the whole pyramid down, the composition suggests.

Opposite, below The murder of Basseville, a secretary at the French legation, in 1793 by the Roman mob expressed the dramatic change in attitude towards the Revolution. At first welcomed in Italy, the French by their rapacity and truculence aroused a hostility which was only temporarily overcome by Napoleon a few years later.

Vittorio Alfieri (1749–1803), the great tragic dramatist and a Piedmontese aristocrat, was repelled by the Revolution's excesses. In his polemical writings he appealed to the national spirit, envisaging an Italy composed of only two kingdoms united under a free government.

Carlo Goldoni (1707–93) was the most successful Italian playwright in an age of theatre. In reaction against the old *commedia dell' arte* tradition, he created a new realistic vein reflecting the society of the time. His comedies of Venetian life are still often performed.

The idea of Italy as a nation, pervasive in the period of the decline through the common culture of the educated classes and common memories of the old well-nigh confederal state system, had received a new impetus at the time of the reforms. Radicati's speeches were dedicated to Charles III as the 'other King' in Italy. Genovesi felt himself to be more Italian than Neapolitan, even while rejoicing at the inestimable advantage of having a King of his own and no longer being a 'provincial' under foreign domination. Carli, who came from Capodistria, felt Italian, not foreign, in every town of Italy. And Alfieri felt Italian, not Piedmontese, not only because he finally left Piedmont to live in Florence or Rome but also in his vision of the future Italy as reduced to two kingdoms and then united by war under a free government. But as the work of reform progressed men's feelings of loyalty to their own individual state were strengthened and people tended to speak of a Piedmontese, Neapolitan, or Tuscan 'nation'. If anyone spoke of Italy at that time it was the moderate conservatives, and they had in mind a confederation: Italy to them was still the Italy of the sixteenth century.

But then the Napoleonic wind passed over Italy blowing away the traditional states; the French were seen re-fashioning the political map of the country as they pleased and even paying some attention to their Italian allies, in so far as they counted for anything; and so a feeling for unity, fostered by geographical and naturalistic ideas of nationhood, began to develop. It developed especially, as was to be expected, among the more radical democrats whose ideas more nearly approached the egalitarian and communist conception of popular sovereignty. Among them were the already mentioned conspirator Buonarrotti, and many southerners who emigrated to Nice or, after the Napoleonic invasion, to the Cisalpine Republic; and secret societies with unitary aims also began to spread, forerunners in their several ways of the Carbonari.

All these movements towards unity had no practical political effect during the Napoleonic era, but they prevented the old local patriotisms from reviving afterwards to anything like the original extent.

Then came the holocaust. With the return of the absolute monarchs, republicans everywhere were severely suppressed. The most violent persecutions were in the south, where in 1799 Cardinal Ruffo's *Sanfedisti*, or army of the Holy Faith, savagely slaught-ered their opponents who had dared to hold out in the provinces, a slaughter promoted by hatred of innovation combined with class hatred and long-standing local disputes between families. Then, after Naples had capitulated with guarantees from Cardinal Ruffo, Nelson and the King disavowed the capitulation and the finest of the republican leaders were sentenced to death, among them the philosopher Mario Pagano, the historian Domenico Conforti, and Admiral Caracciolo. The irreplaceable losses sustained among the educated classes during the days of the reactionary terror in Naples were to have a lasting effect on the Kingdom's future.

Some critics have since maintained that those tragic events proved the theoretical and absurd nature of democratic ideals while others have attributed the catastrophe to inexperience in revolution. But the wisest historicist could not have prevented the situation in Italy from being what it was: a common consciousness and links of common interest between peoples from widely different societies cannot be improvised in a few years. Moreover, even in France there was the Vendée; and there was no equivalent of Paris in Italy. But a humanistic bourgeoisie did exist there, which quickly enlarged its ranks as it became more Jacobin, and later served the new states no less capably and energetically than did the French bourgeoisie after the Revolution; of all the countries occupied by France, Italy, together with the Rhineland, had the greatest affinity with French society, as was shown in the next fifteen years.

This is not to deny the fact that the ordinary populace took a large and enthusiastic part in the repression of Jacobinism, especially in the south, though it was true of the peasantry practically everywhere. But these 'armies of the Holy Faith' had not the same traditional aristocratic leadership as in the Vendée or, even more, in Spain. They burst upon the scene, only to be then chased or withdrawn from it; they made no further appearance except as a negative element, a potential danger to be neutralized. Not even the traditional institutions dared to place any permanent reliance on them; when the old regimes came back provisionally they were supported solely by military occupation.

Thus when, in 1800, Napoleon again descended upon Italy, there were no efficient Italian forces ready to withstand him, but quite a number of potential allies. The country offered all the opportunities for a new development.

Giorgio Spini

Napoleonic domination, by making the country virtually dependent on a single master, foreshadowed Italy's unification; rational and uniform systems of administration were introduced while special privileges for the nobility and clergy were abolished. Napoleon's betrayal of revolutionary democracy aroused opposition which led to the organization of secret societies like the Carbonari and eventually, in the final phase of the Risorgimento, to the creation of two main parties: the democrats, heirs to the French Revolution, were strong among the lower middle class and the junior army officers; the moderate liberals, who admired English constitutional democracy, had their following among the progressive nobility and the upper middle class. Before these policies were clearly established, the Napoleonic débâcle brought the return of the absolutist governments after the Congress of Vienna. Any expression of Italian individuality—Leopardi's verse, Manzoni's novel or an opera by Verdi—resounded like an affirmation of nationality. The revolution of 1820 was a fiasco; but in 1848 and 1849 republics, though short-lived, were proclaimed in Venice, Florence and Rome, the last headed by Mazzini, messianic nationalist and radical democrat, and defended by Garibaldi with his red-shirted legion. Reaction again followed, but a rallying point for national aspiration was Piedmont's constitutional monarchy, a situation which Cavour adroitly manipulated to drive Austria out of Italy. Garibaldi's amazing capture of Sicily and Naples in 1860 completed Italian unification except for the remnant of the Papal State, which was finally taken ten years later. As Cavour had hoped, but sooner than he intended, Italy was unified under the Savoy monarchy— a solution which neither Garibaldi nor Mazzini cherished.

The Risorgimento

From the beginning of the nineteenth century to 1870 Italy experienced the culminating phase of her national rebirth, the Risorgimento, in which she achieved unification as an independent national state administered on liberal lines. This was something new and truly revolutionary in a country inured for centuries to foreign domination, divided into a number of small states and weighed down by political despotism and religious repression.

Italy was not alone in this venture, for the search for a national identity was common to all Europe at that time. Indeed the leaders of the Risorgimento were the first to regard their own struggle as part of a great international movement towards liberty and human progress, as well as an expression of national consciousness. However, the struggle in Italy undoubtedly represented one of the most dramatic episodes in that international movement, for here was a nation striving to regain its place within the main stream of modern Western civilization from which it had been forcibly severed for generations by the Counter-Reformation and by foreign domination. Above all, the unification of the Italian peninsula involved the destruction of the local centres of interest and power represented by the earlier

Opposite The Sleep of Sorrow and a Dream of Joy: an allegory of the Italian Risorgimento. Italian national aspirations aroused the sympathy of the English public, and this detail of a marble statue by Raffaele Monti (1818–81) was one of the most popular exhibits at the London International Exhibition of 1862.

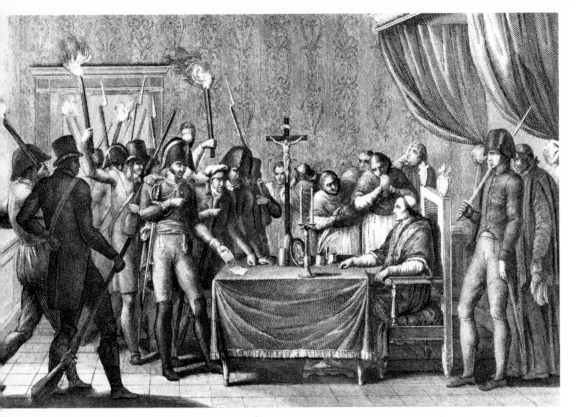

On 5 July 1809, at the height of Napoleonic power in Italy, the French General, Radet, forced his way into the Quirinal, and demanded that Pope Pius VII sign a retraction of a bull asserting papal supremacy over all temporal sovereigns. The Pope refused and was deported next day.

A portrait of Joachim Murat wearing a plumed hat, lavish court dress and cloak, by François Gérard, a pupil of David and official painter to Napoleon. Murat was a brother-in-law of Napoleon, who made him King of Naples (1808–14) during the French occupation of Italy.

Napoleon I reviewing Italian and Polish troops at Montechiaro (1805). The Republic he had formed in 1801 after crushing the Austrians at Marengo was renamed the Kingdom of Italy, with himself as King, when he became Emperor. Italy was a useful source of money and manpower; in return the Napoleonic states were a first step towards Italian unity and independence.

Elisa, Napoleon's sister, faces her Italian husband, Felix Baciocchi, on a superb medal coined in their principality of Lucca. In 1805 Napoleon made them rulers of this former republic and, always ambitious to create a House of Bonaparte, gave them the titles of Prince and Princess.

petty states; and one of those centres, the Papal State, was identified with the supreme authority of Catholicism. It was not only a liberal and national revolution but also a spiritual revolution in the sphere of moral and philosophical principles. Hence the sympathy aroused by the Italian Risorgimento in many European countries and in the United States, and hence, too, the ardent idealism it awakened among contemporary Italians.

Italy under Napoleon

Italy's experiences, good and bad, during the Napoleonic domination had a decisive influence on the future course of the Risorgimento. The nineteenth century opened almost symbolically with the triumph of First Consul Bonaparte over the Austrians at Marengo, which reopened northern Italy to French influence. Besides re-establishing French hegemony beyond the Alps, Napoleon also revived the vassal government of the Cisalpine Republic which he had already once installed in Milan and which had been overthrown in the reaction of 1799. He intended by this means to engage the newly-aroused Italian patriotism; and he even changed the name from the Cisalpine to the Italian Republic. But his chief aim was to ensure for himself the rulership of the new state; and when he decided to become Emperor of the French, the Italian Republic had docilely to transform itself into an Italic Kingdom, of which Napoleon assumed the crown. In the following years the rest of Italy fell easily into Napoleon's hands; among local dynasties the Savoys and Bourbons alone survived the storm, taking refuge in Sardinia and Sicily, which were British protectorates in all but name.

In the fluctuations of imperial policy, the Italians were constantly changing hands. The Grand Duchy of Tuscany was promoted to be the Kingdom of Etruria, then abruptly reduced to the rank of a French province; Joseph Bonaparte was appointed King of Naples one day and next day transferred to the Kingdom of Spain, his post in Naples being given to the Emperor's brother-in-law, Joachim Murat. Even Pope Pius VII was at first invited to confer respectability on the new regime by means of a Concordat between the Catholic Church and the Empire and Napoleon's solemn coronation in Notre Dame – only to be summarily expelled from Rome later because he had failed to exact observance of the imperial decrees on the Continental Blockade. Nevertheless, the old political fragmentation of Italy was replaced by only three large divisions: in the north-west an area annexed to the French Empire, comprising Piedmont, Liguria, Tuscany and Latium; in the south, the Kingdom of Naples; and in the north east, the Italic Kingdom, from the Ticino to the Julian Alps and from the Trentino to the Marches. The Italic Kingdom had little autonomy, but the mere existence of an embryonic national state, with its own administration, its green, white, and red tricolour, and its own army marching victoriously through Europe behind the Emperor was in itself an exciting experience for many Italians.

A factor for unification, despite the formal existence of three governments, in Milan, Naples and Paris, was the country's virtual dependence on a single master. Throughout Italy the rational and efficient methods of the Empire were introduced in administration, the army, law and education. Napoleon's Civil Code established equality of rights and duties for all citizens, irrespective of birth, religion, or social condition, thus destroying the remaining privileges of the nobility and clergy. In the formerly Austrian-ruled Lombardy and Tuscany, the reforming princes of the eighteenth century had already accomplished a good deal. Elsewhere the Civil Code represented a revolutionary innovation – for instance, in the former Papal States, where laymen had always been kept in a state of inferiority in relation to the clergy, or in the Kingdom of Naples, where the relics of feudalism had withstood even the Bourbons' efforts to destroy them. In the south, King Joachim's officials worked so energetically to eliminate feudal ties, convert communal and crown lands into private property, and reduce Church ownership of land, that they actually changed the social structure of the country, creating a large class of bourgeois landowners in the provinces in place of the old nobility.

Italy was still an agricultural country, almost untouched by the industrial revolution, and everything connected with landed property had an enormous importance. Social prestige was almost invariably related to the ownership of land; and the aristocracy and clergy under the old regime were also the biggest landowners. But Italy was also a country of many towns, especially in the central and northern regions. Often small, these towns were still proud of their civil traditions, especially as compared with the rough rural population with its perpetual poverty and ignorance, its superstitions and supine attitude towards the clergy and landowners. But the towns themselves also existed by agriculture, as markets, and administrative and religious centres for the surrounding countryside, and as residence for many of the landowners. In the south, apart from Naples, they were not so much towns as big rural villages, in which a large part of the population was connected with farming. Each town had a good many public officials, merchants, and professional men such as lawyers, doctors and teachers, as well as craftsmen and their dependent workers. But the towns-men also tended to acquire land as much as they could; and the static situation with regard to land ownership resulting from feudal ties and ecclesiastical mortmain made these classes especially favourable to the new ideas of equality and liberty. The only towns relatively indifferent to agriculture were ports – such as Genoa, Ancona, Messina or Leghorn; and this fact together with their cosmopolitan character made them centres of democratic enthusiasm. On the whole, though, the defence of private ownership and easy transfer of land under the Civil Code had great appeal in Italy; even for the nobility there were benefits in converting their lands to unencumbered personal ownership.

Agriculture was also conditioned by the nature of the land itself, often marshy and malarial, needing drainage and modern techniques to make it fruitful, or moun-tainous and unproductive. Farmers and traders were hampered by the numerous frontiers and customs duties, and the lack of good communications. Tech-nical progress and freedom of movement had long been the chief aspirations of the more dynamic landowners; and the better eighteenth-century governors – the Lorraines in Tuscany or the Austrians in Lombardy – had responded. Elsewhere these demands remained unsatisfied until the Napoleonic regime, with its legis-lation, its public works, and its unification of vast areas of Italy. The regime also opened up careers in its army and bureaucracy to the sons of professional men, of medium and small landowners, and even to the more energetic among the nobility, offering greater gain and social prestige than could ever have been derived from the poor soil of Italy. The better part of Italian society for several years wholeheartedly supported Napoleon.

The supporters of the imperial regime were generally educated people who also appreciated the patriotic appeal of the Italic Kingdom. The literary language of Dante and Petrarch symbolizes Italian nationality; but outside privileged Tuscany, the local dialect is still often very different from literary Italian, and only educated Italians were fluent in the language that was the badge of their nationality. Hence the political as well as the literary importance of the great Italian writers of the early nineteenth century; and hence, too, the apathy of the illiterate peasantry towards patriotism. For the educated, however, *italianità* became synony-mous with all that was most noble and attractive in intellectual life, and also with social status.

The peasants saw the Napoleonic regime less favour-ably, since it reinforced the town's dominance over the countryside, and conscripted their sons to die in Spain or Russia for incomprehensible reasons. Moreover, the transfer of the land from indolent nobles or monks to more active and greedier bourgeois owners seldom benefited the peasants. Especially in the south the rural bourgeoisie, instead of imitating the improvements of the Lombard or Tuscan landowners, strove for higher yield by harsher exploitation of the peasants, wresting from them even such miserable resources as the right which they possessed on the communal lands to pasture their animals and to gather wood and fruit. The peasan-try often reacted by the traditional primitive methods of revolt, banditry, smuggling or evasion of military service. In Calabria it reached the point of fierce guerrilla warfare that lasted for years, but the French hanged and shot the brigands without mercy.

Napoleon raised up spirits he was unable to control. The intellectuals who supported his regime lent it an attractive aura of patronage of the arts, with their vogue for neo-classicism as officially exemplified in the art of Canova and the Arcadian verse of the poet Vincenzo Monti. But they were also attracted by Vittorio Alfieri's tragedies, woven around the struggle for liberty and heroism in the face of tyranny, and by Ugo Foscolo's poetry exalting, as in *I Sepolcri*, Italy's great past. In Alfieri and Foscolo they saw not only great artists but also great teachers of morality and patriotic feeling. Patriotism could not be content with the embryonic independence of the Italic Kingdom, while moral conscience remained unsatisfied by the mixture of Voltairian utilitarianism and military brutality which seemed to be the philosophy of the regime. Cultivated Italians were interested also in the new ideas burgeon-ing in Europe. Madame de Staël's famous book *De l'Allemagne* initiated them into the philosophy and poetry of Romanticism which inspired the German patriots in their struggle against Napoleon. Sismondi's *Histoire des Républiques Italiennes* taught them to

Opposite The scene records a harbinger of Italian unification. In 1798, following the French occupation, Italy briefly became a group of republics. The Jacobins celebrated the new dispensation by erecting a temporary classical triumphal arch at the foot of Ponte S. Angelo, just as they put up an Altar of the Nation under the windows of the Vatican in the midst of St Peter's Square. The painting, on panel, is by Felice Giano.

glory in the memory of the ancient liberties of the medieval communes and to hope for a rebirth of freedom and national identity. Meanwhile the Continental Blockade damaged Italy's trading interests and Napoleon's struggle against Britain emerged increasingly as a struggle of despotism against freedom. In 1812 the British envoy in Sicily, Lord William Bentinck, himself a Whig, fostered the introduction of a constitution on the English model. The demands for equality and liberty aroused by the Napoleonic regime could not in the long run be satisfied merely by a good Civil Code.

Italian troops returning from Spain told of the Spanish guerrillas' heroic struggle for independence and of the Constitution of Cadiz, also proclaimed in 1812. Napoleon, while ingratiating the clergy through the Concordat, had also encouraged Freemasonry among his officials and soldiers. But even in these circles nostalgia for a revolutionary democracy was reviving, and secret societies, such as the Carbonari, were organized in competition with Freemasonry.

This opposition to the Napoleonic regime was the seed of Italian liberalism in the succeeding decades, and it also contained the beginnings of the two main parties in the final phase of the Risorgimento. On the one hand were the democrats, heirs of the French Revolution, strong among the lesser bourgeoisie and the junior army officers; on the other hand, the moderate liberals, admirers of the English Constitution, whose following came from the progressive nobility and the upper bourgeoisie. Among the former, Carbonarist ideas spread chiefly at first in southern Italy, among the new provincial middle class opposing Murat; the ideas of the latter produced the *Italici Puri* Party, especially strong in Milan, which aimed at a national Italic Kingdom not subservient to France. The collapse of the Napoleonic Empire in 1814 certainly embittered the partisans of the regime, but the restoration of Austria and the former absolute rulers by the Congress of Vienna was no less bitterly disappointing to the regime's liberal opponents. During the Hundred Days Napoleon sought liberal support, as did Murat when he advanced northwards against the Austrians and issued his 'Proclamation of Rimini', in which he championed Italian independence. Napoleon ended at St Helena and Murat ended before a Bourbon firing squad, but the old adversaries and partisans of the Napoleonic regime now made a common front against Austria and the Restoration. Their reconciliation left little prospect of tranquillity for Italy's rulers.

Italy under the Restoration

The Congress of Vienna aimed to restore a balance of power that would prevent new imperialistic adventures, but it ignored popular national aspirations, and considered solely the interests of the dynasties. The British Tory Government under Lord Castlereagh was especially anxious to establish a barrier against Russia and France. He therefore favoured the consolidation of Austria, which secured most of northern Italy under the name of the Kingdom of Lombardy-Venetia, thus obtaining virtual dominance over the peninsula; and he also favoured the extension of the Savoy Kingdom, through annexation of the Genoese Republic. At the same time he unconcernedly disowned what Bentinck had accomplished in Sicily, which thus lost its liberal constitution. For the rest, Italy returned to its old rulers and its earlier fragmentation into a number of small states, in accordance with the principles of the Restoration proclaimed at Vienna.

Metternich further consolidated this situation, exploiting the Holy Alliance sponsored by the romantic Tsar Alexander I. Rigid absolutism was the political creed of the Austrian minister, who believed that the peoples needed only peace, good administration and justice. The Restoration therefore imposed a frankly reactionary regime, reinforced by an alliance between throne and altar, in which Catholicism was to be an antidote to the ideological poison of the Revolution. This regime varied somewhat according to the local governments. Lombardy-Venetia had a sternly authoritarian – though efficient and just – police regime strictly dependent on Vienna. In the more retrograde Kingdom of Savoy, under Victor Emmanuel I, solemn debate was held on whether a bridge over the Po should be demolished because it had been built by Napoleon. Also the privileges of the nobility and clergy were restored. This measure created permanent tension not only between feudal and militaristic Piedmont and seafaring and mercantile Genoa but also between the Piedmontese aristocracy and the bourgeoisie, thus propelling the latter towards radicalism. The regime in Tuscany was tolerant under the Lorraines, but the Papal State reduced laymen once more to a legal status inferior to that of the clergy. The Kingdoms of Naples and Sicily were combined as a single Kingdom of the Two Sicilies, thus depriving the island of its centuries-old autonomy and making it a permanent potential rebel.

Opposite Two women clandestinely sew an Italian tricolour and a third stands guard at the door. The emblem of the patriots fighting for a united Italy, the flag originally was that of the Cisalpine Republic (1797), and combined the red and white of Bologna with green to symbolize liberty.

In the years immediately following 1815, the Restoration governments proceeded with moderation, respecting, for example, the property transfers of the Napoleonic era and retaining many of the officials. Conservative country people welcomed the return of peace and respect for their religion. However, the more dynamic sections of society were alienated by the rejection of their liberal and patriotic aspirations and by the stolid indifference towards anything savouring of modernity. Even the spread of Romanticism so obviously implied a liberal protest that Austria hastily suppressed its main organ, *Il Conciliatore*, founded in Milan by a group of patricians and intellectuals, former members of the *Italici Puri* party. The revival of the old states, and hence of their customs barriers, paralysed economic life; the active middle class was humiliated by the disappearance of the Civil Code and the return to power of the ridiculous relics of the old regime. By a natural reaction, even more secret societies than before sprang up in Italy. Filippo Buonarroti, a Tuscan, survivor of the French Revolution and Babeuf's conspiracy, became a sort of patriarch of European conspiracies from his exile in Geneva. In northern Italy, especially, secret sects like the Adelfi and the Perfect Sublime Masters embraced democratic, republican and even communist ideas.

The Restoration was shaky. In January 1820 a mutiny of the Spanish army forced the reinstatement of the Cadiz Constitution of 1812. In July the Carbonari in southern Italy provoked a similar military uprising that forced Ferdinand I also to adopt the Cadiz Constitution. Metternich persuaded the Holy Alliance to approve of intervention and Ferdinand was delighted to forswear his constitutional oath and welcome Austrian troops. Sicily in the meantime staged a separatist revolution of her own against Naples. The northern secret societies planned to provoke an insurrection behind the backs of the Austrians while the latter were advancing on Naples, and they were supported both by the liberal patricians of Milan and the young officers from the nobility in the army of Savoy. The officers hoped that the House of Savoy would eventually agree to head the national struggle, and they put their faith in Prince Charles Albert of Savoy-Carignan, who would succeed Victor Emmanuel I and his brother, Charles Felix, neither of whom had heirs. In March 1821 the Piedmontese garrisons rose, demanding the Cadiz Constitution and war against Austria.

The revolutionary force was composed mainly of the secret-society democrats, from the middle class or lesser officialdom, who had demanded the Cadiz Constitution. For the sake of respectability, they had put in the forefront persons of greater social prestige, such as former supporters of Murat in Naples or the Prince of Carignan in Turin, who however were bound to fear a democratic constitution as a potential revival of Jacobinism. Murat's former generals from Naples after an encounter with the Austrians at Rieti disbanded their army rather than resist. The Savoyards refused the role of champions of Italian independence; and the Prince of Carignan deserted his noble friends. One of them, Santorre di Santarosa, nevertheless attempted to lead the Piedmontese forces on Milan but was defeated by the Austrians at Novara.

Thus the revolution of 1820–21 was a fiasco, all the more disastrous because the various governments, apart from the gentle Grand Duke of Tuscany, set aside moderation and embarked on stern repressions. There were few executions, because the insurgent leaders fled in time. But exiles and prisoners could be counted in thousands; among them members of the liberal *Conciliatore* group in Milan, whom the Austrians kept in chains for years in the gloomy Moravian prison of the Spielberg. The brief venture had dissipated any illusion that the Austrians and the Italian despots might hope to govern except by force. Subsequently the presence of so many Italian exiles in the free countries or in countries fighting for their freedom – Santarosa himself fell fighting for Greek independence – afforded proof to Europe of the intolerable conditions in Italy.

Italian Liberalism

The absolutist governments inevitably regarded every aspiration for improvement as revolutionary. Any moral or material progress achieved in Italy therefore became identified in Italian minds with liberal principles and patriotism. Everything that was good or fine rang out like an affirmation of liberty and nationality: the sorrowful verse of Giacomo Leopardi, expressing the anguish of the human state, or the stirring operas of Giuseppe Verdi. Even the work of such men as Alessandro Manzoni, in *I Promessi Sposi*, far removed from revolutionary intention, took on the significance of an act of opposition to the obscurantist regime.

Opposite, above A cross-section of the temple at Possagno, near Treviso, designed on the lines of the Pantheon by the most important of Italian neo-classical sculptors, Canova (1757–1821). The building was completed some years after his death and contains his tomb as well as some of his works.

Opposite, below The Triumph of Religion, one of a series of engravings by Pinelli, represents Pope Pius VII's return to Rome in 1814, after five years in exile. His giant figure, aided by the faithful, upholds the tottering Church, while statues of Justice and Sanctity look on with approval.

33

IL TRIONFO DELLA RELIGIONE

F. Pomares inven.

B. Pinelli del. et sculp.

Questo fatto è allegoricamente rappresentato da un Tempio, che mostra di vacillare. Vi si veggono ai lati dell' ingresso principale le Statue della
Fede, e della Religione. Tornato l'immortal Pio VII. alla sua libertà alza le mani, e fa riparo al Tempio, che sembra di vacillare, rianima la Religione nel cuor dei fedeli; e questa che si tentava di opprimere, trionfa singolarm.te in Roma col ritorno del S.P., e in Spagna col ritorno dell' adorato suo Sovrano.

Ferdinand IV's return to Naples on 7 June 1815, after nine years of exile in Sicily, is commemorated in a contemporary engraving. Below Ferdinand and Pius VII is the fleet which brought him from Palermo. Two weeks earlier, Ferdinand's son, Leopold, had ridden into Naples welcomed by crowds waving branches.

The unrest which ultimately led to unification is illustrated in an early nineteenth-century print. In July 1820, two Carbonarist lieutenants and a priest named Don Minichini, who is seen on horseback, prepared with some hundred odd mutinous troops to march on Naples.

Below A meeting of the Carbonari, the most active and successful of early nineteenth-century secret societies, which aimed to overthrow despotic governments. In 1820, its membership included most of the patriots and the intelligentsia of Italy. This print, published by John Murray in 1821, reflects sympathy in England for the rebel movement in Italy.

Pope Gregory XVI (1831–46), reactionary in politics, was also unenthusiastic about advances in technology. He rarely made public appearances, but in May 1835 travelled with his court on a French steamboat from Civitavecchia up the coast to Corneto, now Tarquinia. Although the use of steam power for ships received papal approval under Gregory XVI, he opposed the construction of a railroad.

Italy's first railroad, which ran from Naples to Granatello, near Portici, was inaugurated in 1839.

Banditry has been a perennial problem in southern Italy until recently. Here, a mid-nineteenth-century print shows government troops of the Kingdom of the Two Sicilies, armed with muskets, putting to flight a group of bandits with blunderbusses at Luco, in the Abruzzi.

'God wants Italy free' says the inscription on a medal coined by the Provisional Government of Lombardy after the expulsion of the Austrians from Milan in 1848. The figure of Italy, holding a spear and wearing a mural crown, points to the legend. Only a few months later, however, Radetsky recaptured the Lombard capital for Austria.

An early nineteenth-century Roman street scene in a water-colour by Achille Pinelli. Water melons are still sold in Piazza Navona; the square with its grandiose fountains by Bernini has remained unchanged, and except for the dress of the animated group, the tableau could be duplicated today.

Around *L'Antologia*, a cultural review published by Vieusseux in Florence, a fine group of liberals was formed, including Capponi and Lambruschini, who discussed problems of Swiss methods of education, historical studies and agricultural improvement. One of the survivors of the Spielberg, Silvio Pellico, recounted his prison experiences in a book, *Le Mie Prigioni*, which avoided all reference to politics and simply gave testimony of a Christian faith restored through suffering. But it was at once said that this book, so imbued with Christian forgiveness, had done as much harm to Austria as a lost battle.

The French revolution of 1830 provoked a fresh repetition of the drama of 1820-21. The Carbonari believed that France had reverted to its old policy of revolutionary expansion and they plotted a new insurrection, this time in the Duchies of Parma and Modena and in the Romagna, trusting in the support of the ambitious Duke of Modena, Francis IV. But the Duke betrayed the conspirators, taking good care not to endanger his throne for the sake of the Italian insurgents, and the revolt had barely begun in February 1831 before it found itself isolated and faced with yet another Austrian military intervention. The rebel forces were defeated at Rimini and reaction returned to vent its fury, perpetrating such excesses in the Papal State as to incur even Metternich's displeasure.

Metternich, however, continued to believe in the authoritarian formula. In the two most important independent states of the peninsula, the Kingdoms of the Two Sicilies and of Savoy, younger rulers, better intentioned than their predecessors, were preparing to put this theory into practice: these were the erstwhile Prince of Carignan, Charles Albert (1831–49), and Ferdinand II of Bourbon (1830–59). Charles Albert, after his unhappy experiences in 1821, had succumbed to a streak of mysticism which induced him to abhor the liberals and convinced him that he had been called by God to strive against the impious spirit of the Revolution. Because of this he worked hard to strengthen his military machine and modernize his state. Ferdinand was a strange mixture of plebeian cynicism and superstition, energy and intelligence, who endowed his kingdom with well-framed laws and attempted to introduce industry – the Bourbon Kingdom possessed Italy's first steamship and first railway (from Naples to Portici). But good administration was not a valid substitute for freedom, and material progress increased the longing for independence.

Italy's progress in economic spheres served to emphasize still further the inconvenience of her political disunity. Thus the building of railways became one of the main targets for the liberals' efforts, for they rightly anticipated that political unity would be encouraged by improved communications and increased trade. The development of the textile industry in Lombardy and Venetia and mineral mining in Tuscany, and the increase of traffic in Genoa and Leghorn strengthened the middle class, and created the first Italian proletariat. Progress in agriculture strengthened the moderate-liberal landowners. Paradoxically, while the worst absolutist governments, such as that in the Papal State, created discontent and hence revolution, the better absolutist governments created the conditions for the very success of the revolution.

Giuseppe Mazzini

The missionary zeal also needed for Italian independence was largely provided by Giuseppe Mazzini (1805–72), a young Genoese who had gone into exile after conspiring in the ranks of the Carbonari. For Mazzini the basis for political action was faith in God, although he regarded Christianity as outmoded. He held that God revealed Himself to humanity through the peoples, to each of whom He entrusted a mission to accomplish on earth; thus in contrast to the French Revolution's tenet of the vindication of rights stood the religion of duty, the sole true basis of freedom itself. Every people has a right to freedom only because it must be free to accomplish its own mission on behalf of humanity according to the universal law of progress and fraternity. The Italian people had a great mission from God: just as once a universal word went out from the Rome of the Caesars and later from the Rome of the Popes, so a Third Rome should send forth a universal word of emancipation and brotherhood among the nations. Hence the two watchwords, *Dio e Popolo*; *Pensiero e Azione* (God and People; Thought and Action), which Mazzini throughout his life commended to his followers.

From faith in God and in humanity, in fact, should flow sustained action, readiness for any sacrifice. Only through duty and sacrifice could a people make itself worthy of liberty. Such faith was characteristic of the young with their instinctive generosity and idealism; so Mazzini named the organization he founded on the morrow of the failure of 1831 *Giovine Italia*—Young Italy. The Carbonari's repeated failure, according to Mazzini, was due to their Masonic mystifications which left their own members in the dark as to their aims, and to their insistence on a few initiates guiding the masses from above. *Giovine Italia's* programme was clear to all: the independence and unification of Italy in a unitary and democratic republic. The method of struggle was popular insurrection, on the lines of the Spanish guerrilla war against Napoleon. Democracy should be built up from below through long struggle. Behind his romantic language Mazzini's political views were highly lucid. He was the first to create a political party in Italy, rather than a secret society, and thereby gave Italians their first experience of democratic struggle.

Mazzini, however, was less explicit on the economic and social problem. He was convinced that political equality should find its completion in economic and social equality, through the principle of association, and he had felt the influence of the dawning French socialism, especially of Saint Simon. But he believed that national democratic independence should take precedence over debate on the future structure of society. He did not hesitate to break either with Sismondi, whom he thought too moderate, or with the old communistically inclined Filippo Buonarroti. Mazzini was able to win enthusiastic support from groups that would never accept a socialist programme; and in this he showed his undoubted realism. As for the Catholic and land-hungry Italian peasants, Mazzini opposed his own humanitarian religion to that of the priests and made no explicit promise of land distribution. Consequently, his success among the rural masses was limited, and his programme of popular insurrection remained confined largely to the towns.

Among the students, intellectuals, artisans and workers of the towns, however, Mazzini's message took hold with such strength that it was able to survive every set-back. *Giovine Italia* spread rapidly, especially in central and northern Italy, and tried to organize revolt in the Kingdom of the Savoy. Charles Albert nipped the plot in the bud in 1833 with a number of executions, and in 1834 he easily averted Mazzini's attempt to organize an expedition of exiles from Switzerland into Savoy as well as an insurrection in Genoa. The attempt served only to increase the number of victims and exiles. Among others forced to flee on pain of death was Giuseppe Garibaldi (1807–82) then an obscure sailor from Nice. He went to South America and fought with an Italian legion for the Republic of Uruguay against the Argentine dictator, Rosas. Mazzini went to London, where he worked as a revolutionary organiser, the bane of the police but also the ascetic symbol of noble ideals.

In the following years the various insurrectionary outbreaks that shook the peninsula were usually ascribed to Mazzini, for the government's fears and his followers' enthusiasm had made him into an ubiquitous revolutionary myth. The homesick exile had become a force to make kings tremble on their thrones.

The Moderates

Mazzini's constant revolutionary hammering roused the moderate liberals who sought a middle way between absolutism and democracy and wanted to avoid a violent revolution. Thus a creative competition developed between the moderate liberal right wing and the democratic revolutionary left wing of the Italian Risorgimento, which was eventually to bring about the country's unity.

A Piedmontese priest, Vincenzo Gioberti (1801–52), a follower of Mazzini and an exile in youth, provided the moderate liberals with a programme in his work, *Del Primato civile e morale degli italiani* (1843. *Of the Civil and Moral Superiority of the Italians*). Gioberti accepted the idea of Mazzini that political action should stem from religious awareness and that God had given Rome a universal mission. But he thought that Catholicism itself if renewed and reconciled with freedom could provide the basis. The papacy in their midst gave Italians an ideal primacy; Italy's regeneration should therefore make that presence its starting-point. The Pope himself should promote Italian freedom and independence, setting the example for the other rulers in the country. Gioberti saw Mazzini's idea of unifying Italy and destroying the local states, with their strong historical traditions, as purely utopian. The Italians should eschew insurrection which had also proved utopian and go forward in agreement with their rulers to create a federation under the presidency of the Pope.

Immediately after publication of the *Primato* came the failure of yet another insurrection in Calabria and the tragedy of the Bandiera brothers, two young Venetians who in 1844 attempted to land in Calabria with a small following and on the orders of Ferdinand

Opposite A popular print shows the symbolic figure of Italy surrounded by the rulers of Italy shortly before several of them granted constitutions to their states in 1848. Above, Pope Pius IX (1846–78). On the left, Charles Albert, King of Sardinia; Archduke Francis of Modena; and Marie Louise, Duchess of Parma and Piacenza, widow of Napoleon. On the right, the Duke of Lucca, whose Duchy was ceded to Tuscany in 1847; Leopold II, Grand Duke of Tuscany; Ferdinand II, King of the Two Sicilies; finally Archduke Ranieri, Viceroy of Lombardy.

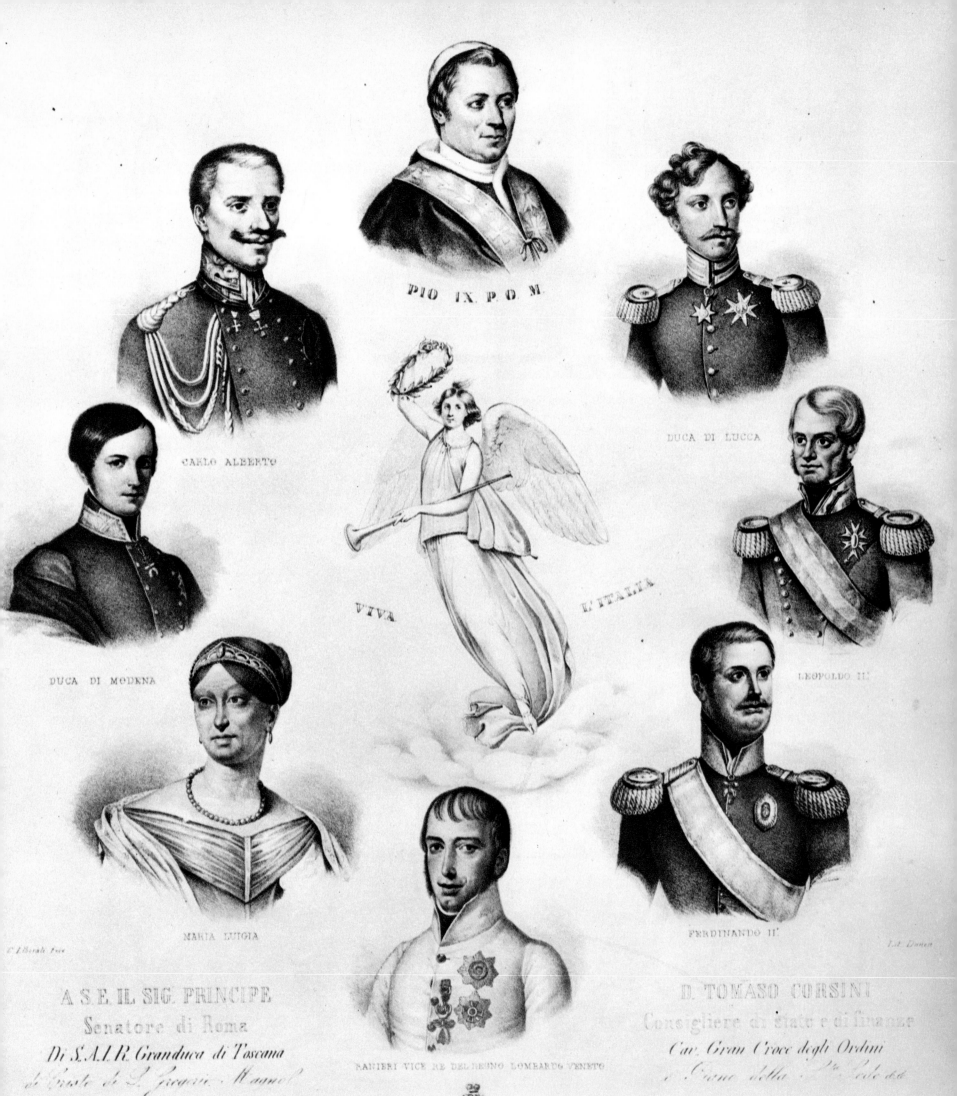

PIO IX. P. O. M.

CARLO ALBERTO

DUCA DI LUCCA

DUCA DI MODENA

VIVA   L'ITALIA

LEOPOLDO II

MARIA LUIGIA

FERDINANDO II

A S. E. IL SIG. PRINCIPE
Senatore di Roma
Di S. A. I. R. Granduca di Toscana
di Cavaliere di S. Gregorio Magno el.

RANIERI VICE RE DEL REGNO LOMBARDO VENETO

D. TOMASO CORSINI
Consigliere di stato e di finanze
Cav. Gran Croce degli Ordini
di Cione della Pia Sede ec.

Pius IX, who later turned reactionary, began his reign in a liberal spirit by amnestying some four hundred political prisoners jailed by his predecessor Gregory XVI. He is shown in a night scene on the balcony of the Quirinal Palace, being acclaimed for the amnesty by the enthusiastic Roman public.

Revolutionary movements have always numbered women among their protagonists. But an unexpectedly daring innovation in the Papal State was the training of a women's auxiliary of the National Guard, organized by the Liberals in 1848 for 'love of country'. Pius IX at the time seemed a possible champion of Italian independence against the Austrians.

Right The triumvirs of the short-lived Roman Republic of 1849 were Giuseppe Mazzini (centre), Carlo Armellini (left) and Aurelio Saffi (right). Mazzini, a radical democrat and mystic, fought tirelessly in Italy and in exile for unification. He embodied the republican conscience of the nation which lost out to the monarchy created by Victor Emmanuel II and Cavour with the aid of Garibaldi.

Opposite, below The Year of Revolution, 1848, began with the Sicilian uprising, when the Neapolitan garrison was driven out of Palermo. The extent of popular support for the revolt is indicated by this print which shows a woman and a priest fighting among the rebels outside Palermo Cathedral.

Below Austrian dominion over northern Italy was the main obstacle to unification. In the wake of Metternich's fall, the Milanese rose in March 1848 and in the famous Five Days forced the Austrian troops to evacuate the city. The print shows the fighting at Porta Nuova, Milan, during the uprising.

Nuovi Stati Costituzionali   *Di Europa nell' Anno 1848.*

A caricature of Leopold II, Grand Duke of Tuscany (1824–59), portrays him as old and stout, an interesting contrast to his youthful portrait on page 209. Though the least reactionary of all Italian despots, he was weak, unintelligent and so somnolent that his subjects called him the Tuscan Morpheus.

Above left Encouraged or frightened by the Sicilian uprising the rulers of many Italian states granted constitutions in 1848. In this contemporary engraving the balloons in ascension represent those states, while the collapsing balloons stand for the Dukes of Parma and Modena, who refused to yield and fled from their capitals. Meanwhile Lombardy and Venetia remained under Austria.

Tira tira, tira tira ... Alla fin si strappera.

After the uprisings in northern Italy against Austria, England and France sought to mediate and also extend their own influence in the country. The cartoon shows the two powers alongside Austria, striving to get a leg into the Italian Boot. The legend warns that if they pull too hard the boot will burst.

II were shot with most of their companions. A large body of opinion in Italy regarded the Giobertian programme as the only way out of the blind alley of continual and useless bloodshed. That programme, moreover, offered a way out for the many Italians who did not want to renounce either their national sentiments or their traditional religion. The trend of Gioberti's followers, the 'neo-Guelfs' as they were called, soon became an important political force in Italy.

Not all the moderate liberals were neo-Guelfs, though they accepted in principle an Italian federation based on agreement between rulers and subjects. The Tuscans of the Vieusseux, Capponi and Lambruschini group were too strongly influenced by Swiss Protestant liberalism to have confidence in Papal Rome. The Piedmontese trusted above all in the strong army of Charles Albert to eliminate Austrian influence; and they found their interpreters in Cesare Balbo with his book *Le Speranze d'Italia (The Hopes of Italy*, 1844) and in Massimo d'Azeglio, a Turinese patrician who contrived to be a romantic painter and recognized novelist as well as an orthodox moderate politician. Not all the Catholics, on the other hand, were Giobertians, for Gioberti himself sharply disagreed with the most reactionary wing of Catholicism, the Jesuits. But his programme seemed to be confirmed when Pius IX (1846–78) was elected and inaugurated his reign with an amnesty for political prisoners. The delirious popular demonstrations that greeted this gesture induced him to grant some reforms. Austria by a clumsy attempt at intimidation gave the Pope the attractive aura of a victim, and 'Long Live Pius IX' became the cry of all Italian patriots. Seeing that the priests themselves were joining in the general enthusiasm, even the countryside began to awake from its political lethargy.

As Gioberti had foreseen, Charles Albert and the Grand Duke of Tuscany, Leopold II, were induced by the Pope's example to grant liberal reforms. The idyll between rulers and people received the blessing of Britain, with Palmerston – at loggerheads with Metternich – encouraging the Italian rulers to transform themselves into constitutional monarchs. Ferdinand II, prodded by a revolt in Palermo, hastily granted a constitution. Charles Albert, Leopold II, and lastly Pius IX had to follow his example; by 1848 all the Italian states were under constitutional rule.

The constitutions of 1848, however, represented a gracious concession by the rulers rather than an expression of popular will. The concession, moreover, was sufficiently restricted not to create any danger of democracy; for instance, Charles Albert's Statute (which became the constitutional charter for the whole of Italy after unification and lasted until the Fascist era) envisaged a Parliament consisting of two Chambers, only one of which was elective, the other being appointed by the King. Furthermore, suffrage was limited, on a basis of income, to a very small number of voters. These constitutions were a success for the moderate liberals, whose members came largely from the progressive propertied aristocracy. In Turin, Florence, Naples and Rome, the constitutional governments of 1848 all consisted of moderate liberals such as Balbo and Capponi; the representatives of the middle class, the professions and trade, even if wealthy, formed the left-wing opposition, the champion of democratic claims. For the moment, however, concord and exultation dominated over every other feeling.

The Upheavals of 1848–9

In February 1848 revolution broke out in Paris, overthrowing Louis Philippe, and thence spread through Europe to Berlin and Vienna. When the news came that Vienna had risen and turned out Metternich, the people of Milan, led by the democrat Carlo Cattaneo, rose too and fought during the famous 'Five Days' (18–23 March) against the Austrian general Radetzky, forcing him to withdraw. Throughout northern Italy provisional governments arose and volunteer corps were organized to fight the Austrians. This time it was Mazzini's doctrine of popular insurrection that received confirmation from the facts. And the moderate liberals, though delighted to see the Austrians evicted, were far from delighted at this revolutionary success. The revolution in Paris had installed a democratic republic in which even socialists had entered the government. As Karl Marx had written shortly before, in London, the spectre of revolution hung over Europe. No Italian in 1848 had read the Communist Manifesto, but there was no need of such literature for the liberal landowners to feel alarm. Behind the volunteer corps crying 'Long Live Pius IX!' they discerned the dreaded image of Giuseppe Mazzini with his republic; and behind the democratic republic they discerned still more fearful dangers for their well-cultivated properties.

It was therefore urgent for the Italian sovereigns to take the initiative from the volunteer bands and lead their regular armies against the Austrians. Charles Albert moved his army towards Milan on 23 March – a little late to help the Milanese, who had already liberated themselves, but timely enough to be able to order his troops to replace the blue flag of Savoy by the Italian tricolour. Popular pressure also induced Leopold II and Ferdinand II to allow regular and volunteer forces to set out from their states; the forces of the Papal State crossed the frontier on their own initiative without awaiting their sovereign's approval. The first war of Italian independence could thus begin as a federal war of the local princes.

But Pius IX was a kindly man anxious to be beloved by the Italians, rather than a man with a mind capable of solving the arduous problem of relations between Catholicism and modern liberalism, religious universalism, and patriotism. So the Pope announced that his position as universal father of all believers compelled him to stay outside the war, though desiring independence for Italy. Ferdinand II, who had sworn the constitution in perfect bad faith, seized the first pretext to let his Swiss mercenaries shoot the Neapolitans and also withdraw from the war. Tuscany's little army was destroyed while fighting a sortie of Radetzky's from Mantua; however this gave Charles Albert time to arrive and defeat the Austrians the next day at Goito. The federal war of the rulers thus became the war of Charles Albert alone, although Neapolitan and papal contingents remained to fight against the orders of their governments.

Charles Albert forced the annexation of the north Italian provisional governments by threatening otherwise to abandon them to the Austrians. His move disgusted those who believed that the political reorganization of Italy should wait until a free vote could be taken in a Constituent Assembly. The Piedmontese generals were honest reactionaries who had accepted their king's sudden conversion to liberalism more by discipline than by conviction. But they were too mistrustful of popular initiative not to curb its original impetus. Their slowness to move gave Radetzky time to get reinforcements from Austria which enabled him to crush the volunteers of the Papal State defending Vicenza, thus isolating Venice, and so to defeat the Piedmontese at Custoza (23 – 25 July). After a feeble attempt to defend Milan which raised doubts as to whether he wanted to save the city or merely to prevent a republican rising, Charles Albert signed an armistice with the enemy and returned to Piedmont amid the indignation of the Lombards.

The defeat shattered the moderate liberals' prestige and left the field to the democrats, who favoured an out-and-out revolutionary war and the convocation of an Italian Constituent Assembly. Venice, to which the remains of the Neapolitan forces had withdrawn, proclaimed itself a republic under the dictatorship of the democrat Daniele Manin (August 1848). In Rome, the moderate Prime Minister Pellegrino Rossi was stabbed to death in November; the democrats came to power and Pius IX took refuge in Gaeta under the protection of the Bourbon King Ferdinand II. The Roman Republic was then proclaimed (9 February 1849) and Mazzini hastened thither to take charge. In Florence, too, a democratic government was installed; it was soon followed by the flight to Gaeta of the Grand Duke Leopold II and the assumption of dictatorship by the Leghorn writer, Guerrazzi. Only the Bourbon King survived the storm, using his army to crush a revolt in Calabria and then embarking on the reconquest of Sicily, which meanwhile had proclaimed independence. The terrorist bombardment of Messina which initiated this reconquest earned him the nickname of 'King Bomba' by which he was henceforth known. Unfortunately the Sicilian government, in the hands of the moderate liberal aristocracy, was too afraid of arming the people to organize an effective defence.

The radicals in the Turin Parliament demanded and obtained that the armistice be broken and war resumed. But throughout Europe the revolutionary wave was ebbing before the reactionary counter-offensive. The Piedmontese army was defeated at Novara, and Charles Albert abdicated and went to die in Oporto, the romantic death of a broken heart which redeemed in Italian eyes the many blunders of his mistaken life. The Austrians retook Brescia, which the democrats had caused to rise behind their backs, after ten days of fierce street-fighting; they established a reign of terror in Lombardy and Venetia, shooting and hanging without mercy; they bombarded Leghorn – the democrats' centre in Tuscany – into submission, and Leopold II resumed his throne. Pius IX, who had now gone over to the reactionaries' camp, appealed to the Catholic Powers to send forces to restore him to Rome. Prince Louis Napoleon, who had become President of the French Republic, had a strong army landed in Latium; the Austrians stormed Bologna and laid siege to Ancona;

Opposite To obtain any sort of arms the Milanese made an assault on the Ibaldi Armoury, the ancient arms collection of a Milanese nobleman, during the revolution of 1848. Spurred by revolution all over Europe and the fall of Metternich, the Milanese in their Five Days uprising drove Radetzky and the Austrians from their city. Tempera by Carlo Bossoli (1815–84).

Spain and Ferdinand II joined in the attack on the Roman Republic.

Although the fate of the Roman Republic was sealed, volunteers rushed to defend it from every part of Italy, among them the legion of Giuseppe Garibaldi, back from South America, wearing as their uniform the red shirt that was to become famous. The defence of the Roman Republic had a decisive political significance in the history of the Risorgimento – possibly because it was now simply a question of being killed for the sake of a principle rather than of winning. Mazzini showed that democracy could govern with wisdom and energy without recourse to the violence of revolutionary terror. Garibaldi performed miracles, holding the French in check, putting the Bourbons to flight, and finally defending hand to hand the ruins of the patrician villas, transformed into fortresses, on the Janiculum Hill. Beneath those ruins was buried the Giobertian illusion that Italian unity could be achieved with the agreement of the Pope. The death at Rome of the young poet Goffredo Mameli, author of the present national anthem 'Brothers of Italy', and the many other deaths in fighting the temporal power made it clear to even the moderates that the Risorgimento must end by making Rome the capital of a free Italy, as Mazzini had prophesied.

When the republic was forced to capitulate, Garibaldi left Rome at the head of a column of die-hards, accompanied by his South American wife, Anita, who throughout had shared the dangers of battle. Pursued by the Austrians, Garibaldi continued his fight across central Italy until, having lost all his men, he found himself alone with but one wounded companion and his dying wife in a hut among the woods of Ravenna. Even then he managed to escape, protected by the support of a people who now regarded him as an almost superhuman being, and arrived safely on the shores of the Tuscan Maremma. Manin, too, for his part held out unyielding in besieged Venice despite bombardment, hunger and cholera until in August 1849 the last army still fighting the Hapsburgs – the Hungarian army under Kossuth – capitulated. Though beaten physically, the democrats emerged morally triumphant from the test of 1849.

Unbridled reaction set in after 1849. Ferdinand II filled his prisons with the best men of southern Italy, so earning for his kingdom Gladstone's famous indictment: 'The negation of God erected into a system of government'. In Lombardy-Venetia, under Radetzky's military government, men were executed for the possession of a patriotic manifesto or a certificate of Mazzini's clandestine loan to finance his movement, and even women were flogged for protesting. The reign of terror, in its turn, provoked new desperate attempts by the followers of Mazzini, such as the revolt in Milan in 1853, which was at once repressed with bloodshed.

Mazzini's personal prestige remained high among the workers, but criticism was growing even among the democratic left. Some, like the Neapolitan, Carlo Pisacane, went over to socialism, finding sterility in Mazzini's ideas for a republican revolution instead of a rising of the starving proletariat based on definite economic aims. Similarly, Carlo Cattaneo, the most lucid mind on the Italian Left, countered Mazzini's romanticism with a positivist philosophy, and attributed recent reverses to the failure to direct the masses towards the conquest of social reforms. He visualized an autonomist and federalist Italy on Swiss and American lines, and even her inclusion in a European federation like the United States of America.

The moderates, caught between reaction and radical revolution, had lost hope in Pius IX, Leopold II and Ferdinand II after their reactionary measures and the suppression of the constitutions they had granted. The only ruler who had respected the Statute was Victor Emmanuel of Savoy (1849–78). Though authoritarian and scarcely the archetype of a constitutional sovereign, he saw that the House of Savoy had everything to gain from championing the liberal national cause. He was a courageous, vulgar, good-natured and highly popular king, who expressed himself better in Piedmontese dialect than in literary Italian and had an ex-washerwoman for his official mistress. Though no political genius he was endowed with enough good sense to steer a successful course during the difficult times after the war. As a matter of fact, after 1849 his kingdom showed the habitual tension between Turin and Genoa, and between the aristocracy and the middle classes. The defeat of Novara was followed by a republican rising in Genoa and a conflict between the Crown and the parliamentary majority, which did not want to approve the peace with Austria. The King had dissolved the Chamber and addressed a manifesto to the voters which barely concealed a threat of a *coup d'état*. Liberal institutions were saved, since the electorate swerved to the right and a moderate cabinet was formed under Massimo d'Azeglio. But even the moderate d'Azeglio found himself at loggerheads with

Opposite Angelo Brunetti, called Ciceruacchio, proclaims the Constitution Pius IX granted to Rome and the Papal State on 14 March 1848. Brunetti, popular leader and follower of Garibaldi, is shown in this painting by Antonio Malchiodi as he addresses the crowd of attentive Romans from the base of the obelisk in Piazza del Popolo.

the powerful Piedmontese clergy when he attempted to deprive them of their anachronistic privileges.

From d'Azeglio's cabinet emerged the most gifted Italian statesman of the Risorgimento, Camillo Benso, Count of Cavour (1810–61), an aristocrat, but a younger son who had to make his fortune in business like any bourgeois. Supplanting the authority of d'Azeglio, Cavour contrived a parliamentary majority by arranging his skilful *connubio*, the 'marriage' between the moderates of the aristocratic Right and the bourgeois Left, and in 1852 became Prime Minister. In the next seven years he transformed the Kingdom of Savoy into one of the most advanced countries of the day. Son of a Genevan mother and thus inheriting the Swiss liberal spirit, and an indefatigable traveller and observer in Western European countries, among them England, which he admired so enthusiastically as to be nicknamed 'Lord Camillo' in the salons of Turin, Cavour combined a magnificent practical sense and exceptional capacity for work with a religious belief in freedom. He adopted the principles of free trade, abolishing the old protectionist legislation, and built up railways, shipping, trade, industry and agriculture. The Kingdom of Savoy became a part of the system of European capitalism, creating a modern banking and public finance system.

An admirer of Vinet's ideas on the independence of State and Church, Cavour aimed to free the State of clerical interference and to abolish legislation whereby the State controlled the Church. A sworn enemy of Mazzini and the radicals, he was nevertheless convinced that the only antidote to revolution was not blind, violent repression but a policy so daringly liberal as to wrest followers from the Left. A true European, he believed that Italy's problems could be solved only within the framework of relations between the great Powers. He therefore sought, on the one hand, to secure the friendship of Britain, the stronghold of European liberalism, and on the other hand to exploit the ambitions of Napoleon III, who was eager to consolidate his position by brilliant military successes. He risked following Britain's cautious directives so literally as to lose the possibility of radical change in the Italian situation; on the other hand, if he adhered too closely to Napoleon he would lose British support. The skill with which Cavour conducted this daring game was the masterpiece of his policy.

In the Crimean War (1854–5) the Western Powers sought Austria's support and Cavour found himself within an inch of the abyss. Austria demanded that her rearguard should be guaranteed against Cavour's intrigues, and the Western Powers promised to compel the Kingdom of Savoy to enter the alliance against Russia and to send, almost as hostages, some troops to the Crimea. Logically, Cavour should then have been replaced as Prime Minister by some old Piedmontese nobleman conservative enough to cause no trouble to Vienna. Moreover Cavour's ecclesiastical policy was encountering particular difficulties just then, including opposition from the King, who had no great sympathy for the brilliant minister who threatened to relegate his sovereign to a subordinate role.

But Cavour turned the tables by himself urging the alliance and offering an even greater contribution for the Crimea. Public opinion failed to understand why Italians should die in the Crimea, and Mazzini inveighed furiously against helping to preserve Turkish tyranny over the enslaved peoples of the Balkans. The expeditionary force to the Crimea met with more deaths from cholera than military glory. But when the Congress of Paris met in 1856 to negotiate peace, Cavour won the support of the British and French ministers and isolated Austria diplomatically. Italians began to regard the Piedmont of Victor Emmanuel II as their chief hope.

Mazzini's response was to organise, in 1857, insurrections in Genoa and Leghorn and an expedition in southern Italy led by Pisacane. But the insurrections were stillborn, and Pisacane's expedition after landing at Sapri and advancing inland was mistaken for a band of brigands and massacred by the populace. After the tragedy of Sapri, a number of democrats deserted Mazzini to form the National Society, aiming to unite patriots of all parties around the slogan of 'Italy and Victor Emmanuel'. Two heroes of the 1849 republics, Manin and Garibaldi, became respectively its president and vice-president. Cavour meanwhile cunningly worked on British sympathies, even playing on evangelical beliefs that the Risorgimento would destroy Papal Rome and open Italy to the Protestant faith; he also worked on Napoleon III's fears of his republican opponents, suggesting that if he wished to render Mazzini harmless he should give Victor Emmanuel II support for a fresh war against Austria.

Napoleon III wavered between the ambition to make himself arbiter of Europe, playing the card of nationality – after all, in youth he had been a Carbonaro and had taken part in the Italian revolution of 1831 – and the need to keep the influential French clerical party

After his defeat at Novara, in 1849, Charles Albert of Savoy-Carignano, King of Sardinia, refused the peace terms of the Austrian Field-Marshal, Radetzky, and abdicated in favour of his son, Victor Emmanuel, who was later to become the first King of a united Italy.

After a heroic defence by Garibaldi, Rome fell to a French Army on 4 July 1849. This followed an appeal by Pope Pius IX, exiled in Gaeta, to destroy the Roman Republic and restore papal governement

The Piedmontese writer, Silvio Pellico (1789–1854), accused of organizing a Carbonarist lodge in Milan, was imprisoned by the Austrians in the notorious fortress of Spielberg, Moravia, from 1822 to 1830. His memoirs of these years, published under the title of *Le mie prigioni*, became a classic.

The column surmounted by a statue of the Virgin in Piazza di Spagna, Rome, was erected to commemorate the proclamation of the dogma of the Immaculate Conception in 1854 — a concrete affirmation of the mystique of Catholicism.

Opposite, left The meeting of Garibaldi and Manzoni. When the guerrilla leader went to visit the 77-year-old author of *I Promessi Sposi*, Manzoni threw himself at Garibaldi's feet and said, 'It is I who should pay homage to you, for I am less than the least of the Thousand, let alone their leader.'

Right A contemporary photograph of the Emperor Napoleon III, in the uniform of a Major-General. His Italian policy was devious, but naturally in his own and the French national interest. His bayonets and chassepôt rifles kept the Pope on his temporal throne until Sedan, but his alliances with Piedmont eventually resulted in Austria's withdrawal from Italy.

Below right A lithograph portrait of Count Camillo Cavour (1810–61), the Prime Minister of Piedmont during the crucial years of the Risorgimento. The main architect of the unification, by international diplomacy and adroit encouragement of the talents and fervour of Garibaldi and the patriots, he gave Piedmont the hegemony in Italy and secured the Italian throne for Victor Emmanuel II and the House of Savoy.

Below left Victor Emmanuel II, Cavour and Napoleon III cut the claws of the Austrian Bear, the Emperor Francis Joseph. By the Pact of Plombières (July 1858), Napoleon and Cavour agreed to an alliance between France and Piedmont aimed at liberating north Italy from Austrian rule.

on his side. Then an Italian republican, Felice Orsini, threw a bomb at him, hoping that his death would let loose revolution in France and thence in Italy. Napoleon III was unharmed, but decided Cavour must be right, and at a secret meeting at Plombières in July 1858 settled terms of an alliance against Austria.

Italian Unity

The Plombières agreements provided that France intervene in support of Victor Emmanuel II if he should be attacked by Austria. In the event of victory, France was to obtain Nice and Savoy; Italy would be divided into three kingdoms, the whole of northern Italy going to the House of Savoy, while the possibility was left in the air that one of the two kingdoms of central and southern Italy might go to a Bonaparte and the other to a Murat. Finally, an Italian Confederation was to be created, under the presidency of the Pope, who would be left with the domain of Latium.

Cavour's dangerous game risked letting Italy come under French hegemony. He had also to provoke an Austrian attack to create a *casus belli*. He ostentatiously allowed Garibaldi to enrol volunteers against Austria, but the plot nearly failed because England offered mediation and Napoleon III seemed ready to accept. But international high finance had by now reacted and Austrian shares collapsed; Cavour seems to have played the falling market and utilized his winnings to finance Garibaldi. Austria then obligingly sent Turin an arrogant ultimatum which Cavour could legitimately reject, thus securing the desired aggression. So, in April 1859, the second War of Italian Independence began.

Risings immediately followed in Tuscany, the Duchies of Modena and Parma and the papal domains of Bologna and the Romagna. If Napoleon III had counted on installing a Bonaparte over central Italy he was swiftly disillusioned, for the insurgents created provisional governments which supported union with Victor Emmanuel's Kingdom. In the meantime the vast confused battle of Magenta ended with the Austrians' retreat, allowing the allied rulers to enter Milan (9 June); Garibaldi, the only skilful commander in the field, reached Bergamo and Brescia. The Austrian Emperor, Francis Joseph, assumed command of operations in Italy and confronted Napoleon III and

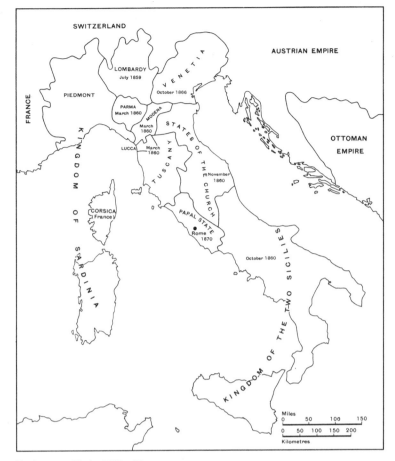

Unification of Italy: 1859–70

Victor Emmanuel II on the heights of San Martino and Solferino (24 June). The carnage among the 300,000 men engaged at Solferino was terrible; incidentally, its horrors inspired a pious Swiss trader, Henri Dunant, to organize the International Red Cross. But once again, the Austrians retreated and the liberation of Venetia seemed imminent.

Suddenly Napoleon III decided to break off a war which promised fewer advantages and more complications than anticipated, and an armistice was signed at Villafranca on 11 July. Cavour resigned in a fury, and the provisional Tuscan and Emilian governments risked seeing their old masters return.

This danger was resisted, notably by Bettino Ricasoli, the 'Iron Baron' of Florence, a follower of the Capponi and Vieusseux group. In Britain the Liberals came to power with Lord Palmerston and Lord John Russell, who were openly convinced of the need for an independent Italy as a counterpoise to France and Austria. Assured of British support, Cavour returned to the government and negotiated an agreement with Napoleon III by which France obtained Nice and Savoy

Opposite, above Italian forces captured Perugia on 14 September 1860. This contemporary painting shows the final engagement in Piazza del Municipio, the main square of the city. The victory avenged the severe repression of Perugia's rebellion against papal rule the previous year.

Opposite, below Austrian troops being thrown into the canal at Palestro, 31 May 1859. The battle, in which the Piedmontese were victorious, was one of a number fought in north Italy during the 1859 War of Independence between Piedmontese and French troops on one side and Austrian on the other. A contemporary print.

but agreed to Piedmont's annexation not only of Lombardy but also of Tuscany and Emilia. Inspired by Bonapartist fashion, early in 1860 a series of plebiscites set the seal on these agreements.

Meanwhile, Ferdinand II had died and the Sicilians profited by the weakness of his successor, Francis II, to renew their agitations. After the unhappy experiences of the moderates in 1848–9 the democrats, led by Francesco Crispi, gained the upper hand among the Sicilian conspirators and political émigrés. For Sicily's traditional independence demands they substituted the National Society's programme for a united Italy under Victor Emmanuel II. They therefore urged Garibaldi to lead an expedition of volunteers to Sicily. Cavour distrusted the complete unification plan: partly because of the tangled international problems that an attack on the Kingdom of the Two Sicilies and the Papal State would create; partly because he was even less enthusiastic about prospects of the King coming to agreement with Garibaldi behind his back, thus weakening the parliamentary regime, or of Garibaldi leading the democrats to triumph over the moderates. However the volunteers gathered in Genoa practically without interference, and on the night of 5 May 1860 Garibaldi embarked with about a thousand Red Shirts from the rocky shore of Quarto.

Managing to evade the Bourbon fleet en route, Garibaldi landed at Marsala and marched inland, assuming command in the name of Italy and Victor Emmanuel. His tiny army's first success near Calatafimi was enough to spread revolution throughout the island. To the simple peasants of the desolate Sicilian countryside Garibaldi seemed a saint with his long flowing hair and fair beard, his patriarchal simplicity, and his inexhaustible capacity to perform miracles. Garibaldi's tactics disorientated the enemy, thus allowing the Red Shirts to hurl themselves on Palermo, which rose and overthrew the Bourbon garrison. The island's liberation was completed by a further victory at Milazzo, while Britain's open support discouraged any intervention in favour of the Bourbons by other Powers such as France or Russia. Moving to the mainland, Garibaldi defeated one after the other the Bourbon generals who blocked his advance in Calabria and reached Naples on 7 September amid delirious popular enthusiasm.

Garibaldi's astounding success made the complete unification of Italy inevitable, and was a triumph for the democratic Left. Cavour had tried in vain to thwart

it by sending agents to Naples to persuade the moderate liberals to take over power before the Red Shirts arrived. It also represented a success of Garibaldi's own policy of a reconciliation between radical democracy and the monarchy of Victor Emmanuel II. Even Mazzini, who in the meantime had rushed to Naples, was resigned to the choice of a monarchy rather than a republic, provided the decision was reached by the democratic method of a Constituent Assembly, instead of by the equivocal system of plebiscites.

For the same reason, the wealthiest people in southern Italy demanded immediate plebiscites seeking in the monarchy and its regular troops a shield against the popular hero's irregular Red Shirts. Cavour put strong pressure on Napoleon III to allow Victor Emmanuel II and his army to come down through the Papal State to Naples in order to check the Red Shirts on the route to Rome and crush Garibaldian democracy. Napoleon III finally became convinced that a democratic success in Italy might lead to a republican rising in France. Victor Emmanuel II invaded the Marches and Umbria, overcoming the resistance of the papal forces. Francis II, who had taken refuge with the greater part of his army in the fortresses of Capua and Gaeta, tried to forestall the arrival of the Piedmontese and engaged Garibaldi in a big battle on the Volturno, which ended in another victory for the Red Shirts. But Victor Emmanuel II reached southern Italy immediately after this, and the volunteers were unceremoniously set aside. Garibaldi withdrew from the scene, his heart full of bitterness, and went to live in proud poverty on the little island of Caprera, off Sardinia, refusing all honours or rewards.

There followed the inevitable plebiscites and the capture of the last Bourbon fortresses by the regular army. Finally, on 17 March 1861, the Parliament in Turin voted a law conferring on Victor Emmanuel II the title of King of Italy. The unity of Italy had been ratified, as Count Cavour wished, by the decision of Parliament; part of Cavour's deep aversion to Garibaldi lay in the fear that parliamentary government after the British model might be endangered by the dictatorship of a *caudillo* on South American lines. At the same time this triumph of a moderate liberal parliament of patricians and wealthy *bourgeoisie* cast back into the shade humble people like the Sicilian and Calabrian peasants who had come to political awareness for the first time because they had faith in Garibaldi as in a benevolent saint. The very fact that Victor Emmanuel

Overleaf The Italian language was the single greatest national bond and Dante, as the supreme master of the language, became a symbol of nationalism; statues of the great poet rose in every town. Of particular patriotic significance was the inauguration of the monument to Dante on 14 May 1865, the six hundredth anniversary of his birth, in Florence. Painting by Vincenzo Giacomelli.

Opposite The second War of Independence, 1859, began when Cavour goaded Austria into an attack on Piedmont which under the terms of his alliance with Napoleon III automatically brought French military intervention in Italy. The Grand Duke of Tuscany and other Austrian princes fled. The painting shows the quiet substitution of the national tricolour for the Archduke's flag.

II did not feel it necessary to change his title to Victor Emmanuel I, as if Italian unity was merely an expansion of the old Savoy Kingdom, underlined the humiliation of those democratic forces which had played so decisive a part in the Risorgimento.

United Italy and its Problems

Cavour died soon after the conquest of the south, but the 'marriage' he had arranged between the progressive landed nobility and the rich middle class of trade, industry and finance survived. Intelligent landowners took an interest in railways and the stock exchange, and the *bourgeoisie* invested capital in land reclamation and in vineyards. The ranks of Cavour's followers were joined by liberals from the new provinces such as Ricasoli from Tuscany or Minghetti from Emilia, and the liberal Right became a solid governing class, homogeneous if restricted, sustained by high ideals of devotion to the public good and an almost fanatical personal probity.

Talent and courage were needed to meet the disastrous state of affairs in Italy after 1861. The whole military and administrative apparatus of a vast state had to be created afresh. The census of that year revealed that 75 per cent of Italians were illiterate, and in southern Italy the percentage rose to 90. Roads, railways, schools, and often even drinking water were lacking; malaria and pellagra were prevalent in much of the country, and cholera periodically claimed many victims. The starving and illiterate masses, who had understood little of the Risorgimento, now had to submit to military conscription and higher taxes than the old governments exacted – just because they did little or nothing for the taxpayers. In addition, the government faced violent hostility from the democratic Left, exasperated at the conclusion of Garibaldi's enterprise and insistently urged on to republican revolution by the indomitable Mazzini, and virulent opposition from the clergy stirred up by Rome against the Italian State.

Many people prophesied the young state's downfall. The iron-willed men of the liberal Right succeeded in saving it, using drastic measures to transform one of the most backward countries of Europe into a civilized modern state.

The democratic Left had not the same habit of command or the same homogeneous character as the Right. Moreover the Left was divided between intransigent republicans and supporters of Victor Emmanuel II, between orthodox followers of Mazzini and more or less socialist radicals; and between autonomists after the fashion of Cattaneo and out-and-out unitarians. They all agreed, however, on wishing to see Rome and Venetia join Italy, an easy ground for dispute with the Right. While the moderates recommended diplomatic methods, the democrats demanded revolutionary action, for this reason assuming the name of the 'Action Party'. The Right, furthermore, was divided on the Roman question. Besides the heirs of Cavour's formula 'A free Church in a free State' there were those who dreamed of reforming Catholicism, like Ricasoli, temperamentally puritanical and close to the Swiss *Reveil*; and lastly there were those who held by the old formula of state control over the clergy. The Left, solidly and fiercely anti-clerical, found a powerful ally in the Masonic Lodges, which became widespread in Italy after 1860 with Garibaldi at their head. Finally, the Action Party had the incomparable advantage of being identified with Garibaldi.

The Right's weakness lay in its concentration in the Po Valley and in Tuscany. In the south the landed nobility was anything but progressive, the wealthy bourgeoisie almost non-existent; and the groups which might have formed a moderate party, and which had in fact demanded annexation to get rid of the followers of Garibaldi, were strongly imbued with local patriotism. The moderate Right, fearing the destruction of unity, wanted to give Italy a highly centralized administration on Napoleonic lines. They thus alienated their natural allies in Sicily and Naples, at the same time summarily setting aside the followers of Garibaldi, the political force that had considerable following among the southern middle class. The new regime in the former Kingdom of the Two Sicilies found itself without political support, surrounded by universal dislike for the 'Piedmontese' and reduced to relying on force alone. Giuseppe Garibaldi, with his apparent simplicity, had cleverly managed to achieve a hold on Sicily and southern Italy. He promised state and church lands to the peasants while reassuring the landowners against the danger of a *jacquerie*. He encouraged anti-clerical Freemasonry while so successfully fascinating the clergy that he had a whole 'ecclesiastical legion' of priests and friars among his Red

Opposite In the Battle of Custoza, 24 June 1866, during the third War of Independence, the Italians under La Marmora were defeated by the Austrians. Navally and diplomatically the war was also not a success, and Italian claims to the Trentino were not given consideration, but Venetia was at last united to Italy. Painting by Giovani Fattori (1825–1908).

Shirts. By creating a big army of volunteers, moreover, he had armed the patriots, in a region where the followers of the Bourbons were by no means a negligible quantity. Cavour had excellent reasons for dissolving Garibaldi's army, but this inevitably created a void in military power, aggravated by the collapse of the Bourbons which filled the countryside with thousands of disbanded soldiers. The resulting 'brigandage' was actually a fierce civil war of the poor against the rich, conducted under the banner of Bourbon legitimacy and encouraged by the Bourbon court which had taken refuge with Pius IX in Rome.

The terrifying guerrilla warfare in southern Italy between 1861 and 1864 engaged almost half the Italian army and exacted a toll of several thousands of human lives, or more than some of the wars of the Risorgimento had cost. Anti-Bourbon feeling in Sicily prevented legitimist 'brigandage', but resistance to military conscription was rife and ruthless military operations were conducted to round up deserters—methods better suited to excite the Sicilians' indignation than to win them to the new order of things.

Venice and Rome

In 1862 the Prime Minister, Rattazzi, imagined he was making an astute move in giving Garibaldi the opportunity to attack the Papal State, counting on a repetition of Victor Emmanuel's intervention in southern Italy in 1860. Garibaldi went to Sicily, gathered an army of volunteers and crossed into Calabria, planning to advance on Rome. But a threatening message from Napoleon III frightened Rattazzi, who sent troops to stop the expedition; in the ensuing encounter in the mountains of Aspromonte Garibaldi himself was wounded.

The indignation aroused by this episode caused Rattazzi's fall and his replacement as Prime Minister by Minghetti, who tried to solve the Roman question by diplomatic negotiation. In September 1864 he signed a Convention with Napoleon III under which the Emperor agreed to withdraw the French troops he had sent to protect Pius IX. Minghetti was convinced that the Pope, once deprived of the troops, would be less unyielding towards the Italian government. But the September Convention seemed tantamount to a re-

nunciation of Rome, the more so since it included a promise to move the capital of Italy to Florence. Riots broke out, quelled only after bloodshed in Turin, and forced Minghetti also to resign. Pius IX, far from becoming more yielding, chose this moment to issue an Encyclical with an attached 'Syllabus' which condemned every liberal principle and declared that Catholicism could never come to terms with modern civilization.

The possibility of obtaining Venetia presented itself in 1866 in the hostilities between Prussia and Austria, and Italy allied herself with Prussia, embarking on the third War of Italian Independence against Austria. There could be no doubt of the outcome, given the inferiority of the Austrian forces. But the Italian commanders' incompetence succeeded in transforming the war into a fresh source of humiliation and internal tension, for the army was defeated at Custoza and the fleet at Lissa by an army half the size of her own. The Left could boast by comparison of further successes for Garibaldi, achieved by his volunteer units in the mountains of the Trentino. It could also blame the government for having prevented Garibaldi from following up these successes with his entry into Trento by hastily concluding an armistice. When Palermo heard the news, an insurrection broke out which was quelled only after several days of fighting.

Victor Emmanuel II therefore handed back the government to Rattazzi, who reverted to his illusory dream of giving Garibaldi a free hand against Rome with a view to intervention by the regular army later on. In 1867 bands of Garibaldi's followers invaded the Papal State at various points and Garibaldi hastened from Caprera to put himself at their head. Napoleon III protested so vehemently that Rattazzi had Garibaldi arrested and sent back to Caprera under guard of the fleet. But the indomitable old man escaped and after reappearing in Latium advanced on Rome at the head of his volunteers, while in the city itself an insurrection was preparing. This time the affair came to a dramatic finish, for the papal troops crushed the conspirators in Rome and destroyed a small column of Garibaldi's men who were bringing them arms. Garibaldi vanquished the papal army at Monte Rotondo, only to find himself faced immediately after, at Mentana on 3 November, by a French army sent in haste by Napoleon III. Not even Garibaldi could do anything against the new long-range *chassepôt* rifles, and the volunteers were routed.

Opposite, above News of the Armistice of Villafranca (in 1859) by Girolamo Induno paints the despondency and consternation of Italians on hearing that Piedmont's ally, Napoleon III, despite military successes, had signed an armistice with the Austrians. It was a bitter, though temporary, setback to Italian unification.

Opposite, below Manifestation in Piazza della Signoria, Florence, 15 March 1860, for the plebiscite held in Tuscany on union with the Kingdom of Sardinia (Piedmont). Plebiscites were also held in Romagna, Modena and Parma; national feeling had become so strong that everywhere the votes for union were practically unanimous.

Garibaldi with his famous Thousand landed at Marsala on 11 May 1860. In a four-months' campaign the small force of patriots, vastly enlarged by local volunteers, took Sicily, crossed to the mainland and entered Naples in triumph. Cavour, to avoid antagonizing France, prevented Garibaldi from going on to capture Rome. Nevertheless most of Italy, except for Venetia and Latium, was now unified.

Left Alexandre Dumas, *père*, took his yacht to Sicily and followed the progress of the Thousand. At Milazzo, he caught up with Garibaldi and found the Dictator asleep on the ground after the battle. After Naples was taken, Garibaldi appointed Dumas as inspector of antiquities for Pompeii, a rare honour for a foreigner.

Opposite An important training camp for the defence of the Papal State was maintained at the Campi d'Annibale, near Rocca di Papa, in the Alban Hills. In this contemporary photograph squads of troops, against a background of tents, form the words meaning 'Long Live Pius IX'.

LE HANNETON

ILLUSTRÉ, SATIRIQUE ET LITTÉRAIRE

GARIBALDI

PAR GÉDÉON

The admiration and sympathy Garibaldi aroused even abroad is suggested in this friendly caricature in the French satirical review *Le Hanneton* of 25 July 1867. Evidently he approved of being shown as a benevolent lion with the Italian Boot under his paw, for the autograph letter reproduced below the drawing gives the editor permission to publish '*mon portrait*'.

Garibaldi rarely left his island retreat of Caprera in his later years. In the national elections of 1874, however, he was elected Deputy and the following year, though aged and infirm, he visited Rome. The photo shows him at a banquet given in his honour in the Teatro Corea which formerly occupied the Mausoleum of Augustus.

A contemporary photo shows Pius IX giving an audience from the blessing platform of the papal train at Velletri, 1863. His early liberalism long since forgotten, the Pope defended his temporal monarchy, now reduced to the city of Rome and narrow territories to the north and south, by repressive measures and the presence of a French garrison.

Gioacchino Rossini (1792–1868) in an engraving made towards the end of his life. Like Verdi, Manzoni and most Italian artists and intellectuals, this celebrated composer was a patriot, and national aspiration was the theme of some of his operas.

From the Loggia of St Peter's, in 1864, Pius IX blesses the multitude of the faithful, many with carriages standing by. A familiar Roman scene that has bridged all the vicissitudes of the papacy's loss of temporal power and its rapprochement with the Italian State. Every Sunday at noon the reigning Pope still blesses those who congregate in St Peter's Square.

Amid bitterness and frustration the liberal Right had managed to preserve the country's unity and to set in motion the machinery of the State, although the Finance Minister, Quintino Sella, was having to fight the deficit with 'economies to the very bone'. In the face of a hostile clergy, the government took drastic measures, dissolving most of the religious Orders and selling their immense properties. Far from mitigating the peasants' lot as the Left would have wished, the confiscation of church properties served chiefly to enrich the middle class, especially in the south. In the long run, however, this move also consolidated the liberal regime by giving it the support of a large class of new landowners. The government was successful also in improving the State finances, although only through Sella's stern fiscal measures, such as the dreaded milling tax, which in a country of bread and *pasta* consumers, amounted to a tax on the people's hunger. In 1868 riots against the tax raged from one end of the peninsula to the other, and the rifles of the *carabinieri* gave pitiless answer to the cries of the starving, leaving some two hundred dead and numerous wounded. Just when the struggle for the Risorgimento was ending, the class struggle, an even more arduous Risorgimento of the oppressed, was beginning.

Mazzini, though only briefly, and Garibaldi adhered to the First International, but with only a vague idea as to its meaning. Mazzinian republicans, radicals and Socialists still worked closely together in the Masonic Lodges and the democratic organizations. Working men's associations multiplied, but they had no definite political colour; quite a number of them still accepted the paternalistic leadership of philanthropic patrons. Even the more radical workers hesitated to free themselves from the fascination of Mazzini although he insisted on putting the demand for a republic before all economic claims and inveighed fiercely against Socialist 'materialism'.

In 1870, for the last time, Mazzini renewed his efforts to stir up revolution, reckoning that the fall of Napoleon III would bring in its wake that of his ally Victor Emmanuel II; a few republican bands arose and a few victims fell, but the country as a whole hardly stirred. The liberal Right, on the contrary, seized the occasion to cut the knot of the Roman question. After vain attempts to persuade Pius IX to yield without further bloodshed, on 20 September 1870 the Italian guns opened fire against the walls of Rome and opened a breach at Porta Pia. The troops entered at the point of the bayonet; Rome was now Italian and the Risorgimento had reached its conclusion.

But the very last page in the account of the Risorgimento was not written with the breach of Porta Pia and the two hundred slain who paid the price for the disappearance of the temporal power of the Popes. It was written by Giuseppe Garibaldi, now an old man suffering from his wounds, unable even to mount a horse but still capable of great vision. When the iron jaws of Prussian militarism tightened around a once more free and democratic France, the aged hero again called up his Red Shirts and went to fight his last campaign in the Vosges, managing to achieve at least some victories, the most difficult of his career, according to his *Memoirs*. The time had come, as the best men of the Risorgimento had foreseen, to go beyond the problems of national revolutions and to meet the new problems of democratic internationalism.

Elizabeth Wiskemann and Peter Nichols

On 20 September 1870 Italian troops stormed the Papal State, which had remained an enclave in the heart of the nation for ten years. Rome, for the first time since antiquity, became the capital of a united Italy. The right, identified with the unification and a policy of austere probity, but socially unprogressive, lost the 1876 elections to the centre left which, through a series of opportunistic coalitions, ran the country for thirty years. The backward and impoverished south was the most pressing national problem, a problem neglected as Italy sought Great Power status. By warring against Abyssinia and Turkey, and finally entering the First World War on the Allied side, Italy gained her African colonies and an adjustment of her border with Austria. Social maladjustment aggravated by the war led to violence by the communists and socialists on one side and the Fascist extreme right on the other. Intimidated, the government and the monarchy let Mussolini take power constitutionally, after which he eliminated Parliament and set up a dictatorship. Fascist social regimentation and militarism brought in turn the conquest of Abyssinia, the Axis pact with Hitler and consequent military adventures during the Second World War in France, Africa, the Balkans and Russia, none of which ended well. With the Allied invasion of Italy, the Fascist regime collapsed and Mussolini was eventually shot by partisans. After the war the Monarchy was rejected in a referendum and the Republic was constituted. Postwar recovery was so outstanding in all aspects of national life that it became known as the 'Italian Miracle'.

Rome the Capital, and the Left in Power

On 20 September 1870 King Victor Emmanuel's troops took Rome and the capital of the new Italy moved from its provisional seat in Florence to what had been the Pope's city. It was not an easy situation. The fact that Italian unity was finally achieved against the will of the papacy, by forcibly taking from the Pope the last of his temporal domains was one of the problems which the young state was about to face. There were plenty of others. Unity itself was a fact, but as an idea it had scarcely begun to penetrate the nation. Put to the question of whether they wanted to form part of a united Italy or not, most Italians – this is the real point of the plebiscites taken at the time – would vote, or could be persuaded to vote, in favour. Nevertheless much of the enthusiasm for national unity was the child of the dreams of intellectuals, followers of Mazzini. This intelligentsia included members of the liberal middle class and was backed by a number of the younger aristocrats. But the mass of the people was poor and illiterate, dominated by priests who owed allegiance not to any idea of a liberal Italy, but to a Pope who had ultimately shown himself to be as conservative as his predecessors, despite an apparent interest early in his

Opposite Lo Stivale – 'The Boot'. A sardonic vignette summing up the Italian situation in 1866. Figures representing Venice, Piedmont and Tuscany strive to join hands with the South, personified by a Neapolitan Harlequin, but Rome, still an independent state, blocks the way. An illustration by Martelli, from Giusti's satirical verse on the history of Italy, Lo Stivale.

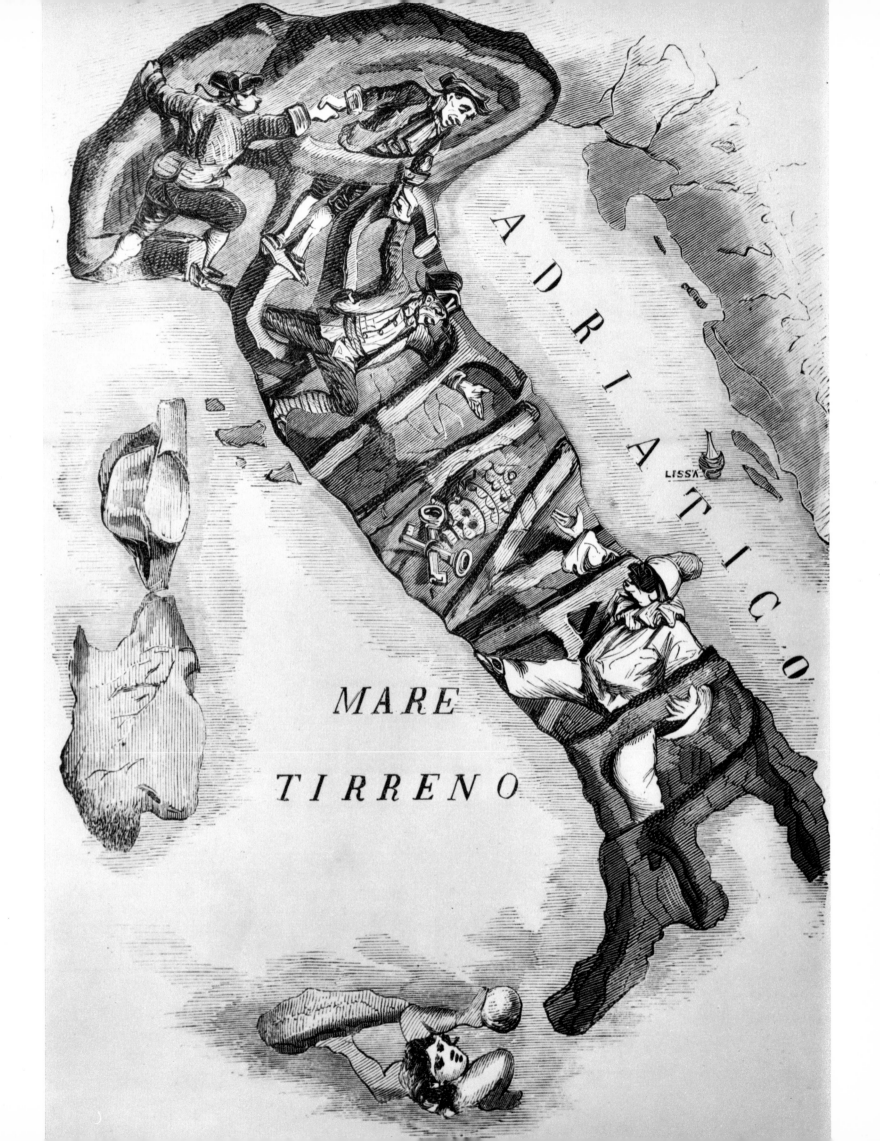

Porta Pia, where on 20 September 1870 Italian Bersaglieri entered Rome following the withdrawal of French troops and the fall of Napoleon III, thus bringing an end to the temporal power of the Papacy. The occupation of Rome was the last stage in Italy's unification. The assault on Michelangelo's city gate, re-enacted for a photographer.

Below The nine-mile long St Gotthard tunnel through the Alps from Italy to Switzerland took ten years to build (1872–82). It was a most important step in developing Italy's international railway communications, which stimulated the growth of Italian industry and effectively made at least North Italy an active participant in European life and commerce.

reign for liberal reform. And only two months before Rome was occupied by the Piedmontese army, the first Vatican Council had proclaimed papal supremacy and infallibility. Even when all allowance is made for the fact that religion is different from politics, this marked as high a point as one could imagine in authoritarianism. Besides the void between these two ways of seeing the world there was also the gap between north and south. The former Bourbon kingdom of Naples was far poorer and more backward than the north and the centre. Reasons deeper than economic differences made – and still make – of the south a place which is different from the rest of the country. To foster the feeling of one nation a careful policy would have been required, giving due recognition to the fact that a Mediterranean not a Western European world opens south of Rome. The south, however, did not receive the special consideration required and the split imposed by religion in one direction was crossed by the geographical division between two Italian outlooks which were to grow inevitably wider apart.

How were such problems to be met? The question of relations with the Pope was not resolved for many years. The young state did however make an attempt to indemnify the Pontiff and define its relations with the Vatican. The Law of Guarantees left the papacy in possession of the Vatican itself, the Church of St John Lateran, which is the Pope's cathedral as Bishop of Rome, and of the summer residence at Castelgandolfo. The Pope was confirmed in his rights and prerogatives as a sovereign, his person was declared inviolable and a sum of £129,000 put aside annually for his maintenance. This measure of course, gave the state a powerful financial hold as papal paymaster. The state also held the right of veto over the temporalities of Italian sees and benefices and had the right to inspect seminaries. The clergy were declared subject to civil law. The Pope would have nothing to do with the settlement, refusing so much as to draw his subsidy. He pronounced the greater excommunication against all who had had a hand in the fall of the temporal power and, declaring himself 'the prisoner of the Vatican', retired to the Apostolic palaces. For half a century no Pope emerged from them. This did not mean, however, that the Popes had no influence on Italian politics. They had after all begun by refusing to allow Catholics to take part in the political life of a state which the papacy refused to recognize. Fear of Socialism eventually brought about the revoking of that prohibition, and Socialism's

successful opponent – Fascism – was in the end to reach a definitive agreement between the Italian State and the Roman Pontiffs.

The early governments immediately after the fall of Rome did at least try in the Law of Guarantees to put the problem of Church and State on a workable basis. They failed but they had made the attempt. On the other great problem of the geographical division they seemed rather to aggravate the differences. The Piedmontese administrative system was applied to the whole country and where possible Piedmontese officials were used to work it. The system was highly centralized. It had served admirably in a small state known for its efficiency and honesty, as well as for its rigorous military tradition which had won for Piedmont the name of the Prussia of Italy. Elsewhere the royal bureaucrats were unpopular with the visionaries, the old followers of Mazzini or Garibaldi, who had dreamt of a republic; they were hated by that section of conservative southern opinion which was opposed so bitterly to the new nation that it was willing to harry its officials with brigandage. Not only was the new state over-centralized, its representative chamber was elected only by the wealthy. This was at a time when the Third French Republic across the frontier had introduced universal male suffrage and the new Germany elected its Reichstag by universal male suffrage, though the franchise for the important Prussian chamber was still severely restricted. As far as the workings of government went, the country began this first stage of unity with an apparently effective start towards the two-party system. This promised development was soon to be cut short by methods which depended on spoils and a blurring of the edges of differences. Yet in spite of the difficulties, the country can be said to have done more than survive. By 1882 Italy's inclusion in the Triple Alliance with Germany and Austria was recognition of her establishment as the sixth great power of Europe.

Party government in the strict sense scarcely lasted half a dozen years. Until early in 1876 it could fairly have been argued that the Conservatives had provided a distinctive contribution by unifying the country, making Rome the capital, defining relations with the Vatican, while the left-wing opposition led by Depretis and Crispi was prepared to offer an alternative administration. In March 1876 the change came. Depretis, who had earlier been a follower of Mazzini, but was now reconciled with the monarchy, took the Premiership.

Opposite As much an engineering feat as a work of architecture, the Galleria Vittorio Emanuele II in Milan, which connects the Piazza del Duomo with the Piazza della Scala, expressed the 'modernism' that accompanied Italy's unification. Built between the years 1865–77 by Giuseppe Mengoni, its sheltered passages and cafés have been the centre of Milanese social life ever since.

He was to remain in power with brief absences from 1876 to 1887, and in that time he destroyed party government. He called a General Election to strengthen his position. The handling of it was the responsibility of Nicotera, the Calabrian revolutionary who had spent three years in a Bourbon prison and was now Minister for the Interior. Official pressure brought to bear through the prefects, corruption, and threats all played their part; in the new Parliament 400 out of 500 Deputies claimed to be supporters of the government. The left, however, had little real unity and no clear programme; the right was splitting into groups. Depretis took the course of constituting his majority wherever he could find it. Political differences were forgotten. The number of votes was all important. Again it was the same process: pressures, bribery, jobs – a constantly shifting majority but a constant one nevertheless. *Trasformismo* had become the essential method of governing the country. Depretis enjoyed manipulation. The country lost interest in what its politicians were doing. Scepticism, already entrenched, prevailed. This situation of workable but uninspiring confusion continued under Francesco Crispi, the Prime Minister who dominated the last thirty years of the century.

Crispi became Prime Minister after the death of Depretis in 1887. He was a Sicilian who in his younger days had fought under Garibaldi. Though high-handed and dictatorial in his methods, he made some admirable attempts at social reform, but even before his accession social troubles were clearly on the increase. Violence followed upon the introduction of revolutionary ideas adapted from the thinking of the anarchist Bakunin. In the early 1890s Syndicalism imported from France began to supersede Mazzinian Socialism. At much the same time German social democracy became a strong influence, particularly in Milan, while at the University of Rome Antonio Labriola was expounding Marxism to his students. Marxism thus began to attract intellectuals in Italy while industry was still in its infancy. By the time that industrialization was in its stride, the intellectuals had already taught many of the new workers to think in terms of capitalist exploitation and to seek defence in the strike weapon. In 1892 the Italian Socialist Party was founded by Filippo Turati. Crispi was hardly the man to deal with explosive innovations. He had a great capacity for work and a firmness which compared well with the methods of his predecessor, but he was inconsistent and impulsive. He spoke of freeing the workers from capitalist slavery, but attempted unsuccessfully to repress Socialism and did not succeed in rallying effective opposition to subversive propaganda among the parties that stood for order.

The failure for which public opinion never forgave him, however, was the colonial disaster which was to force him from office. Italy had found the energy to join in the colonial game, though Italian claims were not pressed with vigour until Crispi was in charge – and then with disastrous results. In 1882 Italy had acquired a station at Assab Bay on the Red Sea. Three years later the harbour of Massawa was occupied. By 1890 the crown colony of Eritrea had been established and at about the same time Italian Somaliland was occupied. Behind this expansion in the Red Sea was the bitter disappointment at the French refusal to permit influence in Tunisia where, in fact, Italians formed the only large body of European immigrants. But East Africa was not to satisfy the ambitions of the Italian public, nor of Crispi himself. Menelik, the Emperor of Abyssinia, accepted Italian collaboration until 1893. He then became hostile and in 1896 at Adowa his soldiers defeated a small Italian army. The defeat was the end of Crispi's colonial dreams and of his career. Because of the great importance which he had attached to Abyssinia the reverse was felt as a particularly bitter humiliation.

Two years later a series of food shortages and labour unrest, which earlier had been acute in Crispi's Sicily, culminated in riots at Milan that resulted in the deaths of nearly a hundred people, the wounding of hundreds more, and arrests on a massive scale. Feelings rose against the authorities, who seemed unable to handle the problems of the nation. In 1900 King Humbert was assassinated by an anarchist, Bresci, who felt he was revenging the casualties of 1898. With the accession of the new king, Victor Emmanuel III, a period of Liberal government was begun by the already elderly Zanardelli and continued by Giolitti, allowing Italy to move into the twentieth century with better hopes.

Giolitti and Liberalism

Although the country lacked the key raw materials of the age – coal and iron – the population was buoyant

---

Opposite, above The transfer of the capital of Italy from Florence to Rome is represented in an irreverent cartoon. Winding away from Florence, the Ministries and branches of the state precede a float in the shape of the Palazzo Vecchio. The procession is headed by Time and the Shades of the Italian Revolutions.

Opposite, below The tricolour flew from the tower on the Capitol from 20 September 1870. But the 'perfect trinity' of the papacy, monarchy and revolutionary nationalism, represented here by Pius IX, Victor Emmanuel II and Garibaldi linking arms was never attained. The King alone fulfilled his role as a national symbol.

Italian emigrants setting out for America, from an engraving of 1879. The new Italy meant hardship and exile for some, since after unification the population rose faster than the number of jobs available, and from then until World War I tens of thousands of Italians, southerners for the most part, left Italy each year to settle abroad, mainly in North and South America.

A public scribe in Rome writing letters for the illiterate. His was a flourishing profession in the mid-nineteenth century, when some 80 per cent of the people could not read or write. The scribes have since vanished, but illiteracy has not entirely disappeared. The small fraction of the population that is still illiterate are offered special courses in the schools as well as instruction on television.

Opposite The poet Filippo Tommaso Marinetti was the leader of the Futurist movement, which avowedly aimed at modernizing Italy's art and attitudes. Romantic gallantry was not rejected, however, as may be read in the dedication to a famous contemporary beauty of Marinetti's portrait by the Futurist painter, Carlo Carrà (b. 1881): 'I give my portrait to the great Futurist, the Marchesa Casati, to her slow eyes of a jaguar who is digesting in the sun the steel cage he has devoured.'

VICTORIO EMANVELE II PADRE DELLA PATRIA

Victor Emmanuel II died on 9 January 1878. His burial in the
Pantheon rather than in the Superga at Turin, like his predecessors
of the House of Savoy, symbolized Rome's new position as the
capital of all Italy. The Risorgimento was coming to a natural
term: only a month later the King's old antagonist, Pius IX, also
died; Mazzini was already dead (1872), and Garibaldi was living out
his last years in the retirement of Caprera.

Left The cholera epidemic of 1884 in Naples. Health conditions in
Naples, notoriously bad under the Bourbons, improved only very
slowly after the unification despite reconstruction of the sewage
system and other public health measures. Living standards
remained such that the Neapolitans composed the proverb:
'Where the sun does not enter, the doctor does'. It is still true for
the thousands of occupants of the ground-floor hovels called the
Bassi.

Opposite, above King Humbert I of Italy and the Crown Prince of
Germany in 1883, observing the illumination of the Roman Forum
from the Tabularium on the Capitol. A year earlier, out of fear of
isolation and on Bismarck's insistence, Italy had joined the Triple
Alliance with Germany and Austria. Alliance with Austria, so
recently an enemy and still holding Italian-speaking areas in the
north, made for an uneasy relationship, but the pact survived
until the 1914–18 war.

Opposite, below Troops embarking at Naples to garrison the Italian
station at Assab Bay, on the Eritrean coast of the Red Sea. The
acquisition of this post, in 1882, marked the beginning of Italy's
colonial ventures in Africa.

Pope Leo XIII (1878–1903),
'prisoner of the Vatican', trying
out Edison's new machine, the
phonograph, and sending him his
blessing incised on a wax
cylinder. Following the tumul-
tuous events of his predecessor's
pontificate, including the loss of
temporal power, Leo XIII had
the problem of coming to terms
with the new spirit of his age.
The realistic social policies of
the Church, which he promoted,
found expression in his many
encyclicals, notably *Rerum
Novarum* (1891).

Right, above Giosuè Carducci
(1835–1907) receiving the
announcement of his nomination
for the Nobel Prize from the
Swedish Minister at his home in
Bologna, 10 December 1906. The
great poet of the period, he
voiced the nationalism of the
later Risorgimento with its anti-
Catholic and pro-classical
flavour.

and seemed, in the north at least, quick to learn industrial skills. In the north too there was capital (some of it German) and from the turn of the century industrialisation was rapid in Milan, Turin and the port of Genoa. The most famous of Italy's modern industries, that of the motor-car, was founded in Turin in 1899 by a group of industrialists headed by Agnelli. It was called Fiat (*Fabbrica Italiana Automobili Torino*) and expanded rapidly. The textile and chemical industries were growing too; and electrical power networks were set up.

The first fifteen years of the twentieth century were remarkably prosperous. Jobs in the new factories absorbed some of the rapidly growing population, though at least half a million emigrated annually, a great many of them to the United States. This period is associated with the name of Giolitti who dominated the final phase of democratic government before the Fascists came to power. Even when not Prime Minister it was Giolitti who kept the majorities together on which successive governments had to rely. He was a Piedmontese whose career had been made in the ranks of the Civil Service, where he had worked hard and shown great ability. He was a Liberal; precise and industrious, he was—a rarity in Italy—completely innocent of political dogma. A devotee of common sense, he moved forward with the times, introducing social reforms to satisfy the working class and extending the franchise so as to integrate this new class into the State. The more moderate Socialist leaders, considered 'revisionists' by their more extreme colleagues on the left, were persuaded to co-operate with him. He believed in bargaining to get things done. In Naples and Sicily this policy easily degenerated into corruption and rule by coercion on the part of the prefects who were responsible to Giolitti in Rome. Unlike Crispi he had no taste for conquest and war, nor for the fine phrases which launched them, but as it suited him to humour patriots and business interests, he set in motion the conquest of Libya in 1911, a decision which further aggravated the divisions within the Socialist Party. The moderate Socialists were willing to support him, but the left wing, led by Lazzari and Benito Mussolini, rebelled at the party congress held in 1912 at Reggio Emilia. The editor of the party's paper, the moderate Treves, was soon replaced by the young and nihilistically-minded Mussolini. This might be regarded as the beginning of the end of the age of Giolitti, a period, be it noted, when

the punctuality of the trains was taken for granted.

It was typical of this highly pragmatic man to make a political arrangement with Roman Catholicism without managing to come to an agreement with the Vatican itself. During his time in power the relationship between Church and State changed substantially. Originally the position, or the problem, was that the Roman Church had not recognized the Italian State, yet the vast majority of Italians were Catholic. The situation was eased somewhat when Leo XIII succeeded Pius IX in 1878, the year of Victor Emmanuel II's death and the succession of his son Humbert. Leo XIII was aware that the Church must recognize the existence of social problems and take more note of the industrial workers. He made this clear in his Encyclical *Rerum Novarum* in 1891. In spite of the papal ban many Catholics who were electorally qualified had in fact voted in parliamentary elections. In 1911 Giolitti extended the franchise, increasing the number of voters from three million to eight million. Pius X, alarmed by Socialist gains, had already lifted the papal ban on voting and Catholic politicians were encouraged to throw their weight against Socialism. When the elections were held under the new law in 1913, Giolitti's candidates negotiated the pact called after Gentiloni, the head of the Catholic Electoral Union. By this agreement Catholics voted for Giolitti's men, who in return tacitly promised to oppose divorce and support private, meaning Catholic, schools.

Turn of the Century Attitudes and the First World War

While common sense characterized the government, patriotic fervour found high expression in the arts. Like most of the Italian artists of the nineteenth century, Giuseppe Verdi was a great patriot of the Risorgimento. His name, indeed, was interpreted as a national symbol standing for *Vittorio Emanuele Re d'Italia*. By the time of the capture of Rome he was 57 and within a year of completing his opera *Aida*, which had been commissioned for the opening ceremonies of the Suez Canal. The great poet of the period, Giosuè Carducci (1835–1907), who was a good deal younger, voiced the nationalism of the post-Risorgimento period with its anti-Catholic, pro-classical flavour.

Opposite The nineteenth century closed in an atmosphere of increasing social unrest and the government's attempts to repress Socialism by force. The general violence reached a climax with the assassination of the head of the State. The print shows the shooting, by an anarchist, of King Humbert I (1878–1900) as he arrived at a gymnasts' meeting in Monza on 29 July 1900. 'The poetry of the House of Savoy has been destroyed', the Queen had said of a previous unsuccessful attempt.

As professor of literary history at the important University of Bologna from 1861 to 1903 he exerted great influence on many generations of students. His junior by five years, the novelist, Giovanni Verga, was a sensitive interpreter of the life of poor peasants in Sicily. One of his tales, *Cavalleria Rusticana*, was afterwards set to music by Mascagni.

In the next generation Puccini continued the great tradition of Italian opera, and literature was dominated by the two contrasting figures of Luigi Pirandello and Gabriele D'Annunzio. Pirandello's plays — still often produced, especially *Henry IV* and *Six Characters in Search of an Author* — dealt in psychological nuances and problems of personal identity.

D'Annunzio's literature, however, cuts across both action and politics. In person D'Annunzio was wild and ebullient, pouring forth a seemingly endless number of poems, plays and novels, and performing dramatic gestures, such as acting out his change of position as a Deputy by crossing the floor of the Chamber from the extreme right to the extreme left. This was the period of the 1898 tumults and their aftermath, and D'Annunzio proclaimed that he could not remain on the right because it was dead. At the time of the Libyan war and in the years preceding the First World War, D'Annunzio epitomized ardent nationalism.

Equally nationalistic, but less neo-Romantic and more 'modernistic', the poet Filippo Tommaso Marinetti launched and led Futurism, principally an Italian movement in arts and letters whose best painters, owing much also to Cubism, were Boccioni, Carrà, Balla and Severini. Futurism was in love with novelty, machines and speed. In revolt against all the ideas, forms and traditions of the nineteenth century, it was opposed to the commonplace and to equality, was proudly irrational, nationalistic and warlike. Thus, the common sense of Giolitti had its antagonists in D'Annunzio and the Futurists. As irredentists, too, they were influential in bringing Italy into the war on the side of the Allies.

An opposite and unique influence was exerted by the philosopher Benedetto Croce, who was first attracted by Marxism, later by Georges Sorel and Vico. By the beginning of the twentieth century his equation of philosophy with history, expressed in his optimistic slogan of *tutt'il reale razionale, tutt'il razionale reale*, had gained much acceptance. He brought a new philosophical background to Liberalism which certainly was attractive to the more leisurely minded intellectuals and anyone seeking an idealistic approach to politics based on rational truth approached by argument. His writings were eagerly followed. Later in 1927 he himself wrote of his book on aesthetics published in this earlier period:

It may be said to have inspired everything of importance that was produced in Italy in the field of philosophical and historical study, criticism of poetry, music and the fine arts, linguistic studies, legal and economic science, the history of thought and civilisation, and religious and educational controversies. Thus after an interval of two centuries, it recovered for Italian thought an active part in the thought of Europe, and even a kind of primacy in certain branches of study.

Together with a slightly younger philosopher called Giovanni Gentile he founded his famous review *La Critica* in 1903.

Italian currents of opinion in the arts and philosophy as yet had little direct influence on politics. The foreign policy of Italy had been cleverly conducted on the whole. Crispi, old Garibaldian though he was, had exaggerated his friendship with Germany and his enmity, involving a costly tariff war, with France. With the Liberal period initiated by Zanardelli in 1900 the sympathies of the Radicals and moderate Social Democrats with the Third French Republic became more evident. Anti-clericals and irredentists disliked the Triple Alliance with Austria, a country which still ruled Italians in Trieste and the Trentino. The leaders of the army and Church and the old aristocracy — often the same people — favoured the Triple Alliance, which, through German financiers, could exert economic pressure. In 1900 and 1902, however, by an exchange of notes with France, a secret understanding was reached which gave Italy a free hand in Libya in return for her acceptance of the French programme in Morocco. Italy attacked Turkey in 1911 and acquired Libya and the Dodecanese Islands by conquest.

When the European war broke out in August 1914, Italy was thus divided in sympathy. According to the terms of the Triple Alliance Austria-Hungary's attack upon Serbia without consultation with Rome left Italy free. The Conservative Salandra-Sonnino Cabinet hoped, however, to obtain some territorial gains from Vienna by negotiation. Like the government and Giolitti, the leaders of the Socialist Party were against intervention. Many Radicals believed with the historian

---

Opposite Giuseppe Verdi, Italy's greatest opera composer was, like most Italian artists of the time, a great patriot of the Risorgimento. His very name was read as a national symbol meaning *V*ittorio *E*manuele *R*e *d'I*talia. His works, including *Aida* and *La Traviata*, are among the most popular operas still regularly performed. The painting is by Giovanni Boldini (1842–1931), a spirited and fashionable Italian portrait painter.

Below Medardo Rosso (1858–1928) the most original Italian sculptor of the turn of the century, created a sculpture of dissolving forms and melting movement like Renoir paintings done in the round. Works such as *The Bookmaker* (1894) influenced Rodin and the whole of twentieth-century plastic art.

In painting, Futurism owed much to Cubism, but in attitude it was impatient with the provincial and traditional aspects of Italian life. The Futurist artists sought to express action and novelty. Gino Severini's (1883–1966) painting *Pan-Pan à Monaco* (1909) conveys the feeling of the bright lights and excitement of cosmopolitan night life.

Salvemini that Italy should be fighting on the side of France and Britain against a retrograde Austria-Hungary and Germany. D'Annunzio and the Nationalists, Marinetti and the Futurists, were vociferous interventionists. So very soon was the dissident Socialist, Mussolini, who once again broke with his party comrades and, with funds from French sources, started an interventionist newspaper, the *Popolo d'Italia*. In addition the Allies – in April 1915 – offered Italy large territorial gains from Austria in the secret treaty of London. On 24 May 1915, 'radiant May' as D'Annunzio called it, Italy declared war upon the Central Powers; public enthusiasm was directed as much against sombre, dull, half corrupt *giolittismo* as against the foreign enemy.

Italy was as ever ill-prepared for war, and the pro-German Chief of Staff, Cadorna, or 'Feldherr' Cadorna as he was mockingly called, had prepared plans for fighting, not against the Central Powers, but with them. By 1917 delays and disappointments had demoralized the soldiers, and in October at Caporetto, where German troops (among them a young officer called Rommel) had joined the Austrians, the Italians were overwhelmingly defeated. Now, however, the nation rallied, and united to resist. The more flexible and humane General Diaz took over from Cadorna, and Orlando became Prime Minister with Nitti as a colleague. With the United States in the war, enlightened leaders such as Carlo Sforza, who urged co-operation with the new Slav nations instead of trying to grab their territory, could push through their policy. A year after Caporetto, the Italians were successful against the Austrians at Vittorio Veneto. Austria-Hungary was by now visibly disintegrating, and on 4 November 1918 an armistice was concluded.

After the elation of victory this first *dopoguerra*, the four years following the armistice, brought nothing but frustration and division. Post-war disorganization and shortages emphasised the sharp differences between the rich and the poor. Many peasants from the south, until they went to the war, had never before seen the better life of the north; now their land-hunger had been whetted with promises that the land should be theirs. In central Italy where the earth was rich and there was co-operative farming or crop-sharing, there had been talk among the peasants of socialist reform even before the war. After the war tension grew between the revolutionary peasants on one side and the big land-owners and constituted authorities on the other. The

industrial workers, most of them opposed to the war until after Caporetto, had been stimulated by the Russian Revolution and now sought to set up workers' councils to control industry. Indeed they hoped to profit by the general disillusionment in order to bring about their own revolution in Italy.

In the elections held in November 1919 proportional representation was adopted for the first time. This system helped the Socialists to emerge as the largest party in the Chamber, including 156 Marxist Revolutionaries and only 19 moderates of the blend which had collaborated with Giolitti. Representatives of a new antagonistic mass party – 100 *Popolari*, the followers of Don Sturzo – appeared in the Chamber at the same time. Sturzo was a remarkable Sicilian priest who had organized a Catholic party approved rather cooly by the Church and not dependent on it. A Catholic party which was anti-Marxist but democratic, the new formation was a serious challenge to the Socialists. One of Sturzo's ablest supporters was Alcide De Gasperi who had become an Italian citizen when the Trentino was ceded by Austria to Italy.

Fascism Takes Over Italy 1919–28

Another new party had failed to make its appearance in the Chamber in November 1919. This was the Fascist Party founded by the renegade Socialist Mussolini in Milan in March of that year. His following included disgruntled ex-servicemen offended by Socialist anti-patriotism, social misfits of various kinds, and a few individualists like Marinetti and even – though only very briefly – the conductor, Toscanini. The programme Mussolini offered his followers was one very near to revolutionary syndicalism. Between March and November the feeling grew among Italians, that despite the acquisition of Trentino, South Tyrol, Trieste and Istria, various Dalmatian islands and Zara, Italy had been cheated at the Peace Conference. (The Treaty of London, published by the Bolsheviks, had promised more, though not Fiume.) D'Annunzio had shown wild courage as an aviator during the war, marrying his talents as writer and man of action by dropping eloquent propaganda leaflets on Trieste and Vienna. In September 1919 with a few hundred black-shirted *Arditi* (as Marinetti had named their dare-devil

Opposite From left to right, the impresarios Gatti-Casazza and David Belasco, the conductor Arturo Toscanini and the composer Giacomo Puccini, on the stage of the Metropolitan Opera House, New York, in 1911. Puccini (1858–1924), the author of *La Bohème* and *Madame Butterfly*, was the last of the great nineteenth-century opera composers. Toscanini (1867–1957), the most celebrated conductor of modern times, started his international career directing opera at La Scala.

squads) D'Annunzio seized the formerly Hungarian port of Fiume from the international forces in occupation. In Fiume D'Annunzio set up what he chose to call his *Reggenza del Carnaro*, and there he tried out picturesque costumes, salutes and other histrionic devices such as the mass intoning of propaganda phrases. In anticipation of one of the fundamentals of Fascism – the corporative State – he also established ten corporations, the first for industrial and agricultural labourers, the second for technicians and managers, and so on. The tenth, however, was 'reserved for the mysterious forces of progress and adventure'. Mussolini, characteristically as it turned out, vacillated between jealous support of D'Annunzio and the fear that D'Annunzio might fail. Thus in November Mussolini, with Marinetti second on his list, polled dismally.

It was after November 1919 that the Fascists began to gain powerful support. On the one hand the magnitude of the Socialist vote, with the Socialists talking Bolshevism, frightened the property-owning classes who began to pay Fascist *squadre* to use physical violence against 'the Reds'. On the other hand, the Socialist leaders showed incompetence. They encouraged strikes and the occupation of factories without achieving anything constructive. In January 1921 the Socialist left-wing broke away, as so often before, this time to become the *Partito Communista Italiana*.

For Mussolini it was fortunate that D'Annunzio had been evicted from Fiume by the Italian authorities at the end of 1920; with the poet dethroned, his followers joined the Fascists at home. Strangely Giolitti had been brought back to power in June 1920 – by now he was 78 – and he decided to hold elections in May 1921. Still more strangely he offered Mussolini an electoral pact. He believed that the Socialists had outlived their usefulness for the moment, and that by using the Fascists they would be absorbed or integrated into the constitutional State. In this way he countenanced the growth of intimidation by Fascist thugs such as Farinacci and Grandi. While the Socialists lost some seats and the *Popolari* gained, thirty-five Fascists were elected, but thirty-five only. How was it that in less than eighteen months the King would invite their leader to form a government?

Briefly the intermediate period was used by the Fascists to step up terrorization of the country by their armed bands, with whom the authorities were sometimes in collusion. At the same time, since the left had stood fairly firm in the election, Mussolini concentrated on appealing to the right. He watered down his natural anti-clericalism, and in September 1922, in order to propitiate the army, he abjured his republicanism in favour of allegiance to the monarchy. Meanwhile Giolitti had resigned for the last time in June 1921, and was succeeded by a series of timid, helpless governments, uncertain of their majorities. When the Fascists, who had developed into a second black-shirted army, concentrated their forces in key positions outside Rome in October 1922, the King vetoed the use of the army itself against them, and on 28 October invited Mussolini, who was in Milan, to become Prime Minister. In justice to the King it should be added that even some of the Liberal leaders favoured this experiment. The Fascist 'March on Rome' was thus a foregone conclusion.

When Mussolini's government was formed it looked harmless enough. He himself took on the Ministry of the Interior and the Foreign Office, and placed Fascist colleagues at the Ministries of Justice, Finance and the 'Liberated Provinces'. But, except for the Communists, all the other parties were represented in the Cabinet; the Under-Secretary for Industry and Commerce was a young *Popolare* called Giovanni Gronchi. Indeed from October 1922 to January 1925 the regime was transitional and almost uncommitted. After the bombardment of Corfu in August 1923 in retaliation for the murder of the Italian General Tellini in Greece, Mussolini had to draw back. In January 1924, however, by the Pact of Rome he induced the Yugoslavs to agree after all to Fiume's annexation by Italy. The King rewarded Mussolini with the Order of the Annunziata and made D'Annunzio Prince of Monte Nevoso. Meanwhile in 1923 an important change had been made at home. A law was passed according to which in future the strongest party in the Chamber was to have two-thirds of the seats, the remaining third being proportionately distributed. This did not sound unreasonable. In the elections of April 1924, despite large-scale Fascist intimidation, nearly three million, almost a third of the electorate, voted for the non-Fascist parties; of these the *Popolari* did best, though the moderate and extreme Socialists together outvoted them, even without the Communists.

When the new Chamber met, a moderate Socialist leader, Giacomo Matteotti, bravely protested against the numerous Fascist outrages during the election campaign. On 10 June 1924 he was murdered; shortly afterwards a Fascist called Dumini, together with his accomplices, was arrested and charged with the crime.

Opposite King Victor Emmanuel III (1900–46), with the royal family behind, waving the Tricolour from the balcony of the Quirinal on Italy's entry into the First World War, 24 May 1915. The secret Treaty of London signed with the Allies a month before, followed by the declaration of war against Austria, marked the breakdown of the Triple Alliance and expressed the nationalists' determination to obtain the territories still under Austrian control.

Guglielmo Marconi (1874–1937) applying his invention of radio telegraphy to practical military use in Italy's colonialist campaign in Libya in 1911. The war, though successful, provoked division at home and revealed deficiencies in Italian military organization. These two factors proved significant when Italy entered the World War four years later.

A look-out post above the Astico valley during the Italian campaign against the Austrians and Germans in the winter of 1917. On 24 October 1917 the Italians were routed at Caporetto and had to withdraw to the Piave. Just a year later they made up for this defeat with their victory at Vittorio Veneto.

Gabriele D'Annunzio (1864–1938) the neo-Romantic writer whose patriotic verse and dare-devil exploits inspired nationalistic sentiment during the First World War and the early phases of Fascism. He was born at Francavilla, on the Abruzzi coast near Pescara, and is here seen at ease among the luxurious and exotic objects with which he liked to fill his villa there.

Luigi Pirandello (1867–1936), a Sicilian, Italy's most famous playwright, who also wrote novels, short stories and essays. A master of psychological nuance and situation, his plays are still regularly put on all over the world. Among his best known works are *Six Characters in Search of an Author* and *Henry IV*.

Opposite Giorgio de' Chirico (b. 1888), one of the best-known twentieth-century Italian painters, owes his world fame to the works of his early career, such as *The Disquieting Muses* (1916). His more or less surrealistic 'metaphysical' paintings seemed like foreshadowings and visual accompaniments of the bleak, blank 'orderliness' and the curious anachronisms—note the castle and the factory in the background—of Fascism.

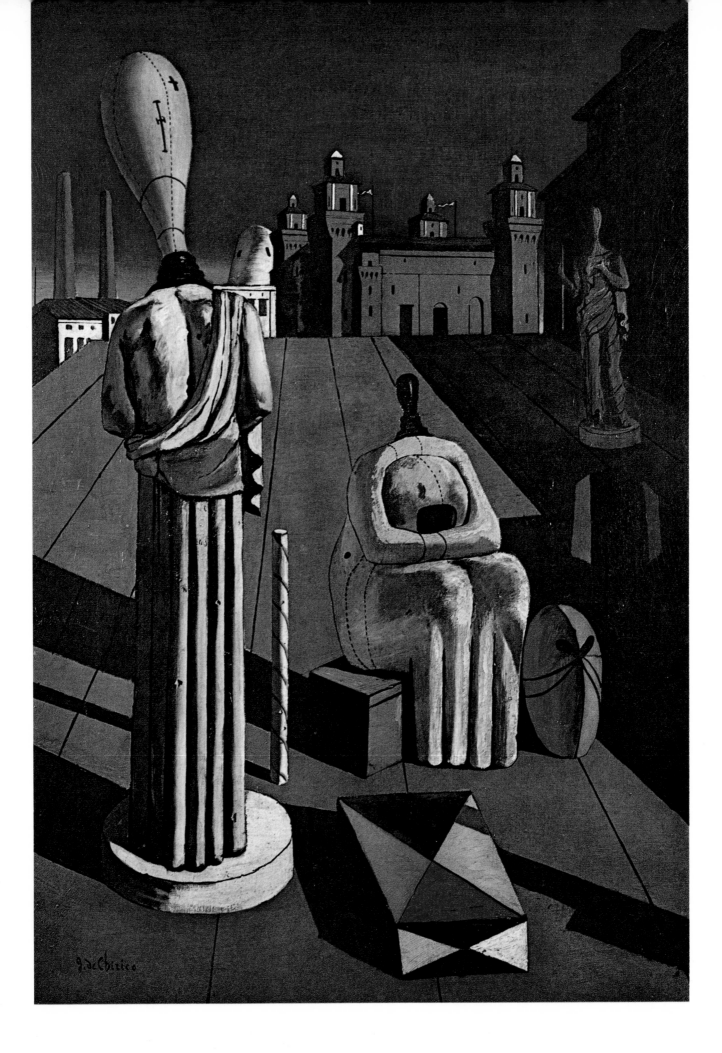

The judge in charge of the case which followed courageously resisted Fascist pressure, but was then transferred to a court in Sicily so that the murderers should not be condemned. Their real trial and condemnation occurred after the fall of Fascism, sentence being pronounced on 4 April 1947. The degree of Mussolini's responsibility is debatable. At the time, the murder of Matteotti outraged public opinion and shook Mussolini's power to its foundations; many people presumed that he had done for himself. It was now that an opposition group of deputies, led by Amendola, withdrew in protest from the Chamber; they were called the Aventine group. After six months' crisis, however, Mussolini took heart; the challenge seemed to stimulate his decision to preserve his power by extending it. On 3 January 1925 he made a speech to the Chamber in which he took responsibility for Fascist violence and announced the creation of the one-party State and the suppression of all opposition. The other parties, the trade unions, the municipally elected mayors and town councils, and the opposition press disappeared; a secret police system with a Special Tribunal was introduced. The Fascist Party with its leader or *Duce*, Mussolini, would have the guidance of a Fascist Grand Council of some thirty members, nominated by the *Duce* himself. In order to create the corporative State of which Mussolini had spoken more and more, twenty-two corporations were set up to represent industry, trades and professions, mining and quarrying, the chemical trades, the clothing trades, cereals and so on. In April 1927 the *Carta del Lavoro* was approved by the Fascist Grand Council. 'Work in all its forms,' it declared, 'is a social duty... the process of production from the national point of view is a single whole; its aims are united and identified with the well-being of the producers and the promotion of national power.' After guaranteeing the workers national insurance, paid holidays and extra pay for night work, Articles VII and IX of the *Carta* declared that 'the Corporative State considers private enterprise in the domain of production to be the most efficient method and the most advantageous to the interests of the nation...; the State intervenes in economic production only when private enterprise fails, or is insufficient, or when the political interests of the State are involved.' Clause XXIII laid down that employers must employ the labour allotted to them by the corporative labour exchanges, which gave preference to members of the Fascist Party.

In practice the corporative State bestowed almost unbridled power on very large concerns such as Fiat, Montecatini (chemicals), and Ansaldo (shipyards); their directors gave big donations to the Fascist Party charities and often in return could dictate policy. Fascism, inherently bellicose, would increasingly need what they produced as war approached; it accepted their industrial monopolies. The working class lost not only all hope of workers' industrial control—even the party's control was half fictitious—but also the right to strike or even to bargain. It gained for certain only the free theatre tickets and holidays provided by the *Opera Nazionale Dopolavoro* founded in 1925. The conscious appeal of Fascism to the youth of all classes was very strong, and highly successful for many years. The class which was most wholeheartedly Fascist was the lower middle class for whom the party provided innumerable jobs, but also a reply to the Marxist apotheosis of the worker.

The Totalitarian State

In the transitional period from October 1922 to January 1925 Italy's economic prospects were extremely uncertain, and American restrictions on immigration intensified unemployment. But by the end of 1924 the Dawes Plan was in operation and Europe heading for prosperity—perhaps Mussolini's acceptance of full responsibility in January 1925 was not wholly unrelated to this fact. From 1925 to 1927 the Italian economic position improved with that of the rest of the Continent. More water-power was produced, and in the textile industry there was a boom in artificial silk. In 1927 Mussolini made the deflationary decision to stabilize the lira high at 90 to the pound sterling. The Great Depression hit Italy less severely than it hit Germany, Austria or Britain. And driving, as it did, each country back upon its own resources, it seemed to justify the Fascist policy of national self-sufficiency or *autarchia*. The Fascist State came to the rescue of the big banks, gladly acquiring complete control of them. The *Istituto per la Ricostruzione Industriale* or *IRI*, founded as a State investment agency, rapidly extended State control of industry.

The policy of *autarchia* was a hopeless one in view of Italy's lack of coal; her gas and oil had not yet been

Opposite The Red Desert of Michelangelo Antonioni's film is both an industrial milieu and a state of mind. One of the latest Italian directors to achieve world celebrity, Antonioni continues Italy's post-war cinematographic realism in an atmosphere of introspection and alienation that the 'neo-capitalist' economic miracle is supposed to induce.

discovered and at that time industry still depended on coal as a source of power. Much publicity was given to 'The battle of the Grain', the Fascist attempt to make the country self-sufficient in wheat. It was unsuccessful, despite big State investment in technical improvements for this purpose. Perhaps the regime's proudest boast was its lavish public works programmes by which unemployment was kept down, marshes were drained and motor-roads were built. In rural localities, such as at Foggia, houses were built for a certain number of newly settled farmers. After a concerted effort, the criminal conspiratorial organization of the Mafia appeared to be suppressed in Sicily, but in fact was expelled to Brooklyn and Chicago, or had simply been forced to lie low. The period since the Second World War has shown that much the same can be achieved without a Fascist police state and its propaganda. Mussolini, moreover, did nothing to solve the problem, or problems, of the *Mezzogiorno*.

In order to 'bury the lie of universal democratic suffrage' a new electoral law was introduced in 1928. It called for the Corporations and certain other associations to present 1,000 names to the Fascist Grand Council, which from these would select 400. The electorate was then to accept or reject these 400 candidates for the Chamber. In 1929 the Chamber was elected in this fashion. As its function had become acquiescence, the change was uninteresting. Ten years later the assembly of the Corporations replaced the Chamber altogether. Oddly enough the Senate established in Piedmont by Charles Albert's *Statuto* of 1848, and extended within the Kingdom of Italy in 1861, remained untouched throughout the Fascist period; it consisted of the King's nominees.

Mussolini's most impressive achievement is sometimes considered to have been the reconciliation of Church and State. Pope Pius XI was himself an authoritarian; the papacy, moreover, approved of the corporate idea, which was related to the attitudes expressed in the Encyclical *Rerum Novarum*. Negotiations were begun in 1926 and bore fruit in three agreements signed at the Lateran in February 1929, the Treaty, the Concordat and a financial settlement. The Treaty recognised the sovereignty and independence of a small Vatican state of 109 acres; Catholicism, as in the *Statuto*, was declared to be the 'sole religion of the State'. By the Concordat the views of the Church on marriage were allowed to prevail and religious instruction was made compulsory in all the schools.

As Richard Webster says, 'Italy became a confessional state, unique among the Great Powers of contemporary Europe'. From the point of view of the Risorgimento the lay State had been defeated and the Church had won.

Looking back now it is hard to see what Mussolini thought he had gained by the Lateran Pacts beyond the prestige of a seeming alliance with the papacy: he had even given recognition to Catholic Action, a militant organization within the Church claiming authority over laymen. He was probably willing to surrender the schools to the Church because the Fascists were planning to submerge the influence of the schools beneath that of their own youth organizations. The young from the age of four to eighteen were indoctrinated with the Fascist philosophy of force in after-school gatherings arranged by what was until 1937 called the *Opera Nazionale Balilla*, and after that *Gioventù Italiana del Littorio* (GIL). From 18 to 21 young people were impressed either into the *Gruppi Universitari Fascisti* (GUF), or the *Giovani Fascisti* if they were not students. As a matter of fact when Mussolini first became Prime Minister he had appointed Croce's friend, Gentile, to be Minister of Education. The result had been a relatively liberal piece of educational legislation in 1923 which, however, had compelled religious instruction in the elementary schools. Now the Concordat did the same for the secondary schools. In ostensible alliance, Fascism and Catholic Action put an end to Gentile's liberalism. In the universities, not only were the students obliged to join the GUF – the majority of them were certainly keen Fascists – but also in 1931 all professors in the universities dependent on the State were obliged to take an oath to 'the King, his royal successors and the Fascist regime'. Eleven professors, most of them distinguished people, refused to comply and were dismissed – including Gaetano De Sanctis, professor of Greek history, and the art historian Lionello Venturi.

The Fascist period stultified intellectual and artistic life, though it was not as paralysing as National Socialism in Germany. Bacchelli wrote one of his greatest novels in 1927, *Il Diavolo al Portelungo*, and Moravia's *Gli Indifferenti* came out in 1929. The poets Montale and Ungaretti continued to work – Ungaretti often in France, after his initial support of Fascism. Fascist architecture was generally heavy, bleak and pompous, like the Milan railway station, but Michelucci's station at Florence was a happier contribution, as were Pier Luigi Nervi's architectural

Opposite Mussolini's newspaper, *Il Popolo d'Italia* for 13 July 1930. Beside a cartoon symbolising '*Mare Nostrum*' ('Our sea' – the Fascist slogan for the Mediterranean), two columns headed 'A Grotesque Anti-Fascist Venture' report the plane crash on the Gotthard of Giovanni Bassanesi, an anti-Fascist émigré, after launching

subversive leaflets' over Milan. Among similar enterprises at this time, the most famous was that in which the poet Lauro de Bosis, on 3 October 1931, flew over Rome and dropped 400,000 manifestos on the Corso and Piazza Venezia. He vanished with his plane, presumably having crashed in the sea on the way back to France.

Mussolini, surrounded by Blackshirts in Piazza del Populo, following the so-called March on Rome, 28 October 1922. On that date, it is true, the Fascists had secured the lines of communication between north Italy and Rome, but Mussolini himself waited in Milan until summoned by King Victor Emmanuel III. He arrived in Rome, by train, only on the morning of the 30th.

Right Giacomo Matteotti (centre), a leading Socialist Deputy after the First World War, is here seen outside his party's headquarters. He eloquently denounced Fascist strong-arm methods in the 1923 election campaign, and on 10 June 1924 was murdered by the Fascists. Mussolini himself appeared to have some degree of responsibility in the killing. The opposition parties withdrew in protest from the Chamber, and Mussolini defiantly increased the use of blackjack and castor-oil squads to silence the anti-Fascists.

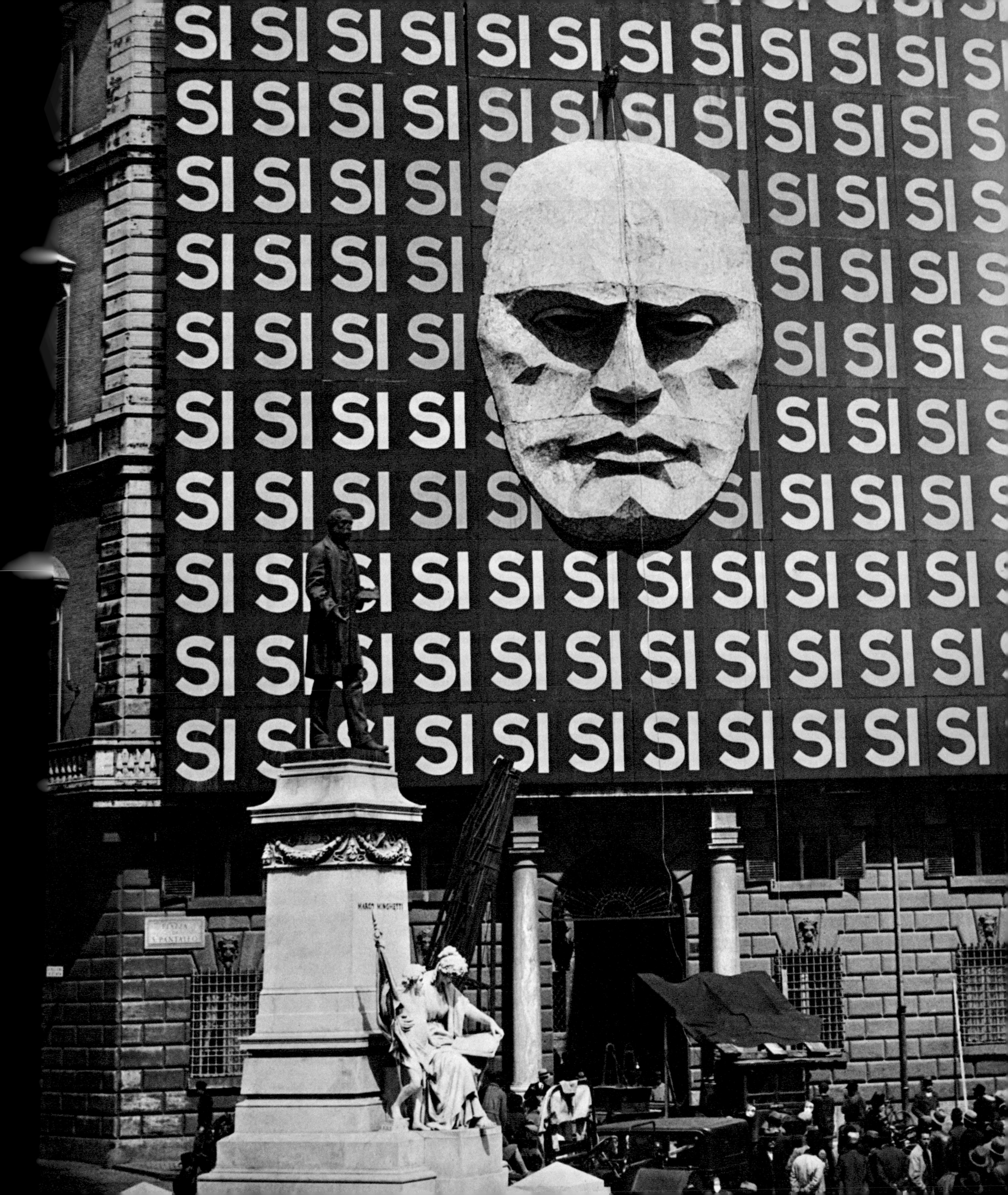
SI

engineering works. Giorgio de' Chirico was the outstanding Italian painter of the day; he, too, spent much of his time in France, having been associated with Apollinaire and surrealism. Croce's home in Naples remained a centre of liberal thought and discussion, and *La Critica* continued to appear. It seems that Mussolini felt Croce's freedom to be worthwhile as good propaganda abroad.

Mussolini's foreign policy was affected by the inclusion of some 250,000 German-speaking South Tyrolese and 400,000 to 500,000 Slovenes and Croats in post-Versailles Italy. The Fascist regime denied all minority rights and tried to coerce these people into becoming Italian; even their tombstones had to be reinscribed in Italian. This caused much bitter feeling against Italy in Austria, the Weimar Republic and Yugoslavia. In this period Mussolini took Albania under his protection and began to champion Hungary's claims against the Little Entente which included Yugoslavia, then the Triune Kingdom of the Serbs, the Croats and the Slovenes. When Hitler came to power in Germany in January 1933, Mussolini sought means to protect Austria from German expansion. For at first he was not attracted by what Hitler liked to regard as the sister revolution in Germany. Mussolini's antipathy towards German National Socialism reached its climax in July 1934 when the Austrian Chancellor, Dollfuss, was murdered by Austrian Nazis. By this time the *Duce* had associated both Austria and Hungary with Italy through economic agreements.

Having built up the conception of the new Fascist Rome and Roman Empire, and having encouraged an increase in population, Mussolini was but to be expected to seek to wipe out the disgrace of Adowa by the subjection of Abyssinia. He attacked that country in October 1935, and did not regret the consequent break with the League of Nations and with Britain. By May 1936 he could proclaim King Victor Emmanuel as Emperor of Abyssinia. All but the staunchest anti-Fascists applauded this success for the Italians, the 'have-nots' to whom the British had seemed to grudge any imperial expansion: now Mussolini and Fascism were at the height of their glory.

In the very next month the first Popular Front Government under Léon Blum was formed in France. Mussolini felt this almost as a personal affront, the more so since a Popular Front had won the elections in Spain in the previous February. When Franco attacked the Spanish Republican Government in July and appealed to Italy for help Mussolini responded with enthusiasm. The Spanish Civil War dragged on for nearly three years and drained away Italy's resources; it also confronted Mussolini with his Italian enemies.

Matteotti had not been the only critic of Fascism; the élite in all the great cities had resisted fearlessly, publishing their anti-Fascist journals as long as they could, and then fighting the regime clandestinely. The Liberal editor of *Il Mondo*, Giovanni Amendola, was savagely assaulted by Fascist thugs, then escaped to Nice where he died of his injuries in 1926. Piero Gobetti, a young Liberal–Socialist of Turin, suffered much the same fate. Antonio Gramsci, very much a pre-Stalin Communist, was arrested in 1927 and died in prison ten years later. Others, like Ferruccio Parri and Ernesto Rossi, defended themselves with great spirit at their trials. Many were banished to the island of Lipari. Others like Sturzo, Salvemini, Sforza, Carlo Rosselli, Saragat and Nenni escaped abroad, and Paris became the main centre of their anti-Fascist activities. This was one reason why Mussolini was hypersensitive about France, particularly when its Prime Minister was a Socialist as well. When the Spanish Civil War began, Nenni and many of his friends volunteered to fight for the Republic. Italian Communists also volunteered in numbers, including Luigi Longo, leader of the Italian Communist Party today. In March 1937 Italian anti-Fascists (among them Nenni) helped to disarray Fascist troops at the battle of Guadalajara. Soon after Carlo Rosselli, a Florentine close in sympathy to Salvemini, predicted in a broadcast from Paris that Fascism would be defeated, 'today in Spain, tomorrow in Italy'. In June 1937 he was murdered at Bagnoles de l'Orne in Normandy, by Cagoulards at the instigation of the Italian government: it was the thirteenth anniversary of the murder of Matteotti.

The Spanish Civil War, in which Hitler also sent help to Franco, paved the way for the Italian–German understanding which Mussolini named the Rome–Berlin Axis in November 1936, an agreement which found formal expression in the Steel Pact signed in May 1939. Hitler had always intended to bring about this constellation, and invited Mussolini to Germany in September 1937. His return visit was paid in May 1938 when he declared eternal recognition of Italy's Alpine frontier. By this he meant the Brenner Pass, renouncing all German or Austrian claims to the South Tyrol. From about this time Mussolini introduced anti-Semitic measures into Italy.

Opposite Posters and a mask of Mussolini covering the façade of Palazzo Braschi in Rome, urging a yes-vote in the elections of 25 March 1934. Voters were asked to vote in answer to the question: 'Do you approve the list of deputies drawn up by the Fascist Grand Council?' This was the last time Italians voted even nominally for a Chamber of Deputies under Fascism: in 1939 it was replaced by the Chamber of Fasces and Corporations.

The Steel Pact was followed in three months' time by the German attack upon Poland which precipitated the Second World War. Italy, exhausted by her intervention in Spain, remained neutral until June 1940 when Mussolini hastily declared war in time to claim some booty from a defeated France. There was little enthusiasm for the war in Italy and much feeling against it and against the Germans. Ciano, Mussolini's son-in-law and Foreign Minister, a futile but entertaining character, had tried helplessly to warn the *Duce.* By the spring of 1943 Italy had been defeated all round, except where the Germans took over the battle on her account, as in Greece. Already in March there had been an astonishing strike at Fiat's in which the directors encouraged the workers. Serious strikes followed in Milan. All these were in effect peace demonstrations. When Mussolini paid one of his routine visits to Hitler in April, Ciano's successor at the Italian Foreign Office told Ribbentrop that the strikes would make it impossible for Italy to go on fighting. In July after the Allies had landed in Sicily, Mussolini was induced to call together the Fascist Grand Council, which had not met since December 1939. Veiled criticism was levelled at the *Duce* and an obscure motion passed in favour of a return to royal authority. The King took the opportunity to dismiss and arrest Mussolini on 25 July 1943, and to appoint Marshal Badoglio as Prime Minster. Fascism seemed to explode like a soap bubble and Italy rejoiced with all her heart.

There now followed the most bitter disappointments of all. Badoglio, while trying to get in touch with the Allies, declared that the war would continue. His aim was to prevent a German occupation of Italy which had already been prepared down to the last detail. Meanwhile the Allies bombed Milan and other cities. Badoglio's government, moreover, did nothing to restore the liberty that was now so much desired, though the restoration of free government in the circumstances would have required the heroism of a Mazzini or a Garibaldi. On 8 September it was announced that Italy had signed an armistice with the Allies. The Germans rushed troops to Rome and beyond. The King and Badoglio hastily left Rome for the south, where the Allies were already in possession. In Naples at the end of the month a spontaneous rising, the *Quattro Giornate*, helped to throw back the Germans before the Allied armies moved in.

One of the worst discouragements of all was the sensational helicopter rescue of Mussolini from the Gran Sasso in the Abruzzi by the Germans on 12 September. Hitler then compelled him to set up a neo-Fascist Republic with headquarters on Lake Garda. This Republic of Salò had a certain appeal just when the monarchy was discredited, and it significantly adopted a Socialist programme including workers' control of industry. Mussolini hoped to attract the industrial workers of northern Italy who had gone out on strike in the spring.

From the time of the armistice small groups of Italian soldiers had escaped with their arms to the mountains. Enthusiastic members of the clandestine *Partito d'Azione*, or of the Communist Party, joined them, and in Venetia and eastern Lombardy Catholics were numerous among the partisans. Gradually the *Resistenza* to Mussolini, now Hitler's puppet, grew into a movement so important that it was spoken of as the Second Risorgimento. There were those, of course, who preferred the Republic of Salò, but it is true to say that the better elements saw in the Resistance the way to cleanse Italy of the evil of Fascism and to advance towards political freedom, which this time should be married to social justice, as Mazzini would have wished. On the whole the partisans were Republicans, though they spurned the Republic of Salò. Most of the peasants as well as the industrial workers tried to help the Resistance, so that the Second Risorgimento had more social substance than the first. A clandestine *Comitato di Liberazione Nazionale* was set up in Rome and established contact with the chief anti-Fascists in the northern cities. Six political parties had emerged and were represented on the CLN: Liberals, Christian Democrats, *Demolaburisti*, Socialists, Communists and *Partito d'Azione* – the last embodied the ideas of Carlo Rosselli and used his device of *Giustizia e Libertà.* When the Allies took Rome early in June 1944, an elderly pre-war politician called Bonomi, formerly a Socialist but now a *Demolaburista*, succeeded Badoglio as Prime Minister. Sforza and the Communist leader, Togliatti, had returned to Italy from abroad and served under Badoglio. Now they joined Bonomi, together with Sturzo's former lieutenant Alcide De Gasperi. In the north the leading figure, both as partisan and politician, was the old anti-Fascist, Ferruccio Parri, or 'Maurizio', according to his *nom de guerre.* In August 1944 the Allies, with partisan support, liberated Florence, but failed to prevent the retreating Germans from destroying the exquisite *Ponte Santa Trinità* across the Arno. It was not until April 1945 that the great northern cities were liberated. A few

Special sale to get rid of goods from countries supporting sanctions against Italy during the Abyssinian war of 1935–6. Mussolini was furious when the League of Nations imposed economic sanctions in November 1935 in response to Italy's aggression against Abyssinia, and he ordered a boycott of such foreign goods. The sanctions were not effective; rather they were a cause of further estrangement from England and, more remotely, a factor leading up to the eventual alliance between Italy and Germany.

Mussolini visiting a boys' camp of the youth organization, the *Gioventù Italiana del Littorio*, at Forlì, near his birthplace of Predappio in the Romagna, July 1939. Regimentation and militarization of Italians under Fascism, while not so thoroughgoing as in Germany, was aimed at all sections of the population and included men, women and children.

The Fascists made a cult of 'manly' toughness. To bring paunchy officials into line with the party image, Mussolini ordered them to keep fit. Here some of them are going through gymnastics at the Foro Mussolini, the sports ground in Rome now known as the Foro Italico.

Mussolini, Hitler, King Victor Emmanuel III, Queen Elena, and their retinues at a review of troops in Via dei Trionfi during Hitler's visit to Rome in May 1938, which returned Mussolini's visit to Germany of September 1937. The exchange of courtesies con-

firmed the close relations that had been established between the two countries during the Spanish Civil War. These relations culminated in the 1939 Steel Pact, an agreement that prepared the ground for the Second World War.

Mussolini and Neville Chamberlain with their Foreign Ministers, Count Ciano (far left) and Lord Halifax in Rome in January 1939 after the Munich Agreement of September 1938. Chamberlain obtained the withdrawal of Italian troops from Spain (only after Franco's victory was assured) but in return recognized Italy's conquest of Ethiopia.

France would not recognize Italy's Ethiopian Empire and had supported the Spanish Republicans. These irredentist posters were put up on 1 June 1940, ten days before Italy's entry into the Second World War and the 'stab in the back' campaign against France. Already in 1938 slogans had been launched proclaiming these territories as Italian by right.

Italian dead during the winter campaign of 1941 in Russia.
Mussolini eagerly agreed to Hitler's request, in June 1941, for
Italian participation in the attack on Russia, and between the late
summer of 1941 and early in 1943 at least ten Italian divisions were
sent to the eastern front. Badly equipped, they suffered tremendous casualties. Italian requests for the return of prisoners were
lackadaisically received by the Russians for years after the war
ended.

On the fall of Fascism, 25 July 1943, the statues and symbols of the
old regime were attacked and destroyed by the public.

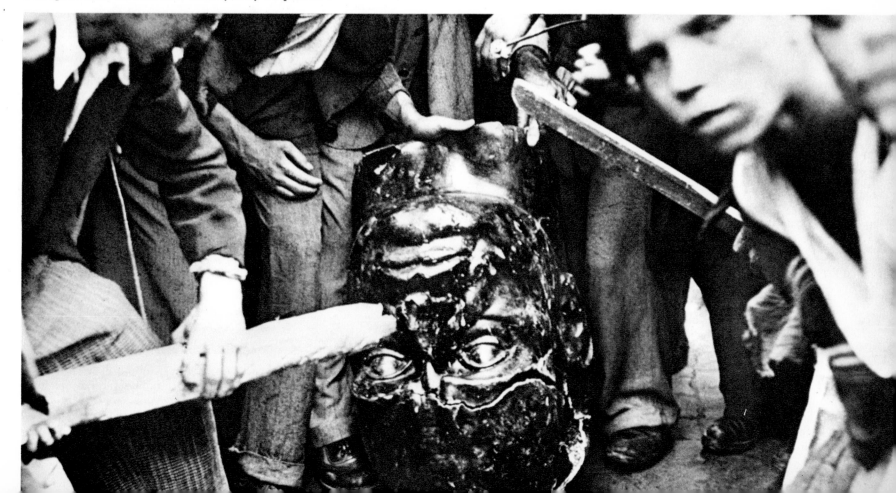

Prince Humbert succeeded his unpopular father, who had abdicated, on 9 May 1946. In the referendum on whether Italy should be a monarchy or a republic, the monarchy was defeated by 12,717,923 votes to 10,719,284. Rome and the south had voted monarchist, but Italy became a republic even though the slim majority did not represent widespread enthusiasm.

Italy's first four Presidents since the establishment of the Republic in 1946. From left to right, Antonio Segni (1962–4); Enrico De Nicola (1946–8); Giovanni Gronchi (1955–62); Luigi Einaudi (1948–55). President Segni resigned owing to ill-health in December 1964 and was succeeded by Giuseppe Saragat, leader of the Social Democrat party and thus the first socialist President of Italy.

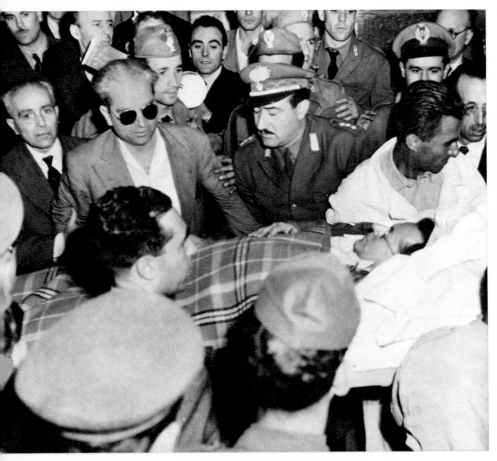

The Communist Party leader Palmiro Togliatti after an attempt on his life by a student, 14 July 1948. The disorders, threatening a Communist take-over of the country, which ensued were firmly repressed by the Minister of the Interior, Scelba. Togliatti recovered to lead the Communist Party for another fifteen years until his death in August 1964.

Alcide De Gasperi, Christian Democrat leader during the crucial post-war years, and Mario Scelba, Minister of the Interior, reading the Communist daily *L'Unità's* acknowledgement of the Christian Democrat election victory in 1948. De Gasperi headed a series of governments which were slow-moving in domestic reforms but kept Italy aligned with the West.

days later Mussolini and his mistress were caught, shot and then hanged by their heels in Piazza Loreto, Milan.

Italy Since the Second World War

For the first time since 1922 Italy could resume the course of constructive democracy. The losses in the war had been hideous. Railways and bridges had been destroyed, but at least the great industrial network in the north had been saved from German destruction, thanks to partisan precautions, as well as to the early surrender of the German armies in Italy. The Marxist parties hoped to use the local branches of the Committees of National Liberation all over the country to impose a Marxist system; they revived the familiar cry for workers' control of industry. The Socialist leader, Nenni, who had early returned from France, was concerned above all to preserve the 'unity of the working class'. A pact he made to this effect with the Communists while in exile in 1934 made it difficult to liberate his party from strong Communist influence – certainly until he joined the government in December 1963. Since the elections of 1948 the Communists, moreover, have polled better than the chronically divided and dividing Socialists.

The country's first problem, after the Allies had provided immediate economic relief, was the drafting of a Constitution. A *Consulta* or Consultative Assembly, consisting of nominees of the six parties and pre-Fascist deputies, met in September 1945 and elected Sforza its President. The Consulta's chief task was to arrange for the election of a constituent assembly and for a referendum on the 'institutional' question as to whether Italy should be a monarchy or a republic. Both the election and the referendum were held on 2 June 1946. Although Prince Humbert had taken his father's place on 9 May, the monarchy was defeated by 12,717,923 votes to 10,719,284, Rome and the south having voted monarchist. On 2 June Italy, therefore, became a republic, though not by a majority representing widespread enthusiasm. Nevertheless, regrets for the monarchy disappeared relatively soon. In the election De Gasperi's Christian Democrats gained 207 seats in the Constituent Assembly; Nenni's Socialists,

115, Togliatti's Communists, 104, and the other parties, insignificant results.

The Allies made formal peace with Italy in February 1947. The African colonies had, of course, been lost. It was decided to preserve the Brenner frontier, but establish a Free Territory of Trieste under United Nations control, with Istria, Zara and the islands going to Yugoslavia. The plan, however, proved abortive, and in 1954 the Free Territory was divided between Italy and Yugoslavia so that the city of Trieste remained Italian.

The Chamber was in future to be elected every five years by universal and direct suffrage and proportional representation. The Senate was to be elected every six years by larger regional constituencies. The way towards future governmental decentralization was prepared by declaring that the nineteen regions of Italy were to have a considerable degree of autonomy. This was accorded to Sicily in May 1946, to Sardinia, the Val d'Aosta (partly French-speaking) and Trentino-Alto Adige (with a German-speaking minority of about 250,000) in February 1948. Much later, in January 1963, the region of Friuli-Venezia Giulia, with Trieste as its capital, was given autonomy. The new constitution provided that the President of the Republic should be elected for seven years by a joint session of the two Chambers, with some extra representatives of the regions.

After Parri had served for a few months as Prime Minister, De Gasperi was appointed to the office by the provisional president De Nicola. Until his death in 1953 De Gasperi was to remain as head of government and the post-war decade with its strengths and weaknesses belongs to him. This is not to say that he was happy about all developments, but the virtues in Italian development were largely his virtues and the defects, which emerged so much more strongly after his death, were the result of mistakes on his part, or simply his lack of interest in certain types of urgent problem.

He inherited a position in some ways similar to that of 1870. He had the problem to face of relations with the Church; the gulf between north and south was wider than ever; the State had been discredited by Fascism and a sense of it had to be encouraged once again from the start. The country's international position needed re-establishing. Where in the previous century industrialization had been an urgent task for the new State, this time the problem was reconstruction after the damage of the war. The essential difference was, of course, that the accession to power of the Christian Democrats marked the taking over of government for the first time in the history of a united Italy by the Roman Catholic forces, which hitherto had played no promoting role in Italian affairs. There was also the difference that the monarchy had gone. Italy was now a confessional republic. There was no rival court to that of the Pope. There was also to be no rival to the Church as an electioneering machine, and this was the first of De Gasperi's discoveries.

Party organisation did not much interest him. He looked upon the Catholic Action movement and the priests as the natural election agents and they brought in the majorities for him. His party had practically no machine of its own. This system was workable with a man of so strong a character as De Gasperi. His refuge during the Fascist period had been at the Vatican Library where he held a humble post. There were a number of people at the Vatican who took it for granted that he would be their employee as Prime Minister. This was not the case. He was devout, but he had what few Italians have, a clear sense of the State. This came from his Austrian origins; his first experience of parliamentary life was after all in the Austrian parliament, and however strongly the Italians of the first Risorgimento felt about expelling the Austrians from Italian territory, they might well have begged them to leave behind them some of their respect for the State. In De Gasperi they did. He brought the lay parties – Liberals, Republicans and Social Democrats – into his coalitions, but he helped to make the position of his own party hopelessly weak in relation to the Church in two ways: by calling in the Church for electoral aid, and by sanctioning the incorporation into the Republican Constitution of Mussolini's Lateran agreements with the Pope. To the dismay of genuine Liberals and Radicals, the Communist Party, following its policy of avoiding to appear anti-Catholic, voted with the Christian Democrats on this issue. Croce rejected what was known as the 'canonization' of the pacts as absurd. The fact that the first elected President, Luigi Einaudi, was not a Christian Democrat and was both intelligent and highly respected did not much detract from the impression that the centre of gravity in Rome had shifted towards the Tiber and the Apostolic palaces. Not all this was of the Vatican's making. There is a tendency among Christian Democrats, lacking the sense of State which De Gasperi had inherited from outside Italy, to act in a manner which they think will please the *Monsignori*; there are times, in such matters as cinema censorship for example, when the party seems more clerical than the clerics. Certainly it is far behind the Vatican in subtlety of approach towards the problem of Communism.

The problem of the south, neglected since unification, had been aggravated by the Allied occupation. There were those who even regretted that the progressive north and centre, materially and spiritually European, should be fettered to this backward area with its fearful poverty that recalled the worst of the Levant. Neglect by absentee landlords was a negative factor, added to the disabilities of poor soil and bad climate. Malaria was rife in the plains and caused the inhabitants to crowd into the hill-towns, from which they walked for hours each day to reach the big estates where they worked. For months in the summer there was no rain and the rivers dried up, while in the winter torrents swept away whole villages. Most of the population had no land, or only small plots, and were idle for over half the days of the year, not because they were lazy, but because there was nothing to do. Earthquakes were quite common, though few were as terrible as the one that destroyed the city of Messina in Sicily in 1908, and killed some 60,000 people. The instability of the very ground as a fact of everyday life has a terrible reality for southerners, including Salvemini who lost his wife and all his children at Messina, and Croce, whose parents both died in an earthquake. In Giolitti's time when the north was briskly progressing, the south made no economic gains and thus became even more backward. In the years of recovery since 1945, in the course of which large sums of money were made available by the government for southern development, the north has still progressed faster, so that the gap has constantly widened.

From the beginning northern capital was unwilling to invest in such an area. From the end of the nineteenth century up to 1915 dissatisfied or unemployed southern peasants solved their problem by emigrating to the United States, North Africa or France. After the First World War emigration was blocked and Mussolini found no comprehensive solution for the region's problems, preferring to dwell on the improvements which he could make in Africa rather than in the south, and holding out the brightest of prospects for emigrants to the colonies. Poverty remained hopeless and was inevitably accompanied by brutality and corruption.

Rioters in Genoa, 1 July 1960, protested against the holding of the neo-Fascist (M.S.I.) party congress, as well as against the Tambroni government's acceptance of neo-Fascist support in Parliament. No government could henceforth contemplate running the country with the aid of neo-Fascist votes; thus the possibility was opened for the creation of a new centre-left alignment.

Flanking the Social Democratic Head of the State, President Giuseppe Saragat, are the two leading Christian Democrats, Aldo Moro (right) and Amintore Fanfani. The centre-left government, which includes Pietro Nenni, leader of the left-wing Italian Socialist Party, is the first attempt to give this party a direct voice in the government.

The veteran Socialist Party leader, Pietro Nenni, speaking at the party's Central Committee in Rome in January 1962. A month later the party gave the government its support in Parliament, a first step towards its eventual entry into the centre-left coalition in December 1963.

Election posters pasted up on temporary hoardings in Palermo — a common practice during election campaigns in most Italian towns. The two-party system does not exist in Italy, and the numerous parties appear here side by side: neo-Fascist, Liberal, Monarchist, Christian Democrat, Socialist and others.

Pomona (in profile) and *Horse and Rider* by Marino Marini (b. 1901). One of the outstanding Italian sculptors who have continued the academic tradition in a modern vein, since the war he has had an international reputation. The figures are here seen in his studio in Milan.

Right, top The Neapolitan philosopher Benedetto Croce (1866–1952). Croce's liberal teaching, equating philosophy with history, had an immense influence and his international reputation was such that he was allowed to continue working relatively unimpeded under the Fascist regime.

When the Allies landed in Sicily and then on the mainland in 1943, they found the south's chronic poverty and squalor intensified by the dislocations and privations of war. It was one of Italy's disasters that from the autumn of 1943, for over a year, the country was cut in half. The progressive northern portion (slowly diminishing it is true) was imprisoned within Nazi–Fascist bonds, while the poor, backward, corrupt south was what the Allies were obliged to launch as the new Italy. The south had no experience of the Resistance movement. Once again it was the north which had, and took, the chance to be dynamic. This meant new differences between the north and south. And yet at the end of it all, in spite of the chaos which recalled the other *dopoguerra*, with disgruntled prisoners of war straggling back from Russia, India and Canada and the new head-on clash of Marxists and their opponents in the local committees of national liberation, the Italians seemed somehow more basically united, their common language and common way of life counting for more than their differences. This time the determination that the problem of southern development should be tackled was both official and sincere. American help made large-scale programmes feasible. A special fund for southern development, the *Casso per il Mezzogiorno*, was set up to finance and execute this development.

Roads were built, re-afforestation put in hand – the great forests of southern Italy had been ruined by cutting for railways and wartime needs – some of the big estates were in part divided into small holdings, and new settlements for the peasant owners were constructed under the land reform. Individual efforts suggested the government's real concern for the south; De Gasperi, for instance, decided when he saw the inhabited caves of Matera in Lucania that a special law must be passed to clear these holes in the rock and provide new housing in blocks of flats. The total effort has been impressive, and in scope and intention unprecedented in Italian history. In the first fifteen years of the Cassa's activities the equivalent of £1,000 million was spent on southern development. Other incentives, such as cheap loans and tax rebates to industrialists willing to set up new plants in these districts have naturally had their effect. Yet even so vast an effort has not convinced the southerner that the north really cares. Land reform was hurried through under pressure of peasant riots guided by the Communists, and in this sense has been a political as much as an economic or social step. This problem has now to be re-thought, as

the beginnings of real planning – absent from much of the expenditure so far – show clearly enough that agriculture in the south, as elsewhere in Italy, must be efficient, specialized, where possible mechanized and, in every case, better organized. Division of land into small plots for private ownership cuts across all of these pointers to the future.

The industrial expansion in the north culminated in the boom years of 1959 to 1963. They were called the *Miracolo*, after the term used to describe the West German boom. Expansion was remarkable, though not difficult to explain. Enrico Mattei played a large part in the discovery of natural gas, mainly in the Po Valley, which provided a fuel and a basic material for petro-chemical works sufficiently valuable to offset Italy's lack of other raw materials. Money for aid and investment poured in from the United States and elsewhere, partly out of human considerations in recognition of the suffering and destruction caused by the war, partly to counteract the influence of Italy's large Communist Party. As an immediate threat to democratic government, the party's strength was often exaggerated – dramatization of any predicament, whether serious or otherwise, is a national trait – still it was the largest in the West and the Communists soon became the second largest group in the Italian Parliament. Labour was abundant and cheap because unemployment was high, though there was a shortage of skilled workers for many years. Opportunity and training, however, helped to overcome this deficiency, but northern demand for labour upset plans for development in the south. Poor southerners who could educate themselves sufficiently had in the past crowded into small official jobs in Rome and the north, jobs too badly paid to interest many northerners. An unfortunate feature of the Italian bureaucracy is that the system was imposed by the north and the personnel was found in the south. Once again the State got the worst of two worlds. With expansion in the north, the demand for labour brought southerners pouring into the factories of Milan and Turin. Their interest in acquiring and cultivating land in their own provinces had waned. Although oil flowed from the new field at Gela, and natural gas was discovered in Lucania, the north continued to progress much faster than the south. In the future tourism may help to equalize conditions. Even the fact that hotels have been built in the southern regions and tourists now penetrate in numbers to Calabria and Lucania offers some guarantee against

Opposite, centre The writer Ignazio Silone (b. 1900), from the Abruzzi, was imprisoned as a Communist by the Fascists but was expelled from the Party in 1929. He then lived in Switzerland, returning to Italy after the war. Some of his best-known books *Fontemara, Pane e Vino* describe the situation of the peasants under Fascist dictatorship.

Opposite, below Self-portrait of Carlo Levi (b. 1902), who became famous after the war as the author of *Christ Stopped at Eboli* (1946), which described peasant conditions in a Lucanian village.

a return to the old neglect and ignorance. The exodus northward was an admission that southern development could not keep pace with the prospects originally offered, even though the post-war governments were doing more in a dozen years than had been attempted in the previous seventy years of unification. But the massive internal migration of peasants eager to work brought north and south literally face to face for the first time.

All these developments were initiated during De Gasperi's period of power. The new respect which Italy gained abroad was also the achievement of De Gasperi. He brought Italy into the United Nations and made her a prime mover in the cause of a united Europe. His successes at home were more limited. It is true that he laid the foundations for industrial expansion, but even in the period from 1948 when his party enjoyed an absolute majority, he made no real attempt to introduce such urgent measures as reform of the Civil Service, or of the school system, which were necessary for the nation's future. He left the country internally as ill-equipped as he left his party, yet his great services in providing stability, respect and the basis for prosperity cannot be gainsaid.

Italian politics did not recover from De Gasperi's death for ten years. The coalition system continued but no great personalities emerged and scepticism about Christian Democratic rule grew. A succession of Prime Ministers – Segni, who was later to be President, Pella, Fanfani, Scelba and Zoli – attempted variants of De Gasperi's idea of coalitions, including as far as possible all the democratic elements in political life, and isolating the Communist opposition. The party had two main difficulties. The first was that its nature as a coalition itself rather than a party became increasingly evident. After De Gasperi's hand was removed the internal divisions were clear. They were partly personal, but there was also a basis of real political conflict. As the centre coalition gradually approached extinction because the smaller parties became incompatible, the Christian Democrats, now without an overall majority, had to choose whether to look towards the moderate left for their allies, or to the right. This brought them to their second difficulty. Some of its leading figures preferred a leftward look and others the right, and whatever decision was taken, there would be serious discontent. But the possibility for some time of having dealings with the extreme right ended in the summer of 1960 when Signor Tambroni attempted to rule with only

the neo-Fascists to support his own Christian Democratic votes, and the result was serious rioting throughout the country. The Resistance movement had not altogether been forgotten. What had been forgotten was that the country, whatever its governments might represent, was moving towards the left. This was obvious enough from election figures: by 1963 one in four Italians was voting for the Communist Party.

The Communist Party had its obvious attractions. For one thing it was the one serious party of opposition. It could gather to it all the grievances rife in a country suffering first from the damage of war, then from the effects of a quick reconstruction, and the social changes resulting from rapid industrial expansion. Many social problems had been left untouched. The traditional anti-clericalism in such areas as Emilia and parts of Tuscany was now interpreted in Marxist terms. The Communists were better organized than any other party and, under Togliatti, better led. In alliance with the Socialists they ruled in many municipalities and provincial administrations in central and northern Italy and made a point of providing efficient administration. They were constantly able to denounce scandals and corruption which were undoubtedly a part of the Christian Democratic regime. From the early post-war period they dominated intellectual life. One of the great Christian Democratic failures was the inability to enlist creative artists, or thinkers of almost any kind. The post-war period has not been marked by great heights of cultural achievement. There has nevertheless been some serious work. The fashion for clear and simple prose in reaction to the exaggerations of Fascist style was set by Carlo Levi when in 1946 he published his *Christ Stopped at Eboli*, an account of his exile in Lucania under the Fascists. It was a landmark in setting not only the fashion in style, but in subject; the south and social problems in general dominated the work of a number of novelists and at the same time, of course, gave the Italian cinema its distinctive voice. Here again writers and directors were inclined to be left wing. Perhaps because they had been denied the chance of extreme-left engagement under Mussolini, or perhaps because they found Christian Democracy an uninspiring concept, they applied themselves to social studies, a critical realism of protest. The cinema from the time of Rossellini's *Rome, Open City* and De Sica's *Bicycle Thieves* to Visconti's attempt in *Rocco and his Brothers* to study the southern problem through the experiences of southern immigrants in

The writers Alberto Moravia (b. 1907) and Pier Paolo Pasolini (b. 1922), seen in front of a painting by Renato Guttuso (b. 1912) at Nuova Pesa Gallery in Rome, 1962. Pasolini and Guttuso share the left-wing views common to many present-day Italian writers and artists; the right wing has not been very productive. Moravia is Italy's best-known living novelist.

Right Sicilian peasants at a Saturday night dance contrasted with *Dolce Vita* poster (*below*) advertising Federico Fellini's film, which purported to give a panorama of the pastimes of Roman life, from the lower middle class and up. The background of the film, the city of Rome, was real and appeared to lend substance to daydream sequences of a Roman life that scarcely exists.

Left The Pirelli building in Milan, by Pier Luigi Nervi and Gio Ponti. Nervi (b. 1891), a distinguished engineer and architect, has a long-standing reputation in Italy and abroad for daring and pleasing solutions to large-scale construction problems. His recent important buildings include two stadiums erected in Rome for the Olympic Games and the International Fair pavilion in Turin.

Right Statue of Camillo Olivetti (1868–1943), founder of the business-machine manufacturing company at Ivrea, Piedmont. The sculpture, by Mirko, which stands in the entrance of the main plant, has a mosaic surface.

Milan, and in Fellini's panorama of high life, *La Dolce Vita*, has offered a constant reminder to a large public that Italian society is far from perfect. This social concern has touched some of the poets; Quasimodo for example, Italy's Nobel prize-winner, disclaims party affiliations but writes of the horrors of war and social inequalities, and is a regular signer of petitions. Moravia, a prolific and engaged writer and critic, would also make little of political labels, but shows impatience with the governing party. Bassani is a Socialist. In the field of the visual arts the left by no means has the whole field. Its most prominent social realist is Guttuso, a member of the Central Committee of the Communist Party, who refused publicly to be moved, as were many of the intellectuals, by the repression of the rising in Hungary. During the past decade or more the internationally recognized forward wing among Italian artists has included the painters Afro, Burri, Vedova, Turcato, Scialoja and Dorazio and the sculptors Marino Marini, Giò and Arnoldo Pomodoro, Andrea and Pietro Cascella, Colla and Somaini. Perhaps the finest book published in Italy after the war was the Prince of Lampedusa's *Il Gattopardo*. This lyrical re-evocation of a noble household at the time of the Risorgimento is set in Sicily. It wins its social significance in an oddly indirect way. The setting of part of the novel is Palma de Montechiaro in the south of Sicily. Danilo Dolci, the writer and social worker, held a congress there which included a study of conditions in the town. It was not difficult to draw the conclusion that southern Sicily was better off a century ago than it is today.

Fortunately for Christian Democracy in particular, and Italian democracy in general, the Communists have had serious difficulties of their own. Togliatti imposed upon the party two precepts: first, that it was to be a mass party, not just a group of activists, and secondly that it was to work patiently to achieve power by constitutional means. Togliatti was an outstanding tactician and was able almost up to his death in August 1964 to maintain absolute leadership. Even in his lifetime, however, there were signs among the ranks of impatience and a feeling that constitutionalism was too weak a prescription. More revolution was wanted. That was why the vigorous intervention in Hungary of the Red Army impressed the rank and file of Italian Communists. At the same time a more moderate section of the party was thinking in terms of less dogmatic Marxism and a broader left-wing front to include all professed representatives of the workers from Communists right round to Social Democrats.

What helped to put the Communists into difficulties and, had it been resolutely followed, might well have cut deeply into Communist support, was the decision of the Socialists at the end of 1963 to enter the government as allies of the Christian Democrats. This move was a slow maturing within the Socialist leadership of the need to break with the Communists and—for the first time—to take a hand in the conduct of affairs. It was made possible by three factors: Signor Aldo Moro, then Secretary of the Christian Democratic Party and later Prime Minister, possessed the necessary skill and tact to bring his party round to accepting alliance with Marxists. Then the atmosphere at the Vatican had changed with the accession in 1958 of John XXIII, who followed Pius XII, and almost immediately showed his dislike of the habit of direct interference by the hierarchy in Italian politics. His successor Paul VI, is generally in favour of a centre-left approach to Italian affairs. The third, and perhaps dominant, factor is that public opinion had shown that right-wing alliances were out and that the country as a whole was certainly more to the left than its governments had allowed. Up to this point it was true enough of the Christian Democratic party. As represented in Parliament it was inclined to be more conservative than the party taken as a whole. This was because the choice of deputies depended first on the drawing up of lists and then on preferential votes; in both these processes pressure groups such as Catholic Action and the industrialists could make their wishes felt.

Signor Moro formed the first full-scale centre-left government in December 1963. Before that the Socialists had agreed to the half step of supporting coalition from outside the governmental benches. By his decision to enter the government Nenni saw his party split again, the extreme left which favoured co-operation with the Communists instead of the Christian Democrats breaking away to form a party of its own. The government was handicapped from the beginning by the economic recession which early put a stop to any fundamental reforms which would have cost large amounts of money. With Christian Democrats and Socialists as the main partners in the alliance, the coalition also comprised the Republican and Social Democratic parties. Indeed, it was Signor Saragat, the former leader of the Social Democratic party who did much to bring the alliance together, and it was a good omen when this life-long

Opposite The Autostrada del Sole, the north-south motor highway which will run from Milan to Reggio Calabria when completed. By 1965 it had reached as far south as Salerno. The Bologna-Florence section, a view of which is shown here, in particular required some remarkable feats of engineering to span the mountainous terrain. Like the railway network in its time, the highway is expected to help stimulate Italian economic development and provide a needed link between the industrial north and the underdeveloped south.

moderate Socialist was elected President of the Republic at the end of 1964, to succeed Segni whom illness had forced into retirement. His election combined with the accession of a careful and moderate Pope provided conditions which might offer greater political stability. There was a consensus of opinion that since the death of De Gasperi the centre-left was the best chance yet devised of firm government, offering some guarantees against extremism. It was inevitable that an agreement talked about for a long time should in practice have seemed rather pallid in achievement. But the alternatives looked worse, and as there is no other party but the Christian Democrats likely to be in a position to govern the country for as far ahead as one can see, it seems well that the Socialists should at least have the chance of gaining experience in power. Until this experiment was begun, of the three mass parties in Italy – Christian Democrats, Communists and Socialists – the first appeared doomed to perpetual government and the others to perpetual opposition. It would be regrettable if the only choice in Italy were between a popular front or a clerical regime, which was how the situation was shaping, and at least the Socialist departure from attitudes of the cold war brought a hope of greater flexibility.

IMPORTANT DATES IN THE HISTORY OF ITALY

from c 1600	Archaeological evidence of Minoan/Mycenaean contact with Italy
c 1000	Beginning of the Iron Age in Italy
early 8th cent.	Renewal of Greek contacts with Italy
8th–6th cent.	Etruscan civilization at its height
753	Traditional date of the foundation of Rome
	Colonization of southern Italy by Greek settlers:
c 750	Cumae founded by Euboeans
c 734	Syracuse founded by Corinthians
c 720	Sybaris founded by Achaeans
6th cent.	Establishment of Carthaginian power in Sicily
c 575	Archaeological evidence for the urbanization of Rome
c 535	Coalition of Carthaginians and Etruscans defeats Greeks in battle off Alalia
510	Expulsion of 'Tarquin the Proud'. The end of Etruscan domination and of the Monarchy in Rome. First consuls appointed, Rome becomes a republic. Traditional date
c 480–290	The expansion of Roman power in Italy. The growth of the Roman confederacy. Wars between Rome and the Latins; wars with Samnites, Etruscans and Gauls
474	Greeks defeat the Etruscans in a sea battle off Cumae
c 450	Roman legal code of the Twelve Tables
406–367	The 'Empire' of Dionysius I of Syracuse
387	Sack of Rome by the Gauls
321	Battle of the Caudine Forks
312	Construction of the Via Appia
c 287	Decisions of the Plebs are given force of law
281–275	Pyrrhus invades Italy and Sicily
264–241	First Punic War
c 254–184	Plautus
218–203	Hannibal in Italy
218–201	Second Punic War
216	Battle of Cannae
202	Elimination of Carthage as major power; battle of Zama
195–159	Terence
149	Death of Cato the Elder
146	Destruction of Carthage
135–132	First slave war in Sicily
133–121	Agrarian reforms of the Gracchi
106–43	Cicero
103–101	Second slave war in Sicily
90–88	Italic or Social War, followed by extension of Roman citizenship and Latin rights
c 84–54	Catullus
82–79	Dictatorship of Sulla
73–71	Slave war in Italy; the revolt of Spartacus
70–19	Virgil
65–8	Horace
63	Conspiracy of Catiline
60	Triumvirate of Pompey, Caesar and Crassus
59 BC–17 AD	Livy
49	Caesar crosses the Rubicon
48	Death of Pompey
44	Assassination of Caesar
43	Triumvirate of Octavian, Antony and Lepidus
42	Battle of Philippi
31	Battle of Actium
31 BC–14 AD	Establishment of the Principate; reign of Augustus
5 BC–65 AD	Seneca
8 AD	Exile of Ovid
	THE JULIO–CLAUDIAN DYNASTY:
14–37	Tiberius
37–41	Caligula
41–57	Claudius
57–68	Nero
68–9	Civil wars on the death of Nero
	THE FLAVIAN DYNASTY:
69–79	Vespasian
79–81	Titus
81–96	Domitian
79	Destruction of Pompeii and Herculaneum
96–8	Public assistance (alimenta) in Italy begun under Nerva
98–117	Trajan
117–38	Hadrian
138–61	Antoninus Pius
161–80	Marcus Aurelius
167–75	Invasion of Italy by Germanic tribes; Marcus Aurelius wages war with the invaders
180–92	Commodus
193–211	Septimius Severus Emperor. Increase in the power of the army. Age of the great jurists and lawyers
204–c 269	Plotinus
212	Roman citizenship granted to most of the inhabitants of the empire by Caracalla
c 235–68	Worsening situation within the empire: numerous usurpers, invasions of Barbarians, debasement of the coinage causing inflation

250	Persecution of the Christians by the Emperor Decius
c 258	Emperor Gallienus forms mobile cavalry defence, drives the Alamanni from northern Italy
268–76	Military recovery under the Illyrian Emperors, Claudius Gothicus, Aurelian and Probus
285–305	Administrative division of the empire under four rulers (the 'Tetrarchy') by Diocletian
303–11	The great persecution of the Christians
311	Galerius, co-emperor, reverses policy of persecution, promulgates Edict of Toleration
312	Constantine becomes sole ruler after the battle of the Milvian bridge
313	Constantine confirms Galerius' Edict of Toleration at Milan, Christianity becomes the official religion of the empire
330	Foundation of Constantinople as the 'New Rome'
337–61	Division of the empire between the sons of Constantine
361–3	Attempt at pagan revival by Julian the Apostate
374	Ambrose becomes Bishop of Milan
376	Visigoths cross the Danube
379–95	Theodosius the Great, Emperor
383	Suppression of pagan rituals in Rome and increase in the power of the popes, under Gratian
386	Augustine converted in Milan
404	Ravenna becomes main residence of Western Emperor Honorius
410	Alaric and the Visigoths sack Rome
426	Augustine writes *The City of God*
452	Attila and the Huns invade Italy
455	Genseric and the Vandals sack Rome
476	Deposition of Romulus Augustulus, Odoacer the Herulian becomes King of Italy
487–93	Theodoric conquers Italy
493–526	Murder of Odoacer by Theodoric. Theodoric King of Italy
523–4	Boethius writes *Consolations of Philosophy*
526–34	Amalasuntha, daughter of Theodoric, rules Italy
527–65	Justinian Emperor of the East
529	St Benedict of Nursia founds Monte Cassino
535–53	Byzantine reconquest of Italy from Goths
536	Belisarius takes Rome
540	Belisarius takes Ravenna
541–52	Totila King of the Goths
568	Lombards under Alboin invade Italy
590–603	Pope Gregory the Great
641–68	Constans II Emperor of the East
663	Last visit to Rome by an Eastern Emperor
717–41	Leo III the Isaurian Emperor of the East
725	Leo III forbids image-worship
751	Lombards capture Ravenna; end of Exarchate
754	Pepin creates Papal State
768–814	Charlemagne
774	Franks under Charlemagne conquer Lombards
800	Charlemagne crowned Emperor at Rome
812	Charlemagne's title recognized by Constantinople
827	Saracens invade Sicily
846	Saracens pillage Rome
849	Leo IV destroys Saracen fleet, fortifies Rome
904–63	Decadence of papacy in Rome
910	Foundation of Cluny
962	Otto I crowned Emperor at Rome
967	Otto II crowned Emperor at Rome
996	Otto III crowned Emperor at Rome
1001	Romans rebel against Emperor Otto III and Pope
1014	Henry II crowned Emperor at Rome
1016	First Norman knights arrive in southern Italy
1030	Norman County of Aversa founded
1038	Aversa recognized by Emperor Conrad II
1046	Henry III crowned Emperor at Rome
1053	Normans defeat and capture Leo IX at Civitate
1059	Pope Nicholas II invests Robert Guiscard with Duchy of Apulia, Calabria and Sicily
1059	Decree regulating papal elections
1061–91	Norman conquest of Sicily
1071	Normans conquer Bari, end of Byzantine rule in Italy
1072	Normans capture Palermo
1073–85	Pope Gregory VII (Hildebrand)
1075	Normans take Salerno, last independent Lombard Principality
1077	Henry IV goes as penitent to Canossa
1081	Henry IV invades Italy
1084	Henry IV crowned Emperor by Antipope; Normans sack Rome; Gregory VII flees to Salerno
1085	Death of Robert Guiscard
1088–99	Pope Urban II
1091	Normans take Noto, last Saracen town in Sicily
1101	Death of Count Roger I of Sicily; succeeded by his son Roger II
1111	Henry V crowned Emperor at Rome
1122	Concordat of Worms
1130	Roger II crowned King of Sicily
1130–43	Pope Innocent II
1130–8	Antipope Anacletus II
1147–9	Second Crusade
1153	Death of St Bernard
1154–9	Pope Hadrian IV (Nicholas Breakspear)
1154–66	William I King of Sicily
1155	Rome under interdict. Execution of Arnold of Brescia
1155	Frederick Barbarossa crowned Emperor
1158	Diet of Roncaglia defines Imperial rights in Italy
1162	Frederick Barbarossa destroys Milan
1166–89	William II King of Sicily
1176	Lombard League defeats Frederick at Legnano
1183	Treaty of Constance
1186	Frederick's son Henry marries Constance of Sicily
1189	William II of Sicily dies; succeeded by Tancred of Lecce
1190	Barbarossa drowned on Third Crusade
1191	Henry VI crowned Emperor
1194	Henry VI conquers Sicily on death of Tancred
1198–1216	Pope Innocent III
1198	Frederick II crowned King of Sicily
1204	Fourth Crusade sacks Constantinople
1216	Dominican Order established
1220	Frederick II crowned Emperor at Rome
1223	Franciscan Order established
1227–41	Pope Gregory IX
1237	Frederick II defeats Lombard League at Cortenuova
1250	Death of Frederick II
1258	Manfred crowned King of Sicily
1260	Cimabue's *Madonna* for S. Trinità, Florence
1265	Charles of Anjou invested with Naples and Sicily
1265–1321	Dante Alighieri
c 1266–1337	Giotto
1266	Charles of Anjou crowned; defeats Manfred at Benevento

1268	Charles defeats Conradin at Tagliacozzo
1268–71	Papal interregnum
1271–6	Pope Gregory X
1274	Death of St Thomas Aquinas; Council of Lyons
1282	Sicilian Vespers
1284	Genoa defeats Pisa at battle of Meloria
1292–4	Pope Celestine V
1294–1303	Pope Boniface VIII
1295	Matteo Visconti becomes tyrant of Milan
1296	Arnolfo di Cambio begins Florence Cathedral
1299–1301	Palazzo Vecchio built in Florence
1302	Treaty of Caltabelotta between Naples and Sicily
1302–10	Giovanni Pisano, pulpit in Pisa Cathedral
1303	Boniface VIII seized at Anagni
1304–74	Petrarch
1305–77	'Babylonish Captivity' of papacy
1309	Clement V fixes residence at Avignon
1309–13	Dante: *De Monarchia*
1310–40	Doges' Palace built at Venice
1311	Duccio: Maesta in Siena Cathedral
1312	Henry VII crowned Emperor at Rome
1312	Can Grande della Scala made Imperial Vicar of Verona and Vicenza
1313–1375	Boccaccio
1314–21	Dante: *Divine Comedy*
1324–7	Marsilius of Padua: *Defensor Pacis*
1328	Lewis IV crowned Emperor at Rome
1341	Petrarch crowned with laurels on Capitol, Rome
1343–81	Joan I Queen of Naples
1347	Cola di Rienzo tribune at Rome
1347–51	Black Death devastates Europe
1348–53	Boccaccio: *Decameron*
1353–7	Cardinal Albornoz re-establishes papal authority in Papal State
1354	Murder of Cola di Rienzo
1362–70	Pope Urban V
1367–70	Urban V temporarily returns to Rome
1370–8	Pope Gregory XI
1373	Death of St Bridget of Sweden
1375–1406	Collucio Salutati chancellor of Florence
1377–1466	Fillipo Brunelleschi
1377	Gregory XI returns from Avignon to Rome
1378–1414	The Great Schism
1378–1455	Lorenzo Ghiberti
1378	Revolt of the Ciompi at Florence
1380	Genoese forces surrender to the Venetians at Chioggia
1381	Peace of Turin between Venice and Genoa
1385–1402	Giangaleazzo Visconti, ruler of Milan
1386–1466	Donatello
1387–1455	Fra Angelico
1395–1455/6	Antonio Pisanello
1397–1475	Paolo Uccello
1400–70	Jacopo Bellini
1401–28	Masaccio
1404–72	Leon Battista Alberti
1409	Council of Pisa
c 1410–92	Piero della Francesca
1414–18	Council of Constance ends Schism
1414–60	Guarino of Verona teaching Greek in northern Italy
1420–36	Brunelleschi builds dome of Florence Cathedral
1420–46	Vittorino da Feltre teaches at the school of La Giocosa
1423–33	Wars of Venice and Florence against Milan
c 1429–1507	Gentile Bellini

c 1430–1516	Giovanni Bellini
1431–1506	Andrea Mantegna
1434–64	Cosimo de' Medici ruler of Florence
1434–41	War of the Visconti with Venice and Florence
1435–88	Andrea del Verrocchio
1439	Council of Ferrara, Florence
1440	Lorenzo Valla proves the Donation of Constantine to be a forgery
1442	Angevins lose Naples to Alfonso of Aragon
1444–1510	Alessandro Botticelli
1444–1514	Donato Bramante
1450–66	Francesco Sforza ruler of Milan
1451	Manetti writes *De excellentia et dignitate hominis*
1452–1519	Leonardo da Vinci
1453	Constantinople falls to the Turks
1454	Treaty of Lodi. Peace between Venice and Milan
1455	The Italian league
1458–64	Angevin and Aragonese war of succession
1458–64	Pope Pius II
1465	Sweynheym and Pannartz establish the first Italian press at Subiaco
1469–92	Lorenzo de' Medici, 'the Magnificent', ruler of Florence
1471–84	Pope Sixtus IV
1475–1564	Michelangelo Buonarrote
c 1478–1510	Giorgione
1478	The Pazzi conspiracy
1478–80	Florence, Venice and Milan at war with the Pope, Siena and Naples
1480–1500	Lodovico Sforza, ruler of Milan
1483–1520	Raphael
1486–7	The Barons' War, Naples
1486	Pico della Mirandola: *Oration on the Dignity of Man*
1487–1576 active	Titian
1490–1523/6	Vittore Carpaccio
1490	Aldus Manutius establishes his printing house
1492–1503	Pope Alexander VI
before 1495–1534	Antonio Correggio
1494–5	Charles VIII invades Italy
1494	The Medici expelled from Florence
1498	Savonarola burnt as heretic
1498–1512	Machiavelli, Second Chancellor of Florence
1499–1503	Cesare Borgia conquers the Romagna
1499–1546	Giulio Romano
1499	Louis XII invades Italy, takes Milan from Lodovico Sforza
1500–71	Benvenuto Cellini
1503–13	Pope Julius II
1508–80	Andrea Palladio
1508–9	League of Cambrai, against Venice
1508–12	Michelangelo paints the ceiling of Sistine Chapel
1509–88	Bernardino Telesio
1512	The Medici return to Florence
1512	Battles of Ravenna and Novara. Milan loses its independence, becomes a Swiss protectorate under Maximilian Sforza
1513–21	Pope Leo X
1515	Francis I invades Italy
1516	Publication of Ariosto's *Orlando Furioso*
1518–94	Jacopo Tintoretto
1521	Leo X excommunicates Luther

1525	Battle of Pavia. The imperialists under Charles V defeat and capture Francis I
1525–94	Giovanni da Palestrina
1526	Treaty of Madrid. Milan restored to Francesco II Sforza. Emilian cities ceded to the papacy. League of Cognac. France and chief Italian states against Charles V
1527	Sack of Rome by Charles V
1527–30	Florence a republic
1528–88	Paolo Veronese
1528	Castiglione: *The Courtier*
1530	Treaty of Cambrai
1530–7	Alessandro de' Medici, ruler of Florence
1534–49	Pope Paul III
1535–44	Renewed hostilities between Charles V and Francis I
1537–41	Michelangelo paints the *Last Judgement*
1537–74	Cosimo de' Medici, ruler of Florence
1540	St Ignatius Loyola founds the Society of Jesus
1542	The Roman Inquisition organized
1545	Pier Luigi Farnese made Duke of Parma by his father, Pope Paul III
1545–63	Council of Trent
1548–1600	Giordano Bruno
1550	Vasari publishes his *Lives*
1555–9	Pope Paul IV
1559	Treaty of Câteau-Cambrésis
1559–80	Emanuele Filiberto, Duke of Savoy
1561	Academy of Drawing founded at Florence
1564–1642	Galileo
1567–1643	Claudio Monteverdi
1571	Battle of Lepanto
1573–1610	Caravaggio
1575	Tasso writes *Jerusalem Delivered*
1590–1669	Pietro da Cortona
1595–1631	Federico Borromeo, Archbishop of Milan
1597	Ferrara annexed by Clement VIII
1598–1680	Gian Lorenzo Bernini
1598	Extension of papal states across the Po
1599–1667	Francesco Borromini
1606–7	Paul V's interdict on Venice
1612–7	Wars of Monferrato and Valtellina
1615–6	War of the Uscocchi
1618–48	Thirty Years' War
1627–31	Second War of Monferrato
1630	Sack of Mantua
1631	Urban VIII annexes Urbino
1633	Condemnation of Galileo in Rome
1641–4	War of Castro
1642–1709	Andrea Pozzo
1647–8	Revolts in Naples and Palermo
1653–1713	Arcangelo Corelli
1659	Peace of the Pyrenees
1674	Insurrection in Messina
1676–1741	Antonio Vivaldi
1684	Genoa bombarded by the French fleet
1685–1751	Domenico Scarlatti
c 1692–1765/8	Giovanni Paolo Panini
1696–1770	Giovanni Battista Tiepolo
1697	Peace of Ryswick
1698–1782	Pietro Metastasio
1700–14	War of the Spanish Succession
1704	French invasion of Piedmont
1706	Battle of Turin
1707–93	Carlo Goldoni
1707	Austrian occupation of Milan, Mantua and Naples
1712–93	Francesco Guardi
1713	Peace of Utrecht
1714	Treaty of Rastadt
1714–8	Venice at war with the Turks
1720	Victor Amadeus II of Savoy becomes King of Sardinia after the Peace of Cambrai
1720–78	Giovanni Battista Piranesi
1732	Don Carlos of Bourbon, Duke of Parma
1735	Don Carlos becomes Charles III of Naples
1737	The Medici extinct, Tuscany passes to Francis of Lorraine
1748	Peace of Aix-la-Chapelle
1749–1803	Vittorio Alfieri
1757–1822	Antonio Canova
1764	Cesare Beccaria publishes *Dei delitti e delle pene*
1764–6	Pietro Verri publishes *Il Caffè*
1770	Leopold, Grand Duke of Tuscany, social reformer
1773	Dissolution of Society of Jesus by Clement XIV
1782–1868	Gioachino Rossini
1785–1827	Alessandro Manzoni
1796–7	Napoleon's first Italian campaign
1797	Treaty of Campo Formio. Venice passes to Austria
1797	Cisalpine, Ligurian and Roman Republics
1798	Naples becomes the Parthenopean Republic under the French
1798–1837	Giacomo Leopardi
1799	Austrian and Russian army drives French out of Italy
1799	Persecution of Republicans in southern Italy
1800–1	Napoleon's return to Italy
1801	Treaty of Lunéville
1801–2	The Italian Republic
1805	The Kingdom of Italy
1806	Joseph Bonaparte, King of Naples
1808	Joachim Murat, King of Naples
1809	Deportation of Pius VII
1812	Constitution of Cadiz
1813–1901	Guiseppe Verdi
1815	Congress of Vienna
1815	Murat executed
1817	Rising at Macerata
1818–9	Publication of *Il Conciliatore*
1820	Rebellions at Nola, Avellino and Naples. Constitution granted
1821	Rebellion in Piedmont. Constitution granted
1821	Repression in north and south
1831	Conspiracy and revolt at Modena and Bologna. Mazzini founds Young Italy
1833	Repression of Mazzini's activities in Piedmont
1835–1907	Giosuè Carducci
1843	Vincenzo Gioberti publishes *The Moral and Civil Primacy of the Italians*
1844	Bandiera brothers' expedition
1846	Pius IX elected
1848	Revolt in Sicily. Five days of Milan. Constitutions in all Italian states
1848	The Republic of Venice established
1848–9	First War of Independence
1849	The Republic of Rome
1852	Cavour becomes prime minister of Piedmont
1855	Piedmontese troops in Crimean War
1856	Congress of Paris

1857	Pisacane's expedition
1858–1924	Giacomo Puccini
1858	Cavour and Napoleon III at Plombières
1858–1932	Guiseppe Peano
1859	Second War of Independence, Battle of Solferino
1859	Peace of Villafranca
1860	Cavour comes to an agreement with Napoleon III. Tuscany and Emilia join Piedmont. Nice and Savoy go to France. Confirmed by plebiscite
1860	Expedition of the Thousand
1861	Victor Emmanuel II, King of Italy
1862	Garibaldi wounded at Aspromonte
1865	The capital moved from Turin to Florence
1866–1952	Benadetto Croce
1866	Third War of Independence. Venetia ceded to Italy
1867–1936	Luigi Pirandello
1867	Garibaldi defeated at Mentana
1868	Riots in Italy against the milling tax
1870	Rome, capital of Italy
1870	Law of Guarantees
1876	Parliament dominated by the left, under the successive leaderships of Depretis, Crispi and Giolitti until the end of the century
1878–1900	Humbert I, King of Italy
1878	Death of Pope Pius IX; election of Leo XIII
1882–1916	Umberto Boccioni
1882	Triple Alliance
1883–1966	Severini
1884–1920	Amedeo Modigliani
1885	Occupation of Massawa
1890	The colonization of Eritrea
1892	Italian Socialist party founded by Filippo Turati
1893	Disorders in Sicily
1896	Battle of Adowa
1898	Riots at Milan and violence throughout Italy
1900	Assassination of Humbert I; accession of Victor Emmanuel III
1909	Filippo Tommaso Marinetti launches Futurism
1911–2	Conquest of Libya
1911	Extension of the franchise
1912	Mussolini becomes editor of the Socialist paper *Avanti!*
1915	Italy joins Allies in World War I
1917	Defeat at Caporetto
1918	Victories of the Piave and Vittorio Veneto
1919	Italy acquires the Brenner line. D'Annunzio seizes Fiume. Proportional representation adopted. The emergence of Don Sturzo's *Partito Popolare*
1919	Fascist group organized by Mussolini
1920	Rapallo conference between Yugoslavs and Italians at Fiume
1920	Mussolini's *Squadristi* appear
1921	Fascist party formed by Mussolini
1922	The Fascists march on Rome; Mussolini becomes Prime Minister
1923	The Corfu incident
1924	Elections in April; the murder of the socialist leader Matteotti in June. The opposition of the Aventine group. Recognition of the Soviet Government
1925–7	Establishment of the 'Corporative State'
1925	Treaty of Locarno
1929	The Lateran Agreements
1935–6	Abyssinian war. Attempted sanctions against Italy by the League of Nations
1936–9	Italian troops aid Franco in the Spanish Civil War
1936	The 'Axis' agreement between Germany and Italy
1939	The Steel Pact between Germany and Italy. Italians occupy Albania
1940	Italy enters World War II on the side of the Germans. Invasion of France and Greece
1941	Invasion of Yugoslavia. Troops to Russian front Anti-Fascist strikes in Italy. Italian defeat in Africa. Allied landing in Sicily. Mussolini arrested. Badoglio Government. Mussolini freed by Germans, sets up Republic of Salò. Badoglio's government declares war on Germany
1944	Allies reach Rome and Florence
1945	Growth of the resistance movement. Liberation of Florence by Allies and Partisans. German surrender
1946	Abdication of Victor Emmanuel III. Succeeded by son, Humbert II, who, as Lieutenant of the Realm, is exiled after referendum on the Monarchy. Establishment of the Italian Republic
1946–53	De Gasperi, leader of the Christian Democrats and Prime Minister for most of the period
1947	Saragat breaks with Nenni, founds Social Democratic Party. Treaty of Paris between the Allies and Italy
1948	Attempted assasination of Togliatti, leader of the Communist Party
1948–55	Einaudi, President of the Republic
1949	Italy joins NATO
1954	Trieste without hinterland returned to Italy
1955	Vanoni Plan
1955–62	Gronchi, President of the Republic
1959–63	Economic boom, the 'Italian Miracle'
1960	Rioting over the Tambroni government's acceptance of Fascist support
1963	Centre-left government, including Christian Democrats and Socialists
1964	Death of Togliatti. Longo becomes leader of Communist Party. Saragat, President of the Republic. Left wing of the Italian Socialist party breaks away to form PSIUP

PHOTOGRAPHIC ACKNOWLEDGMENTS

The illustrations were selected by Milton Gendel.
The maps were drawn by Tom Stalker-Miller.

The Publishers are grateful to the following for their help in assembling the illustrative material and for permission to reproduce photographs:

The names of photographers and photographic agencies are given in italics

INTRODUCTION

page 9 *Gabinetto Fotografico Nazionale*, Rome; 10 *Novarese*, Florence

ANCIENT ITALY

page 17 left and right, 18 top right Museo Pigorini, Rome, *Gabinetto Fotografico Nazionale*; 18 centre right Museo Archeologico Nazionale, Rome, *Gabinetto Fotografico Nazionale*; 18 left Museo Archeologico Nazionale, Cagliari, *Gabinetto Fotografico Nazionale*; 19 *Novarese*, Florence; 20 top British Museum; 20 bottom Museo Nazionale, Naples, *Studio Crea*; 23 Louvre, *Studio Crea*; 24 *De Antonis*; 27 Villa Giulia, Rome, *Gabinetto Fotografico Nazionale*; 28 and 29 *Gabinetto Fotografico Nazionale*; 30 Villa Giulia, Rome, *Gabinetto Fotografico Nazionale*; 31 *Novarese*, Florence; 32 Museo Nazionale, Naples, *André Held*; 35 top left Palazzo dei Conservatori, Rome; 35 right Museo Nazionale, Rome, *Gabinetto Fotografico Nazionale*; 35 bottom left Lateran Museum, Rome, *Gabinetto Fotografico Nazionale*; 36 top Pompeii Museum, *Edwin Smith*; 36 left Museo Nazionale, Naples, *André Held*; 37 Museo Nazionale, Naples, *André Held*; 38 Museo Nazionale, Naples, *Scala*; 41 top and bottom right Museo Nazionale, Naples, *Josephine Powell*; 41 bottom left Museo Nazionale, Naples, *André Held*; 42 top left *Josephine Powell*; 42 top right *Fototeca Unione*, Rome; 42 bottom *Fotocielo*, Rome; 45 top left NY Carlsberg, Glypotek Copenhagen, *Gabinetto Fotografico Nazionale*; 45 top British Museum, London; 45 below *Fototeca Unione*; 46 left Lateran Museum, Rome, *Gabinetto Fotografico Nazionale*; 46 top and bottom right Museo Nazionale, Rome, *Gabinetto Fotografico Nazionale*; 47 Museo Nazionale, Naples, *André Held*; 48 top Museo Nazionale, Naples, *De Antonis*; 48 bottom Sala Nozze Aldobrandini, Vatican, *De Antonis*; 51 bottom left Palazzo dei Conservatori, Rome, *Commune di Roma*; 51 top left Villa Adriana, Tivoli, *Islay Lyons*; 51 top right *Josephine Powell*; 51 bottom right Museo Nazionale, Naples, *Alinari*; 52 Museo dei Conservatori, Rome, *Gabinetto Fotografico Nazionale*; 53 top Museo Torlonia, Rome, *Gabinetto Fotografico Nazionale*; 53 bottom Uffizi, Florence, *Alinari*; 54 Palazzo dei Conservatori, Rome, *Curtis G. Pepper*; 57 Museo Nazionale, Rome, *André Held*; 58 Villa Adriana, Tivoli, *Georgina Masson*; 59 top *Pontefice Commissione di Archeologia Sacra*; 59 bottom Museo Cristiano, Vatican, *André Held*; 60 left *Fototeca Unione*; 60 right Aosta Cathedral Treasury, *Gabinetto Fotografico Nazionale*

BARBARIANS, PRIESTS AND COMMUNES

page 63 S. Apollinare Nuovo, Ravenna, *Scala*; 64 Vatican Library; 67 top left Palazzo dei Conservatori, Rome, *André Held*; 67 bottom left Bibliothèque Nationale, Paris, *Deutsches Archaelogisches Institut*, Rome; 67 right S. Vitale, Ravenna, *Josephine Powell*; 68 Museo dell' Arcivescovado Ravenna, *Anderson*; 69 top left Monza Cathedral Treasury, *Alinari*; 69 bottom left Monza Cathedral Treasury, *Gabinetto Fotografico Nazionale*, Rome; 69 top right Vatican Library; 69 bottom right *S. Saba*, Rome; 70 Monza Cathedral Treasury, *Josephine Powell*; 73 opposite Vatican Library; 74 top Anagni Cathedral, *Gabinetto Fotografico Nazionale*; 74 bottom S. Bartolomeo, Rome, *Gabinetto Fotografico Nazionale*; 75 St Mark's, Venice, *Scala*; 76 Vatican Library; 79 top ENI; 79 bottom *Fotocielo*, Rome; 80 top *Gabinetto Fotografico Nazionale*; 80 bottom right Vatican Library; 83 above *Gabinetto Fotografico Nazionale*; 83 bottom left S. Maria in Trastevere, Rome, *André Held*; 83 right S. Pietro L'Aquila, *Gabinetto Fotografico Nazionale*; 84 Bressanone Museum, *Gabinetto Fotografico Nazionale*; 87 S. Maria dell' Ammiraglio, Palermo, *Scala*; 88 Biblioteca Laurenziana, Florence, *Novarese*; 89 top Vatican Library; 89 top and bottom right Bürgerbibliothek, Bern; 90 top Anagni Cathedral, *Oscar Savio*; 90 bottom left Archivio Segreto, Vatican Library; 90 bottom right Museo Comunale, Barletta, *Gabinetto Fotografico Nazionale*; 93 left St Mark's, Venice, *Josephine Powell*; 93 right Museo Poldi Pezzoli, Milan, *Josephine Powell*; 94 left Prado, Madrid, *Anderson*; 94 right S. Francesco, Pescia, *Anderson*; 94 bottom right Louvre, *André Held*; 95 top left Museo di Castelvecchio, Verona; 95 bottom left Palazzo dei Conservatori, Rome, *Gabinetto Fotografico Nazionale*; 95 right Museo Civico, Bologna, *Alinari*; 96 top Palazzo Vecchio, Florence, *Novarese*; 98 bottom Rocca d'Angera, *Gabinetto Fotografico Nazionale*; 99 Vatican Library, *Scala*; 100 Pinacoteca Civica, San Gimignano, *Scala*; 103 Sala Regia, Vatican, *Anderson*; 104 Sala dei Gigli, Palazzo Vecchio, Florence, *Novarese*

THE RENAISSANCE: ART, HUMANISM AND SOCIETY

page 107 Castello Sforzesco, Milan, *Scala*; 108 Uffizi, Florence, *Scala*; 109 Uffizi, Florence, *Josephine Powell*; 110 top left Museo Medicio, Florence, *André Held*; 110 top centre Uffizi, Florence, *Anderson*; 110 top right S. Trinità, Florence, *Alinari*; 110 bottom Accademia, Florence, *Novarese*; 113 left and right Brera, *Josephine Powell*; 114 left S. Andrea della Valle, Rome, *Gabinetto Fotografico Nazionale*; 114 right *Gabinetto Fotografico Nazionale*, Rome; 115 top Hospital of S. Spirito, Rome, *Anderson*; 115 bottom Museo Mediceo, Florence, *Alinari*; 116 left *Gabinetto Fotografico Nazionale*, Rome; 116 top right Museo Civico, Como, *Josephine Powell*; 116 bottom right Brera, Milan, *Josephine Powell*; 119 Appartamento Borgia, Vatican, *De Antonis*; 120 Palazzo Vecchio, Florence, *Scala*; 121 top Campo di SS Giovanni e Paulo, Venice, *Anderson*; 121 bottom Victoria and Albert Museum, London, *Gabinetto Fotografico Nazionale*, Rome; 122 top left Castello S. Angelo, Rome, *Gabinetto Fotografico Nazionale*; 122 bottom left Archivio Segreto, Vatican; 122 right *Studio Crea*; 125 top left Pinacoteca Ambrosiana, Milan, *Gabinetto Fotografico Nazionale*; 125 top right Museo Mediceo, Florence, *Josephine Powell*; 125 bottom Castel S. Angelo, Rome, *Gabinetto Fotografico Nazionale*; 126–7 Museo Nazionale di Capodimonte, Naples, *Gabinetto Fotografico Nazionale*; 128 top Staatsbibliotek, Berlin, *Arborio Mella*; 128 bottom Pecci Blunt Collection, Rome, *Josephine Powell*; 131 Palasso Schifanoia, Ferrara, *Scala*; 132 and 133 Uffizi, *Scala*; 134 S. Marco, Florence, *Scala*; 137 top Palazzo Farnese, Caprarola, *Gabinetto Fotografico Nazionale*; 137 bottom left Castel S. Angelo, Rome, *Gabinetto Fotografico Nazionale*; 137 bottom right Museo della Zecca, Rome, *André Held*; 138 top

Casa Buonarotti, Florence, *Josephine Powell*; 138 bottom Pecci Blunt Collection, Rome, *Josephine Powell*; 139 top left *Giordani*, Rome; 139 top right S. Francesca Romana, Rome, *Gabinetto Fotografico Nazionale*; 139 bottom Pecci Blunt Collection, Rome, *Josephine Powell*; 140 top left Castel S. Angelo, Rome, *Gabinetto Fotografico Nazionale*; 140 top right *André Held*; 140 bottom *Gabinetto Fotografico Nazionale*; 143 Private Collection, Bergamo, *Mondadori*; 144 Accademia, Venice, *André Held*; 145 top *Anderson*; 145 bottom Private Collection, Rome, *Gabinetto Fotografico Nazionale*; 146 top left Uffizi, Florence, *Josephine Powell*; 146 top right Castel S. Angelo, Rome, *Gabinetto Fotografico Nazionale*; 146 bottom left Brera, Milan, *Alinari*; 146 bottom right Museo della Zecca, Rome; 149 Pecci Blunt Collection, Rome, *Josephine Powell*; 150 top Royal Institute of British Architects, London, *Gabinetto Fotografico Nazionale*, Rome; 150 centre Gabinetto Nazionale delle Stampe, Rome, *Oscar Savio*; 150 bottom Pecci Blunt Collection, Rome, *Josephine Powell*; 151 S. Maria in Trastevere, Rome, *De Antonis*; 152 Museo Nazionale de Capodimonte, Naples, *Scala*

DECLINE AND ENLIGHTENMENT

page 155 *Studio Crea*; 156 top left Museo di Roma, *Gabinetto Fotografico Nazionale*; 156 top right Uffizi, Florence, *Gabinetto Fotografico Nazionale*; 156 bottom S. Anastasia, Rome, *Gabinetto Fotografico Nazionale*; 159 Galleria Borghese, Rome, *André Held*; 160 Milan Cathedral, *Scala*; 163 top Pecci Blunt Collection, Rome, *Josephine Powell*; 163 bottom left Gabinetto delle Stampe, Rome, *Gabinetto Fotografico Nazionale*; 163 bottom right Calcografia Nazionale, *Gabinetto Fotografico Nazionale*, Rome; 164 top left Palazzo Castellani, Florence, *Novarese*; 164 bottom left Pecci Blunt Collection, Rome, *Josephine Powell*; 164–5 Pecci Blunt Collection, Rome, *Josephine Powell*; 166 *Curtis G. Pepper*; 169 S. Ignazio, Rome, *De Antonis*; 170 Galleria Doria Pamphili, Rome, *De Antonis*; 173 top left *Anderson*; 173 top right *Alinari*; 173 bottom Gabinetto delle Stampe, *Oscar Savio*; 174 top left Louvre, Paris, *Gabinetto Fotografico Nazionale*; 174 top right and bottom Pecci Blunt Collection, Rome, *Josephine Powell*; 175 top Biblioteca Storia dell'Arte, Rome, *Oscar Savio*; 175 bottom Vatican Library; 176 top Pecci Blunt Collection, Rome, *Josephine Powell*; 176 bottom *D'Onofrio*; 179 *Scala*; 180 Louvre, Paris, *De Antonis*; 183 top Pecci Blunt Collection, Rome, *Josephine Powell*; 183 bottom Galleria Nazionale, Palazzo Corsini, Rome, *André Held*; 184 Pecci Blunt Collection, Rome, *Josephine Powell*; 187 top Toulouse Museum, *André Held*; 187 bottom left Armide & Oppé Collection, London, *Gabinetto Fotografico Nazionale*; 187 bottom right Vienna Academy, *Gabinetto Fotografico Nazionale*; 188 top left *Josephine Powell*; 188 top right Kunsthaus, Zurich, *Gabinetto Fotografico Nazionale*; 188 bottom left *Mondadori*; 188 bottom right *Studio Crea*; 191 top Istituto per la Storia del Risorgimento Italiano, Rome; 191 bottom Pecci Blunt Collection, Rome, *Josephine Powell*; 192 left *Gabinetto Fotografico Nazionale*, Rome; 192 right Museo di Roma, *Gabinetto Fotografico Nazionale*

RISORGIMENTO

page 195 Victoria and Albert Museum, London; 196 top left Pecci Blunt Collection, Rome, *Josephine Powell*; 196 top right Museo della Certosa di S. Martino, Naples, *Gabinetto Fotografico Nazionale*; 196 bottom left Biblioteca del Risorgimento, Florence, *Novarese*; 196 bottom right Private collection, Rome, *Josephine Powell*; 199 Museo di Roma, *André Held*; 200 Museo del Risorgimento, Milan, *Scala*; 203 top Private Collection, Rome, *Josephine Powell*; 203 bottom Gabinetto Nazionale delle Stampe, Rome, *Oscar Savio*; 204 Istituto per la Storia del Risorgimento

Italiano, Rome, *De Antonis*; 205 top Museo di Roma, *André Held*; 205 bottom Museo di S. Martino, Naples; 206 top left Pecci Blunt Collection, Rome, *Josephine Powell*; 206 bottom left Museo di Roma, *Gabinetto Fotografico Nazionale*; 206 right Ripamonte Collection, Rome, *Josephine Powell*; 209 Gabinetto Nazionale delle Stampe, *Oscar Savio*; 210 top left Pecci Blunt Collection, Rome, *Josephine Powell*; 210 top right Istituto per la Storia del Risorgimento Italiano, Rome, *De Antonis*; 210 bottom Istituto per la Storia del Risorgimento Italiano, Rome, *De Antonis*; 211 top Pecci Blunt Collection, Rome, *Josephine Powell*; 211 bottom *Mondadori*, 212 top left Istituto per la Storia del Risorgimento Italiano, *De Antonis*; 212 top right Biblioteca del Risorgimento, Florence, *Novarese*; 212 bottom Istituto per la Storia del Risorgimento Italiano, Rome, *De Antonis*; 215 Museo del Risorgimento, Milan, *Scala*; 216 Museo di Roma, *De Antonis*; 219 top *Novarese*; 219 bottom Bertherelli Collection, Milan; 220 top Istituto per la Storia del Risorgimento Italiano, Rome, *De Antonis*; 220 bottom left Biblioteca del Risorgimento, Florence, *Novarese*; 220 bottom right Pecci Blunt Collection, Rome, *Josephine Powell*; 221 top right *Mondadori*; 221 bottom left Istituto per la Storia del Risorgimento Italiano, Rome, *De Antonis*; 221 bottom right Biblioteca del Risorgimento, Florence, *Novarese*; 222 top Soprintendenza alle Gallerie, Perugia, *Novarese*; 222 bottom Istituto per la Storia del Risorgimento Italiano, Rome, *De Antonis*; 225 *Novarese*; 226–7 Museo di Firenze Com' Era, Florence, *Scala*; 228 Galleria Moderna, Florence, *Novarese*; 231 top National Gallery of Modern Art, Rome, *Gabinetto Fotografico Nazionale*; 231 bottom Museo di Firenze Com' Era, Florence, *Novarese*; 232 top Istituto per la Storia del Risorgimento Italiano, Rome, *De Antonis*; 232 bottom *Mondadori*; 233 top left Istituto per la Storia del Risorgimento Italiano, Rome, *De Antonis*; 233 top right Museo di Roma; 233 bottom Istituto per la Storia del Risorgimento Italiano, Rome, *De Antonis*; 234 top left Museo di Roma; 234 top right Antologia Illustrata, *Du Foto*; 234 bottom Museo di Roma

MODERN ITALY

page 237 Biblioteca del Risorgimento, Florence, *Novarese*; 238 top left Museo di Roma, Rome; 238 right Antologia Illustrata, Rome; 241 top and bottom Istituto per la Storia del Risorgimento Italiano, Rome; 242 Private collection, Rome, *De Antonis*; 243 top Antologia Illustrata, Rome; 243 bottom Pecci Blunt Collection, Rome, *Josephine Powell*; 244 top L'Illustrazione Italiana; 244 bottom L'Illustrazione Italiana; 245 top L'Illustrazione Italiana; 245 bottom L'Illustrazione Italiana; 246 top left Il Secolo Illustrato della Domenica; 246 top right *Mondadori*; 246 bottom L'Illustrazione Italiana, *Il Messaggero*; 249 Galleria d'Arte Moderna, Rome, *Gabinetto Fotografico Nazionale*; 250 top Private Collection, Paris, *Gabinetto Fotografico Nazionale*; 250 bottom left Galleria d'Arte Moderna, Rome, *Gabinetto Fotografico Nazionale*; 250 bottom right L'Illustrazione Italiana, *Il Messaggero*, Rome; 253 top L'Illustrazione Italiana; 253 bottom left Domenica del Corriere, *Mondadori*; 253 bottom right *Mondadori*; 254 top *De Antonis*; 254 bottom *Mondadori*; 255 Gianni Mattioli Collection, Milan, *Kindler Verlag*; 256 Still from 'The Red Desert', copyright Michelangelo Antonioni; 259 top *Il Messaggero*; 259 centre *Mondadori*; 259 below *Mondadori*; 260 and 263 top and bottom *Foto Italia*; 263 middle *Il Messaggero*; 264 *Foto Italia*; 265, 266, 269 top left and right, bottom left *Il Messaggero*; 269 bottom right *Curtis G. Pepper*; 270 left *Mondadori*; 270 top right *Il Messaggero*; 270 centre right *Mondadori*; 270 bottom right Galleria d'Arte Moderna, Rome, *Gabinetto Fotografico Nazionale*; 273 top left *Il Messaggero*; 273 top right and bottom *Curtis G. Pepper*; 274 top left Pirelli Co.; 274 top right Olivetti Co.; 274 bottom *Il Messaggero*

INDEX Page numbers in italics refer to the illustrations